SO-BWU-925

12-19-77

There is a thread running throughout the cuisines of the world—the noodle—stuffed, sautéed or sauced; boiled, fried or baked; in soups, in casseroles and under stews.

But pity the poor noodle whose name has been so unjustly maligned, shunned by calorie-counters when, in fact, it is the sauce and not the noodle that should take the blame for those extra pounds. At last, Karen Green has written a book that not only defends but glorifies the noodle in all its nutritious, stomach-soothing, and adventurous forms.

In *The Great International Noodle Experience* she has gathered a cornucopia of recipes plain and fancy from the four corners of the world: from Japan, where the noodle is a symbol of longevity, through Italy, where ancient pasta-making equipment is displayed at a museum in Pompeii, and the entire European continent, to the United States, where Thomas Jefferson is credited with the founding of American noodlery.

In addition to more than 100 of her own mouth-watering recipes ranging from the well-loved lasagne in all its adventuresome

(continued on back flap)

Books by Karen Green:

The Great International Noodle Experience   *1977*

How to Cook His Goose (and Other Wild Games)   *1973*
   WITH BETTY BLACK

(continued from front flap)

varieties to the exotic fried won-ton and the traditional kugel, Karen Green has included an entire chapter of prize-winning noodles from the highly respected Durum Wheat Institute's annual recipe contest and a section devoted entirely to the imaginative use of noodles in out-of-doors camp cookery.

In short, hers is an utterly complete compendium to titillate the palates of all lovers of good food, international cuisine and healthful, economical and innovative cookery.

The Great International Noodle Experience

KAREN GREEN

Illustrations by Bill Green

Atheneum

NEW YORK

1977

In memory of my Buba who passed away
while I was writing the final pages of this book.

Library of Congress Cataloging in Publication Data

Green, Karen.
　　The great international noodle experience.

　　Includes index.
　　1. Cookery (Macaroni)　2. Noodles.　I.　Title.
TX809.M17G73　　　641.8′22　　　77–76546
ISBN 0–689–10807–9

First Edition

Acknowledgments

~~~~~~~~~~~~~~~~~~

W H E N I started this book, I decided to leave my thank
you's to the very end. Now, as I write the last sentences,
I do so with mixed emotions. Of course, I am happy to put
the final touches on this project, but I am saddened in a
way because it has practically been my shadow for many
months.

The list of people I wish to acknowledge is enormous and
I apologize if I somehow forgot to mention your name.
Thank you to all who have given their personal recipes for
me to include in this book; to my agent Jane Jordan
Browne and her staff, who encouraged my idea from the
beginning; to Judith T. Kern, my editor at Atheneum, who
worked with me and advised me not to eat too many
noodles; to Patricia L. Sparks, of the Durum Wheat Institute, who aided with an entire chapter; to John William,
of Globe A-1, who sent me cartons of noodles to cook; to
Robert Green, of the National Macaroni Institute, who an-
swered my endless queries; to Joseph Pellegrino of Prince

ACKNOWLEDGMENTS

Macaroni, to Pat Goodrich of Skinner Macaroni, to Deborah Ross of The B. Manischewitz Company, to Ken Tremayne of Nissin Foods, to Lou Arena of Angelus Macaroni Manufacturing Company, to Ralph Sarli of American Beauty Macaroni Company, to Ginny Biddle of The Creamette Company, to Jean P. Sheppard of the Dairy Council of California, to Marcia Cone of the Campbell Soup Company, to Evelyn Berger of the Lipton Kitchens, to Rita Fitzgerald of The R. T. French Company's kitchens, to Dee Munson of the American Egg Board, to Diane Metz Cline of Best Foods, to Catherine J. Dunlap of Golden Grain Macaroni, to Joseph P. Viviano of San Giorgio Macaroni, and to Walter S. McIlhenny, of the McIlhenny Company, who shared with me many recipes and informative booklets; to Gloria Marshall, who sent me lots of printed material; to Page Poore, who offered recipes and contacts; to Carl Sontheimer and Cuisinarts, which cut down my cooking chores; to Annette Disano for her contacts; to Michael Sharp of Williams-Sonoma, who helped me with the loan of two noodle makers; to Klaus Mortimer and to Gary Valenti for the loan of their noodle makers which I adored and purchased; to Sherman Shapiro of Kitchen Bazaar for all his information on noodle–making equipment; to my mother-in-law Mom Hoy and Aunt Neenie, who contacted all their friends for "American" noodles; to all my editors and business associates who extended my deadlines especially during my last weeks of completing this book; to Marilyn Elliott, who kept my son at playschool extra hours; to my Chinese cooking teacher Susan Mozingo, who has given me great confidence in Oriental cooking skills; to my close friend and cooking buddy Ann Osburn who typed my manuscript during the Christmas holidays; and to my illustrator-husband Bill, my son Jonathon, my parents, and all our neighbors, friends and clients who so dearly tasted all my recipes. I love you all.

Preface

~~~~~~~~~~~~~~~~~

I N M Y studies of the cuisines of the world, I have found in all of them a most interesting, reoccuring thread—the noodle. It seems every country has either a noodle in its pride or a sauce or stuffing that would make any noodle proud. Whether for breakfast, lunch, or dinner, as a snack, entree, or dessert, the noodle is an international dietary staple.

But I pity the poor noodle whose name has been maligned in vain. Calorie counters have wrongly sentenced the noodle as an undesirable. For it is not the noodle but the sauce or stuffing that should be credited with those extra pounds.

This book has been written in defense of the noodle. Ounce for ounce, it is high in nutrition and low in cost. It should be rightfully experienced as a comforting, stomach-soothing food, whether you cook it plain or fancy.

Contents

~~~~~~~~~~~~~~~~

CONTENTS

The Great International Noodle Experience

What Is a Noodle?

~~~~~~~~~~~~~~~~~~~~~~~~~~~~~~~

''W H A T is a noodle and how does it differ from a pasta, a macaroni, or a spaghetti?'' I've been asked this question dozens of times. Although the answer would appear to be simple, it becomes something of a problem when we consider the many cuisines of the world.

To simplify matters, let's begin with those products manufactured in the United States. By federal law (Food and Drug Administration), a noodle is a paste made of flour, water, and a minimum of 5.5 percent egg solids, which may be fresh, powdered, or frozen. Macaroni and spaghetti are a paste made of flour and water, no eggs.

Macaroni is tubular, varying in shape and length; whereas, spaghetti is solid, rodlike, varying in width and length. Noodles, sometimes further defined as egg noodles, are ribbonlike, varying in width, length, and shape.

Yet, the generic term ''macaroni'' includes macaroni,

spaghetti, and noodles. Confusing! And, the generic term
"pasta" (originally Italian) refers to both spaghetti and
macaroni products, with noodles considered a kissing
cousin.

The family tree becomes further snarled when we at
tempt to place Oriental noodles in their proper place. Most
do not contain eggs, and besides using semolina or another
hard wheat flour, many are made out of rice, corn, pea,
yam, or mung bean starches.

Because the U.S. government requires the presence of
eggs in the dough for the product to be sold officially as a
noodle, these Oriental products often carry the designation
"imitation noodles" or "alimentary paste" on their package labels. They are, nonetheless, still condsidered noodles
in recipes and at restaurants.

Naturally, the quality of flour determines the quality of
noodle, macaroni, or spaghetti. A premium grade of hard
durum wheat is primarily used for American and Italian
products. From the heart of this high-in-gluten-protein
wheat, a granular, amber-colored flour, somewhat similar
to cornmeal in appearance and known as semolina, is
milled.

Noodles, as well as macaroni and spaghetti, have never been properly appreciated for their nutritional status. Like other bread and cereal foods, they provide a considerable percentage of the daily recommended allowance of protein, carbohydrates, and vitamins. Most manufacturers further enrich their products with additional thiamin, riboflavin, niacin, and iron.

	Protein Content
A. Noodles	13–13.5%
B. Macaroni & Spaghetti	12–12.5%

% U.S. Recommended Daily Allowance for Adults
(Based on approximately 3 ounces, uncooked)

Protein	15%
Thiamin (B_1)	40%
Riboflavin (B_2)	20%
Niacin	25%
Iron	20%

Noodles and pasta, more often, are known for what they lack. True, they do not contain sufficient amounts of two essential amino acids, lysine and tryptophane, to be considered complete proteins. But who eats noodles totally dry? A simple tossing with butter, cheese, or sauce, or a dip in broth complements the protein value.

The reputation of noodles as a fattening food is the result of their toppings—butter and rich sauces. Let the truth now be known: these products are merely worth

about 100 calories an ounce—just about the same as one large apple, but containing many times more protein. That's not a bad trade for their great energy-giving, body-satisfying content.

The New York Times sports pages, June 11, 1976, carried an article which stated, "Spaghetti, mashed potatoes and dried fruit will do more for Olympic athletes this year than steak and vitamins." The story continued to report that the average Olympic athlete needs about 5,500 calories daily. A well-balanced diet, high in calories, provides the needed protein. Foods like steak aren't as effective as people think. Athletes need carbohydrates. A noodle, macaroni, or spaghetti dish was served each day at the 1976 Montreal Olymplics to the 11,000 athletes, coaches, and officials.*

(3 ounces, uncooked)	*Carbohydrate Content*
Noodles	330
Macaroni & Spaghetti	315

Low in sodium and in fat, noodles, spaghetti, and macaroni are good for low cholesterol and low salt diets. They are easy to chew and easy for the body to digest at a moderate speed. And they're nutritionally satisfying for small children as well as for their great grandparents.

(3 ounces, uncooked)	*Sodium Content*
Noodles	3 mg
Macaroni & Spaghetti	1 mg
	Average Fat Content
Noodles	4.5
Macaroni & Spaghetti	1.4

Psychologically, the joy of being physically satisfied by food comes into play. Noodles are associated with warm

* As quoted from the "Macaroni Journal," Vol. 58, No. 6, October 1976, page 14, an official publication of the National Macaroni Manufacturers Association.

thoughts of mother and home. They are soft, soothing, and a pleasure to eat. *The New York Times* Food Editor, Craig Clairborne, says, "I have a theory. I think a lot of my dining preferences are based on nursery habits, and I have an absolute passion for things that are mushy and soft. I love nursery desserts, any kind of custard, tapioca pudding. All these gooey but marvelous creamy things are soothing, sort of like mother's comfort. And I think pasta falls into this category. It's so easy to digest that you feel pacified and enjoy a marvelous sense of well-being." *

When I think of noodles, my mind draws Norman Rock-wellian pictures of family gatherings where everyone feasts on spaghetti and tomato sauce, or of carefree summer picnics where tables are crowded with favorite macaroni salads. Who will deny that the greatest cure for a cold is mother's home-made chicken soup with noodles? And what child hasn't laughed joyously as he grabbed handfuls of noodles and squished them playfully into his mouth?

A great story is told by Johnny Carson. One night he asked his "Tonight Show" guests what one food they would choose to have along if they were to be marooned on a desert island. Of course, they all named their favorite noodles, macaroni, or spaghetti.

If noodles are so good for us and we love to eat them, why have they become the black sheep of the food family? Certainly some ill-advised dieters are at fault. If they couldn't enjoy them, no one would. But they've only succeeded in making noodles more desirable, the forbidden fruit. Dreams are made of such cravings.

* As quoted from "The Pasta Passion," by Lawrence B. Eisenberg, *Cosmopolitan Magazine*, September 9, 1976, pages 184, 198–9, 211.

The History and
Romance of the Noodle

WHEN I was a young girl, one of the romantic stories my
grandmother would tell as she stirred a pot of sauce was
how the Italian traveler Marco Polo had discovered
spaghetti. The tale went like this—One day a Chinese
maiden, while tending to her breadmaking duties, care-
lessly left the dough while she flirted with her lover, a
member of Marco Polo's expedition. The neglected dough
soon overflowed the basket and dried into strings. Noticing
what had happened, the young Italian sailor wished to
cover up the wasteful evidence and carried the dried dough
back to his ship. Like all good cooks, the galley mate saw
this as a challenge to his culinary skills and boiled the
strands in broth for the evening's meal. The crew cheered
the new food. Before returning from Asia, Marco Polo
packed several trunks with these noodles as well as other
Oriental delicacies.

Years later, in my food studies, I learned that though

Marco Polo may have carried spaghetti among his exotic treasures, this was not the first time Italians had seen or tasted it. But, as a child, it was a charming tale to believe in.

Actually, the story of noodles (and all macaroni products) begins with the study of ancient history. Archeologists have proven that one of the staple foods of the Shang Dynasty (1700–1711 B.C.) was a type of noodle. The Chinese have recorded the eating of these products in various forms as early as 5,000 B.C.

From the Orient we move southwest to the Mediterranean where a broad, flat cake of dough, cut into strips, was called "laganon" (close to linguine and lasagne). Bas-reliefs on an Etruscan tomb dating from the fourth century B.C. picture utensils required for the making of noodles—a water jug, ladle, flour bag, edged board for mixing, rolling pin, knife, and pastry wheel. A main dish of pasta stuffed with "agnello," lamb (from which "agnolotti," a round ravioli, has derived), was prepared by the Jews during the century before Christ. The Roman soldiers undoubtedly learned the recipe and brought it with them on their return to their homes.

The pasta of ancient Rome was prepared by baking the kneaded flour and water mixture on large, porous, hot stones. Contemporary translations of several classical texts mention it. Horace tells of a grand supper which included lasagne. And another glorification of pasta is found in the writings of Marcus Gavius Apicius, a renowned gourmand.

Again, as we move on through history, a book of travels by the Arab geographer, Al-Idrisi, whose diary had been commissioned by Roger II, the second Norman ruler of Sicily, mentions tales of the people of Trahia, near Palermo, who made a thread-like food from flour.

"Life of the Blessed Hermit William," dating around 1200, which is displayed in a museum at Pompeii along with several pieces of ancient pasta-making equipment, proves that pasta was known in Italy by the beginning of the century. A translation of this writing finds the sentence, "He invited William to dinner and served macaroni."

About this same time in history, a wealthy nobleman from Palermo is credited with the actual naming of "macaroni." His cook, desiring constantly to please his epicurean master with new tastes, served a plate of tubes dressed with a rich sauce and grated cheese. As the nobleman tasted the new food, he exclaimed ecstatically: "Cari! Ma cari! Ma caroni!"—which idiomatically means "The dears! But the dears! The precious darlings!"

Although this account is not officially recorded, it certainly has more charm than the alternate derivation from the Italian word "maccari," which means "to pound" as when making a paste of flour and water.

But probably the document which most negates Marco Polo's claim to the title "King of Spaghetti" is a will dated 1279. In the archives of the city of Genoa is the notary Agnolino Scarpa's listing of the belongings of a soldier, Ponzio Bastone, which upon his death, included a large basket of dried macaroni—"bariscella plena de macaronis." The famous Italian traveler didn't return from the Orient until 1292, thirteen years later.

Several documents on pasta and noodles, among them an official papal dictum declaring proper quality levels, survive from the thirteenth century. Although by that time pasta had established itself as a staple throughout most of Italy, the preparations were kept simple. During this century and into the fifteenth, pasta was primarily eaten with butter or oil and grated cheese. *De Onesta Voluptate,* by Platina (1485), credits the gentleman Meluzza, from Como, a small town on Lake Como near Milan, for having prepared the first spaghetti with oil and garlic. Tomato sauce was still unknown, but there is some record of a pounded-herb sauce (perhaps pesto) and a white clam sauce. A fourteenth century English cookbook, *The Forme of Cury,* describes a dish close to Fettuccine Alfredo.

Boccaccio describes in the *Decameron* (1350), the idyllic country of Bengodi where the people play and everything is free. The unusual terrain is composed of mountains of grated Parmesan cheese on top of which are workers who make macaroni and ravioli and then cook them in capon broth. The workers toss the cooked pasta down the mountain to anyone who wants to eat.

A stream of light peeked through the Dark Ages and soon burst into the Renaissance. During this rebirth of the classics, there was much creative interest in the culinary arts. Italian cuisine was introduced to France when Catherine de Medici, at the age of fourteen, married Henri II, heir to the French throne. She brought with her from Italy several Florentine chefs. As queen of France during the sixteenth century, she was known for her grand parties and feasts, several of which were designed totally around an Italian theme.

But not until 1772 was pasta commercially exported— from Genoa to London. At this time the word "macaroni" became popular for something other than its tastiness. Well-traveled, rather stuffily dressed gentlemen began to gather at private social establishments known as Macaroni Clubs. At first the term "macaroni" referred to perfection and elegance, but soon it came to be used with pointed wit to describe a dandified man, one who was affected, overdressed, and usually sporting an elaborate wig.

The tune "Yankee Doodle Dandy" was first sung by the British, about the time of the American Revolution, to make fun of the Yankees. Soon, the Yankees took the song as their own to tease the British "dandy." Today, several decades later, children all over the world can be heard singing the melody—often while eating their noodles.

> "Yankee Doodle went to town
> Riding on a pony;
> Stuck a feather in his hat
> And called it 'Macaroni'!"

The Modern Noodle and How to Cook It

BECAUSE of their versatility, taste, and low cost, noodle, macaroni, and spaghetti consumption is constantly increasing world-wide. In the United States, the estimated per capita intake in 1949 was 4½ pounds. Twenty-five years later, it had more than doubled. In 1974, Americans ate 2 billion pounds. If the mere thought stretches your waistline, consider the average Italian who eats between 60 and 70 pounds of noodles and pasta yearly, with the country's total intake weighing in at over 3 billion pounds. According to National Macaroni Manufacturers Association Executive Secretary Robert Green, in a conversation on April 25, 1977, the estimated per capita consumption for Switzerland is 24 pounds; France comes in third with 14 pounds; West Germany, the United States, and Canada tie with 10 to 10½ pounds; the Scandinavian countries, 3 to 4 pounds; and England brings up the rear with about

1½ pounds. In the last 10 years, the fastest growing market has been Japan, where consumption has dramatically increased. A republic soon to be in the running is the Philippines, where consumption has doubled in the past two years ('74–'76) as a result of improved quality and the sudden growth of noodle eat-in and take-out houses. Consumption is also on the rise in Turkey. You're probably wondering where all these products are coming from. Italy, the largest exporter of dried noodles and pasta, shipped about 130 million pounds in 1974, one-third of which went to the United States. The Oriental countries have begun seriously to export their products to American supermarkets and specialty shops. But when we're talking about 2 billion plus pounds annual consumption in the United States, we haven't even begun to make a dent yet. According to the N.M.M.A. Executive Secretary Green, 20 of the 120-plus manufacturer members produce over three-fourths of America's needs. Only about 70 of these manufacturers employ over 20 people; the others all being mom and pop organizations.

A day in the life of a noodle was fairly primitive until quite recently. Less than 150 years ago, all noodles and pasta were made by foot or hand, and then hung like laundry to dry. In most private households throughout the world, they're still mixed, kneaded, rolled, cut, and dried in the manner of our ancestors.

The birth of pasta machinery is credited to Ferdinand II, King of Naples (1830–59). While visiting a pasta factory, he was appalled by the workers' method of treading the dough in a "madia," or large trough, with bare feet as they kept time to mandolin music. The King ordered the famous engineer Cavaliere (Cesare) Spadaccini to invent a more hygienic way to mix the semolina and water. The scientist's creation was a mechanical man with bronze feet for trodding the pasta. Spadaccini was also commissioned to invent a four-pronged fork for the King and his court to eat this pasta.

About a century later, a patent was filed by the Braibanti family for a machine which included all the stages of pasta manufacturing—mixing, kneading, extruding, and drying in one continuous process. Around the same time (1848) a Frenchman, Antoine Zerega, started the first American pasta factory in Brooklyn. The sole source of power for both mixing and kneading machines was a harnessed horse that walked round and round a vertical shaft.

Noodles and pasta, you've come a long way! Modern manufacturing plants are completely automatic. The semolina is unloaded into storage bins and then transferred to press bins where it is mixed with water. Egg solids are added to make noodle dough, which is kneaded, then pressed through rollers into sheets and cut into shapes. Pasta dough, instead of being pressed, is fed into dies, which are heavy metal discs with holes. The size and shape of the holes determine the size and shape of the finished product. If the die has small holes, each with a steel pin in it, the result will be small, hollow, tubular pasta called macroni. If this pin is bent, the result will be elbow macaroni. Rotary knives cut the dough into the desired length. According to one manufacturer of metal dies, a total of 325 shapes can be manufactured in the United States.

Drying, the next step, is the critical part. The cut dough is carefully conveyed to drying units or rooms. Noodles and short or small pasta shapes are spread on belts; longer items are hung. Once properly dried the products are weighed, packed, sealed and shipped.

The economics of the business today, according to Mr. Green, N.M.M.A. Executive Secretary, is that "the wheat is grown primarily in the upper Midwest, milled in Minneapolis, or shipped by boat to Buffalo for the Eastern market, and the flour is sent to metropolitan areas because it is cheaper to ship the raw materials than the finished goods," which bulk up and become fragile. Hence, he explains, "you have regional producers who serve a market of essentially 100 or 200 miles. The largest macaroni manufacturer in the country is in the metropolitan New York area, and his products are not sold in Chicago.''

When buying noodles and pasta at your local market, select smooth, shiny products. If they are crumbly or broken, chances are they're stale. The well-stocked personal pantry should contain several packages. You'd probably consider my cupboards overburdened. Yet, on the practical side, because they are a dehydrated food noodles and pasta can be stored for a long time in a cool, dry place. Once opened, I reseal, or rebag the unused portions. I use all types of shapes of noodles, macaroni, and spaghetti in and on everything from snacks to desserts. As a general guide, the smaller ones are best for soups, but in a pinch I simply break a handful of long strands.

Besides being blacklisted by dieters, the much-maligned noodle and pasta have been woefully mistreated by cooking them in too little water, over-cooking them, rinsing away much of their nutrition, and by keeping them around too long before serving. And yet, they have still survived as one of the world's favorite foods.

A lot of words have been written on proper cooking directions. The golden rule is—boil rapidly in a lot of salted water and serve immediately. But, of course, there are exceptions. For example, lasagne doesn't always have to be precooked before baking; dry pastinas can be added to soups during the last minutes of simmering; rice-stick noodles can be deep-fried and tossed with a salad; and cellophane noodles should be soaked before woking. Since laws are made for the majority, here are my Ten Commandments of Al Dente. If you read carefully and follow these directions, you should never again suffer a soggy, mushy, or limp noodle.

Ten Commandments of Al Dente

1. In a large, deep, heavy pot (10- to 12-quart capacity is best), heat 6 to 7 quarts of cold water.

2. "Comincia a bollire" (Literally translated "starts to boil"), is an Italian expression used to indicate that the water has come to the proper boiling point. Add 2 table-spoons salt per pound of noodles or pasta. The water should now boil angrily.

3. Add noodles or pasta gradually so that you do not lose the boil. To avoid breaking long strands, place one end of the noodles or pasta in the water and, as they soften, gently push those remaining into the water. Again, be sure the water continues to boil rapidly.

4. Do not cover. Stir frequently and carefully. I use a long, wooden chopstick, but a wooden fork is excellent, too.

5. Don't leave the kitchen!

6. Meanwhile, heat your serving bowl, platter, or indi-vidual plates. Rinse your colander (if using one) with hot water.

7. Within a few minutes, begin testing for doneness. There are no rules for the amount of boiling time. Some dried products take 15 minutes, others 5; fresh take little time. The best way to test is to pull out a few pieces, blow on them, then bite. They should be firm but tender, not crunchy or rubbery. This state is called *al dente,* which translates from Italian as "to the tooth." If you plan to

further bake, sauté, simmer, or fry the noodles or pasta,
cut down the cooking time by about one-third. (I occasionally refer to this as precooking or parboiling.)
8. Place the rinsed colander in the sink, and immediately
drain the noodles or pasta into it. If the pot is too heavy
to lift, lighten the load by removing the greater bulk with
tongs to the colander. Now the pot can be turned and the
remaining noodles or pasta drained. Remember to save
some liquid if the recipe calls for it.
9. Or, instead of draining by pouring, you can remove all
the noodles or pasta with tongs or a spaghetti fork. Shake
the liquid back into the pot, and immediately place the
pasta in serving bowls or plate(s). Whichever method you
employ, drain well. Otherwise, the water will continue the
cooking process and dilute the seasoning and/or sauce.
Rinse noodles or pasta in cold water only if the recipe
suggests it. This is done primarily for use in cold salads.
10. Immediately complete recipe and serve.

Noodles (again, there are exceptions) and pasta swell
up with cooking. What looks like a small amount when
dried goes a long way when cooked. Depending upon
whether they are to be served as a first course, entree, or
accompaniment, allow between 2 to 4 ounces, uncooked, per
person.

Product	Dry Weight	Approximate Cooked Yield
Noodles	8 ounces (about 4 cups)	4 cups
Elbow Macaroni	8 ounces (2 cups)	4½ cups
Spaghetti	8 ounces	5 cups
Small Shells	8 ounces (2 cups)	4 cups

Among the problems I have encountered cooking noodles
is the boiling over of the water. "Le Stop," a small, heat-

proof glass disc, which I purchased from a gourmet cookware catalog, solved my problem. I stick this in the bottom
of my water pot (I have another for my saucepan!) and,
magically, it prevents liquids from boiling over. Before
this I was always blowing on the water's surface to cool it
off while I hastily grabbed for pot-holders to help me pick
the hot pot off the stove top.

I've heard many complaints that noodles and pasta constantly stick together. This shouldn't happen if you are
stirring properly. But you can add 1 tablespoon of salad
oil to the pot as a precaution.

Even though it is best to serve noodles and pasta immediately, sometimes your timing may not work out as
you had hoped. There are several secerts to holding them
once cooked. You can drain off most of the boiling water,
retaining just enough to barely cover, then add a touch
of cold water to reduce the temperature. This will prevent any further cooking, yet keep them warm until
serving time. Or, you can transfer your noodles from
the pot to a colander with a long fork; place the colander
on top of the pot of water, and the steam will keep the
noodles warm. You may want to toss the drained noodles
with salad oil or melted butter so they won't stick
together. Chefs from the Culinary Institute of America,

one of the finest cooking schools in the world, suggest that if you want to hold pasta *"al dente"* for 30 minutes, you should rinse it in cool water and drain well, coil the pasta and return it to the pot. Then, cover the pot with a damp kitchen towel and place in a warm oven (200 degrees).

Whichever method you use to keep your noodles or pasta warm, if you find they have cooled off too much, run boiling water over them quickly, drain again, and add your hot sauce.

Making too many noodles or too much pasta isn't actually a problem at all. Leftovers, which haven't been mixed with anything, can be refrigerated and added to soups; frozen with other leftovers in a casserole; tossed with vegetables, meat, and dressing for a salad; even deep-fried and seasoned for a snack. Whether plain or fancy, with a touch of imagination they can be used as the base for an appetizing dish the next day.

Some of the best noodle and pasta dishes I have eaten were prepared in a tiny, hot backroom, crowded with boxes and ingredients. The place looked more like a Chinese laundry than a kitchen. So, it's not really what equipment you have, but how you use it that counts. However, I still prefer my cooking area with space to stretch, and, for making noodle and pasta dishes, these are some items I just couldn't do without:

Baking dishes and casseroles (oven-proof with covers, assorted sizes, including rectangular shape for lasagne)
Boilable bag-sealer equipment
Bottle opener
Camp cooking equipment
Can opener
Chafing dish
Chopping blocks
Chopsticks (different lengths)

Clam opener or knife
Colanders
Cooling racks
Corkscrew
Double boiler
Deep-frying equipment
Dredgers
Dutch oven

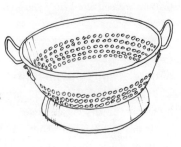

Electric blender
Electric mixer
Electric skillet
Flour sifter
Foil (heavy duty)
Food mill
Food processor
Fondue pot
Forks (wooden and metal)
Freezer containers
Garlic press
Grapefruit knife
Graters (including nutmeg and cheese varieties)
Jar unscrewers
Kitchen scale

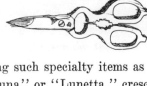

Kitchen shears
Knife sharpener
Knives (variety of, including such specialty items as Chinese cleaver and "Mezzaluna" or "Lunetta," crescent/moon shape for mincing)
Ladles
"Le Stop," boil-over stopper
Measuring cups and spoons (for dry and liquid)
Meat grinder
Meat pounder
Mixing bowls
Molds
Mortar and pestle

Noodle machine (manual and/or electric)
Nut cracker
Oven (including microwave)
Pasta/Noodle machine (manual and/or electric)
Pastry board (wood or marble slab)
Pastry scraper
Pastry wheel (fluted)
Peelers
Pepper mill
Pie crimper

Plastic bags (for storage)
Potholders
Pots and pans (variety, with lids, including large soup ket-
   tle or stockpot)
Ravioli cutter
Ravioli stamp
Ravioli tray
Rolling pin (extra long)
Salad bowls (wood and glass)
Sieve
Skimmers
Slotted spoon

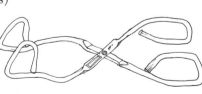

Soufflé molds (assorted sizes)
Spaetzle maker
Spaghetti fork (wood)
Spaghetti pot (with perforated lines)
Spatulas (assorted, including a very heavy metal one for
   stir-frying)
Spoons (wood and metal)
Steaming rack
Strainers (assorted sizes)
Timer
Tongs
Tortellini cutter
Tube pans
Turners

Wax paper
Wire racks
Wire whisks
Wok
Wrap (plastic)

The Basic Noodle

~~~~~~~~~~~~~~~~~~~~

O F A L L the foods I have made from scratch in my kitchen, my favorite is unquestionably the noodle. In about a hour, a simple combination of flour, eggs, some liquid, and an occasional vegetable purée can be turned into a beautiful creation. After a little mixing, kneading, stretching, pulling, resting, rolling, and cutting—"shazam," like magic—I have fresh, light noodles.

I have made noodles by hand—mixing and kneading with my fingers and the heels of my hands, rolling the dough with a long, heavy pin, and cutting the thin sheets into desired sizes and shapes with a sharp knife. And I have made noodles with the aid of machines—mixing the ingredients into a ball in a food processor (within seconds!), then kneading, rolling, and cutting with a noodle or pasta machine. Though I enjoy cooking at the basic level, let the truth be known: I'm very much in favor of these culinary conveniences. Not only do they save time and energy, but the resulting noodles are gorgeously smooth and silky.

There are several noodle machines currently on the market. I have been fortunate to be loaned two manual Atlas models, by Klaus Mortimer of Gourmet Specialties, and by Gary Valenti of Gary Valenti Import-Export. Made in Italy, the Atlas is chrome-plated steel, 6 inches high, 7 inches wide, and weighs 8 pounds, 12 ounces. The noodle cutter attachment is removable to facilitate cleaning and storing. An optional cutter for round spaghetti and curled lasagne can be purchased. The Ampia noodle machine is also imported from Italy. Its basic concept is similar to the Atlas but its roller and cutters are all in one piece. The Italian Altea model, made of heavy chrome-plated steel, is a little larger, $6\frac{1}{4}$ inches in height, $8\frac{1}{2}$ inches in width, $9\frac{1}{2}$ pounds in weight. It kneads dough and rolls it to a choice of 8 thicknesses. (Although the Atlas has only 6, I find them sufficient.) The Altea comes with fine and broad cutters and will even cut soup squares. Other similar metal noodle machines include the Schiller and Asmus unit, the Noodle Chef with extra cutter blades, the Invento unit, and several more specific ravioli and spaetzle makers.

About four times the price of these manual machines is a sleekly-designed electric one, the Bialetti model, also made in Italy. Chuck Williams, owner of Williams-Sonoma, one of my favorite cookery stores, shares with his customers the joy he has had with this machine. ''The rollers on this fancy new machine have a very slight—almost imperceptible—pebbled surface, which gives the finished noodles a correspondingly very slight texture, just enough to hold the sweet butter and freshly grated cheese, or freshly made sauce, whatever it may be . . . Using this electric pasta machine is undeniably great fun.'' *

* Chuck Williams, ''*The Cooks' Almanac*,'' Vol. 3, No. 2, June 1976.

Renowned American cookbook author, lecturer, and teacher James Beard has called this same machine a "revelation." Within 10 or 15 minutes, "it turns out the thinnest, most tender pasta you ever tasted . . . You just make your dough and then knead it by putting it through the plain rollers several times until it is very smooth and the thickness you want. By changing the gauge of the rollers, you can start thick and gradually roll thinner and thinner. Then you change over to the cutting roller and presto, you have pasta!" **

A small, fairly inexpensive unit which I have enjoyed is the Torchio Pasta Maker, by Rawoco, imported from Italy. Made of bright-colored plastic with metal trim, it looks like a food grinder. You feed a small ball of dough into the top, turn the handle and out comes one of four shapes— ravioli or lasagne, macaroni, flat egg noodle, or spaghetti— depending upon your choice of discs. The Barry-Ware Pasta Machine is quite similar.

However you decide to make home-made noodles, the general rule I follow for dough is 1 egg, a scant ¾ cup of flour, a sprinkle of salt and a few drops of warm water, per person.

BASIC NOODLE

SERVES 4 TO 8, DEPENDING

ON COURSE

4 large eggs, lightly beaten
3 cups all-purpose flour (Or you can use your own favorite
flour such as semolina, soy, or whole wheat.)
1 teaspoon salt
4 to 6 tablespoons warm water

** James Beard, "Plugging in a Pasta Machine," as appeared in *The Los Angeles Times*, Food Section, 1976.

If using a food processor: With the plastic mixing blade in place, turn on the machine; add the eggs. Sift together the flour and salt and add to the machine through the feeder. Continue to process, adding water as needed, until you have a smooth, firm ball of dough.

If doing by hand: Sift the flour and salt together into a bowl or onto a board. Make a well in the center of the flour and add the eggs. Gradually work the eggs into the flour, adding water as necessary, until you have a stiff dough. With both hands pulling and pressing, knead the dough until it is smooth, or for about 20 minutes. Cut the dough in half, form each half into a ball, and wrap each ball with wax paper to keep air out. Let the dough rest for 30 minutes. Note: Some recipes instruct you to roll out these balls, then cover them with a kitchen towel and allow to rest.

Work with one ball of dough at a time, keeping the other wrapped. Roll out on a floured surface as thin as possible. Cut into desired shapes and sizes.

To cut noodles by hand: Some noodles, such as tagliatelli, require you to roll up the dough jelly-roll style and slice with a sharp knife into thin strips (⅛ inch for tagliatelli). Other noodles may require that you roll out the dough and cut into sheets (ravioli), strips (lasagne), rectangles or

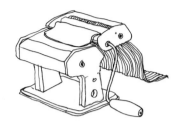

squares (cannelloni).

If using a roller-style machine: Attach or clamp it to your kitchen counter, and set the rollers as wide apart as possible. Divide the dough into smaller balls. Keeping the unused portions covered, run one piece through the first stop, 5 to 10 times, to knead until smooth, folding in half each time. I keep a small bowl of water and a pile of sifted flour handy. If the dough becomes sticky, sprinkle it with flour as you fold it in half. If it is too crumbly, work with some water, pushing the dough together. Continue at the first setting until the dough becomes smooth and elastic. Get all the dough up to this stage, sprinkling flour on each sheet and stacking them. Then, bring the rollers together one notch and roll the dough through the machine again. Continue this process until all the dough has passed through this width. Reduce the space again one notch and put the dough through the roller again. Continue until the dough is as thin as you desire it. At this point, some recipes suggest that you dry the dough on kitchen towels for up to 30 minutes before cutting it. Now, put the silky sheets of dough through the cutter blades. You can catch the noodles as they fall or let them pile up.

When all are cut, take your hand- or machine-made noodles and toss them with your fingers onto a lightly floured surface (the kitchen counter is fine!) to separate them and to allow them to dry.

You can use the noodles immediately, but they are best when allowed to dry slightly. For fresh noodles, let dry up to an hour, then boil them very quickly or quick-freeze them for later use. To dry them for storage, let the noodles sit on a lightly floured surface for 12 hours, or overnight. Then package in air-tight containers.

Vegetable purées are used to make colored noodles. The most popular is spinach, for green noodles, although I've also used beets for pink noodles. When adding a vegetable purée make sure it is as dry as possible. Otherwise, you will be adding much more flour than you really want, resulting in pasty noodles lacking the proper spinach flavor.

BASIC GREEN NOODLE
SERVES 4 TO 8, DEPENDING
ON COURSE

2 eggs, lightly beaten
One 10-ounce package frozen, chopped spinach, defrosted,
*   puréed, and thoroughly drained*
2 to 2½ cups flour
½ teaspoon salt

If using a food processor: First combine the eggs and spinach, then add the flour and salt to make a dough. If doing by hand: sift the flour and salt together, make a well and add the eggs and the spinach. Proceed as in the Basic Noodle recipe.

PROBLEM SOLVING FOR HOMEMADE NOODLES

1. If you're a beginner, don't try it in damp weather. The extra moisture in the air causes lots of problems.
2. As a general guide to follow, don't use more than 1 cup of flour per large egg. Some recipes even call for extra whole eggs or egg yolks.

3. If the ball of dough is hard, crumbly, and not smooth, it usually means that there is too much flour for the number of eggs. Don't panic. To establish a proper balance, add warm water, a little at a time.

4. When making green noodles, don't worry if the color is not evenly distributed at first. Proper kneading and rolling will take care of this.

5. During the kneading, lightly flour your hands and board frequently.

6. After the dough is rolled out paper thin, you can hang it or let it sit to dry slightly, but do not let it become too brittle to cut.

7. To clean noodle machines, most manufacturers suggest using only a long brush, no water or soaps. I use a baby bottle brush to clean my machines. Then I let them sit on the kitchen counter for several hours and check later to see if any excess dough has escaped my first cleaning. If any dough has dried to the machine, it can easily be shaken off.

If you are unable to locate a store which carries these noodle and pasta machines, write to:

Klaus Mortimer
Gourmet Specialties
2250 McKinnon Avenue
San Francisco, Ca. 94124

O R

Gary Valenti
55–72 61st Street
Box 151
Maspeth, Queens, N.Y. 11378

The directory on pages 321–24 lists several gourmet cookery stores which have catalogs and mail order departments.

The Oriental Noodle

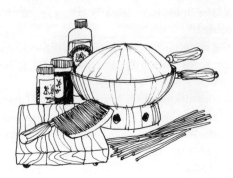

NOODLES are as basic to Oriental cuisine as pasta is to the Italian and macaroni to the American. Beyond their importance as a food staple, noodles symbolize longevity to the Chinese and good luck to the Japanese. They are traditionally served at Chinese birthday parties instead of cake. A soba (noodle) course is festively prepared for a Japanese New Year feast.

Oriental noodles are manufactured in a variety of widths, from flat ribbons to very thin, delicate strings. They are always very long, often coiled like scouring pads. American markets generally display an extensive array of dried and fresh Oriental noodles. An Oriental specialty market will offer you an even greater selection.

To cook Oriental noodles, follow the package instructions, which generally suggest that you add the noodles slowly to rapidly boiling, salted water, separating the strands with a pair of chopsticks. Test frequently for doneness. Most will be tender within a few minutes. If other ingredients are to be added, or the noodles are to be recooked, set them aside before they are fully done. Leftover noodles can be used in many dishes, including soup and chao mein (fried noodles). With the exception of transparent noodles, which are soaked in hot water to soften, and rice stick noodles, which are often deep-fried in oil without previous cooking, you will find Oriental noodle preparation similar to the more familiar spaghetti.

Unlike those of other cuisines, Oriental noodles traditionally do not have to be served immediately when cooked. They may be sauced and eaten at once, or you can store them for later use. To save, drain and rinse noodles in cold running water, add 1 tablespoon of oil per pound to prevent sticking, and refrigerate in an air-tight container.

Since many Oriental noodles have several formal names, this glossary will help explain which to use in different dishes. The following abbreviations are used to distinguish noodles of various nationalities:

Chinese (C)
Japanese (J)
Korean (K)
Philippine (P)
Thai (T)

Bai Fun (*C*) : Translucent noodles.
Banshu Somen (*J*) : Noodles made from wheat flour. Each 1-pound commercial package generally contains five smaller packets of noodles.
Bijon (*P*) : Thin rice noodles, also called rice sticks, long rice, mai fun, maifun.
Cellophane Noodles (*C*) : Also called translucent noodles, shining noodles, silver noodles, transparent noodles, bean threads, and vermicelli. Made from mung bean

flour (sometimes wheat). Hung in the sun to dry as last stage in factory production. Look as if made from cellophane. Sold packaged in quantities generally from 2 to 8 ounces. To cook: Place in cold water, bring liquid to a boil, cover and set aside for 10 to 30 minutes. Drain. Become gelatinous, moist, and slippery when cooked.

Chao (Chow) Mein (C): Fried noodles.

Chiaotze (C): Dough for wrappings.

Chow Fun (C): Wide, flat noodles, traditionally made of rice. Also called Foon Tiu Mien.

Dang Myun (K): Dried vermicelli.

Dim Sum (C): Steamed dumplings.

Fan Si (C): Translucent noodles.

Haar Chee Mein (Meen) (C): Resembles spaghetti. Flavoring is usually added to basic noodle dough, for example, shrimp.

Harusame (J): Translucent noodles. Very small yam thread.

Higamugi (J): Thin udon. (See p. 33)

Jao-Tze (Jaotze) (C): Similar to a ravioli or dumpling.

Kishimen (J): Wide, thin udon (See p. 33). To cook: boil 1 minute, then simmer about 10, stirring constantly.

Lo Mein (C): Fresh egg noodles. Uncooked 4 inches x 8 inches, closely wound together. When cooked, shoelace appearance. Whitish color, doughy. Will keep several days in refrigerator, months in freezer. Available in refrigerator section of markets.

Mai Fun (Maifun, Mi Fun: My Fun) (C): Also called rice sticks and thin sticks. Opaque white noodles. Similar to spaghetti. Brittle, dry and hard, but become smooth and shiny when cooked.

Mee Krob (T): Crunchy noodles.

Mein (Mien) (C): General word for noodles. May be preceded with another word to indicate particular variety.

Menrui (J): General word for noodles.

Ning Fun (C) : Translucent noodles.

Pancit (P) : Rice stick noodles.

Saifun (J) : Very small, thin yam noodles.

Shirataki (J) : Translucent noodles. Also called ''Devil's Foot Noodle.'' Made from root plants, such as yams. Resemble Chinese bean thread noodles.

Soba (J) : Buckwheat noodles. Slender, green. Flavor and color from buckwheat flour.

Somen (J) : Thin, straight, threadlike vermicelli. Made from wheat. Available in a variety of colors—yellow (egg yolk), pink (strawberries), green (powdered green tea), white, gold (citron). Cooking time generally 2 to 3 minutes.

Suey Gow (C) : Sui Maai skins or wrappers (circles).

Sui Maai (Mai) (C) : Similar to won tons. Generally steamed ''flower buds.''

Udon (J) : Wide, flat, straight ribbonlike noodles. Made of wheat or corn flour. Cooking time generally 10 to 12 minutes. Come in several widths.

Won Ton (C) : Dumpling or skin wrapper. Twelve-ounce packages of fresh squares available in refrigerator or freezer section of most markets.

Yee Fu Mein (Meen) (C) : ''Picnic'' or ''Tourist'' noodles. Instant, dehydrated noodles, come in blocks that are twisted or coiled, packaged with envelope of dry soup seasoning. Ready to eat within a few seconds to minutes.

If you are having difficulty finding local stores to purchase your Oriental ingredients and cooking utensils, check pages 321–24 for a list of several stores that will fill mail orders. When writing to them, you might ask if they have a catalog and price list for future use.

Basic Noodle Dough recipes (pages 25–28) can be used to make most Oriental noodles. These are some more specific recipes.

CHINESE EGG NOODLES

SERVES 4 TO 8, DEPENDING
ON COURSE

4 eggs
2 cups all-purpose flour
Cornstarch

In a large mixing bowl, lightly beat the eggs with a fork. Gradually add the flour, and mix well. Knead this mixture into a soft dough. Cover the dough with a damp kitchen towel, and let it stand about 15 minutes. Knead again for several minutes. Sprinkle board and rolling pin with cornstarch. Roll dough out as thin as possible. Fold dough over several times. Cut across the folds, slicing noodles into desired widths. (A noodle machine can be used for kneading, rolling, and slicing. See pages 23–29.) Cook for approximately 2 minutes in boiling, salted water.

JAPANESE UDON

SERVES 4 TO 10, DEPENDING
ON COURSE

4 cups all-purpose flour (or whole-wheat flour)
1 teaspoon salt
1 egg yolk
Cold water
Additional flour

Sift the flour and salt together into a large bowl. Add egg yolk and enough water to make a stiff paste. Knead thoroughly. Cover the dough with a damp kitchen towel, and let it stand 30 minutes. Sprinkle board and rolling pin with additional flour. Roll out dough until it is paper thin. Fold into a long roll and cut into strips, $\frac{1}{10}$-inch wide. When unrolled, the dough strips should be at least 12 inches long. Cook 3 to 4 minutes in boiling, salted water.

WON TON SKINS

APPROXIMATELY 6 DOZEN SKINS

2 cups all-purpose flour   *½ cup cold water*
1 teaspoon salt   *Cornstarch*
2 eggs, lightly beaten   *Additional flour*

Sift flour and salt together onto a board or into a mixing bowl. In a small mixing bowl, beat the eggs and water together. Blend the eggs into the flour. Knead until the dough is very smooth and elastic. Divide the dough into four pieces. Work with one piece at a time. (Keep the others covered with plastic wrap.) Roll the dough on a floured board (or sprinkle cornstarch on the board) with a lightly floured rolling pin. Roll out dough into rectangles $\frac{1}{16}$-inch thick, and cut into 3-inch squares. Stack the squares, sprinkling cornstarch between each layer. To save, wrap in plastic and refrigerate for about a week, or freeze for considerably longer. Brush off the cornstarch before using.

STUFFED NOODLES

In Northern China, where the staple is wheat flour, deep-fried won tons are generally dipped in a vinegar sauce, while in Southern China they are deep-fried and served with mustard and sweet-and-sour dressings; braised; shallow-fried; steamed; or boiled in soups. Here are a variety of fillings for stuffed won tons:

SHRIMP-AND-PORK-FILLED FRIED WON TON

TO FILL 35 TO 40 WON TON SKINS

(SEE PAGE 37)

SERVES 6 TO 10, DEPENDING ON COURSE

2 tablespoons cooking oil
½ pound ground pork
3 scallions, chopped fine
1 teaspoon fine-chopped
  fresh ginger
½ pound raw shrimp,
  cleaned and chopped
  fine
2 tablespoons fine-chopped
  water chestnuts

2 tablespoons soy sauce
1 tablespoon sake (rice
  wine) or dry sherry
1 tablespoon Chinese oyster
  sauce
¼ teaspoon salt
Dash sugar
1 tablespoon cornstarch,
  dissolved in 1 table-
  spoon water

Set wok over high heat; pour in cooking oil. When hot, add pork, scallions, and ginger. Stir-fry * until the meat loses its raw color. Add shrimp, water chestnuts, soy sauce, sake, oyster sauce, salt, and sugar. Continue to stir-fry another 2 minutes, then thicken with the cornstarch. Remove to a bowl and cool.

PORK AND SPROUTS WON TON

TO FILL 24 WON TON SKINS

(SEE PAGE 37)

SERVES 4 TO 6, DEPENDING
ON COURSE

½ pound ground pork
5 scallions, diced
¼ pound fresh bean
  sprouts, chopped
⅛ teaspoon cayenne pow-
  der

¼ teaspoon salt
1 tablespoon minced fresh
  ginger
1 tablespoon soy sauce
1 tablespoon sake
2 tablespoons cooking oil

* If you are not familiar with stir-frying, check page 60 for instructions.

Place all the ingredients except the cooking oil in a mixing bowl; mix well with your fingers. Set wok over high heat; add oil. When hot, add meat mixture and stir-fry * in wok about 5 minutes. Remove to a bowl and cool.

BEEF-FILLED WON TON

TO FILL 30 TO 35 WON TON SKINS

(SEE BELOW)

SERVES 6 TO 10, DEPENDING

ON COURSE

¾ *pound ground beef*	*1 clove garlic, minced*
½ *cup fine-shredded*	½ *teaspoon salt*
cabbage	*2 tablespoons oyster sauce*
¼ *cup minced scallions*	*2 tablespoons cooking oil*
¼ *cup chopped fresh*	
mushrooms	

Follow instructions for Pork and Sprouts Won Ton, (page 36).

TO STUFF WON TONS:

When filling is cool, place 1 teaspoon in center of each skin. Fold one corner up over the filling at an angle to make two triangles slightly askew. Pull bottom corners of

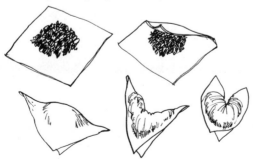

* If you are not familiar with stir-frying, check page 60 for instructions.

the triangles gently down below the base. Overlap the tops of the two corners slightly and pinch them together, using cold water to seal tightly.

To deep-fry, heat a quantity of cooking oil in a pot or wok. When hot (375 degrees), drop in 5 or 6 won tons at a time and fry until golden brown. Drain on paper towels, and serve with Plum Sauce and Chinese hot mustard, both of which are available at most markets.

Similar to won tons, Sui Maai (Mai) are steamed, not fried, "flower buds." They are delicately mild in flavor and, therefore, are classically served with a spicy hot chili sauce. Their skins are circular rather than square, but if "suey gow" wrappers are not available they can be approximated by trimming the corners off the 3-inch square won ton skins into slightly smaller circles.

SUI MAAI WITH SHRIMP,
PORK & VEGETABLE FILLING
(Steamed Dumplings)

TO FILL 30 SUI MAAI SKINS
SERVES 6 TO 10, DEPENDING
ON COURSE

½ *pound raw shrimp, cleaned and chopped fine*
½ *pound ground pork*
4 *large Chinese dried mushrooms, soaked 30 minutes in warm water, drained and chopped fine*

½ *cup bamboo fine-chopped shoots*
1 *tablespoon sake*
1 *teaspoon salt*
Dash white pepper
½ *teaspoon sugar*
1 *tablespoon soy sauce*
1 *tablespoon cornstarch*

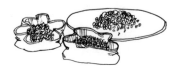

In a large mixing bowl, place all the ingredients (except the skins) and use your fingers to combine all the flavorings. Place 1 teaspoon of filling in the center of each skin. With your fingers under the skin, squeeze the top together to make a flower-bud shape. Place about 10 to 15 dumplings on an oiled platter. Fill your wok or large steaming pot with about 2 inches of water; place a steaming rack in the center. Bring water to a boil and place plate with dumplings on rack. Cover pot and steam for 10 minutes. Continue until all dumplings are cooked. Serve as an appetizer, snack, or luncheon dish with Szechwan chili sauce.

Another member of the Chinese dumpling family is "Jao-Tze." The wrappings must be made by hand. Although they require a lot of time-consuming labor, Jao-Tze can be made a day in advance, placed on a tray sprinkled with cornstarch, covered with a damp cloth, and refrigerated until final cooking. They are popular both fried, "Guo-Tieh," and steamed, "Shui-Jiao," but I prefer them crispy with a vinegar-soy sauce for dipping.

JAO-TZE

MAKES APPROXIMATELY 3 DOZEN

WRAPPING:

2 cups all-purpose flour	*⅔ to 1 cup boiling water*
¼ teaspoon salt	

CABBAGE & PORK FILLING:

⅔ pound Chinese celery	*½ teaspoon salt*
cabbage	*½ teaspoon sugar*
½ pound ground pork	*1½ teaspoons fine-chopped*
1 tablespoon sake	*fresh ginger*
2 tablespoons sesame oil	*3 scallions, chopped fine*

To make wrapping: Place flour and salt in a large mixing bowl, add boiling water and mix as you would a pie crust. Knead until smooth, about 5 minutes. Cover with a damp kitchen towel and let stand in a warm, not hot, place for at least 30 minutes.

After filling has been made, remove dough from bowl and knead again on a floured board for 3 more minutes to smooth it out. Divide into 4 parts. Roll each part like a sausage, about 10 inches long and 1 inch wide. Cut each ''sausage'' into 10 pieces. Flatten each piece with the palm of your hand and roll it out, from the center to the edge, into a thin circle, about 3 inches in diameter.

The filling requires several hours of preparation: Cut off tough end of cabbage. Cut cabbage lengthwise into 2 sections. Bring a large pot of water to a boil, drop cabbage in and cook for 1 minute. Rinse immediately with cold water and drain. Dry the cabbage uncovered for 2 hours, then chop fine.

Place pork in a mixing bowl and add sake; mix together. Add sesame oil, salt, sugar, ginger, scallions, and dried, chopped cabbage. Mix thoroughly and set aside.

Place a heaping teaspoon of filling in the center of each circle of dough. Fold dough into a half-moon shape, gathering the open edge like curtain pleats. Make certain each dumpling is tightly sealed.

To fry: Place wok over high heat and add enough oil to coat the surface. Arrange about 12 dumplings in the wok, pour in ½ cup hot water, cover, and cook over medium-to-high heat for 5 minutes, or until water evaporates. Once steamed, uncover; add another tablespoon of oil around the edges and fry dumplings for 2 more minutes, or until nicely browned. Carefully turn upside down on a plate and serve with soy sauce and vinegar.

To steam: Place a steaming rack in your wok; fill wok with water. Place dumplings on a greased plate. Bring water to a rapid boil, set in plate with dumplings, cover, and steam about 10 minutes. Transfer to a serving plate and serve with soy sauce and vinegar.

S O U P S

Although American tastes prefer the soup course as one of the first to whet the appetite, Oriental soups are served traditionally at the end of the meal to promote proper digestion; as the main dish for a light meal or luncheon; or, occasionally, as a mid-meal course to clear the palate.

Probably the most famous of Oriental soups is composed of won tons simmered in chicken broth. Unlike fried won tons, those for soup are stuffed with raw filling. Place a teaspoon of your favorite won ton stuffing (uncooked) in the center of the wrapper and fold according to instructions on page 37.

WON TON SOUP

SERVES 6

2 to 3 dozen filled won tons
4 to 5 cups chicken broth
2 teaspoons soy sauce
3 scallion tops, sliced thin

Add stuffed won tons, a few at a time, to a kettle of boiling water. After they rise to the top, simmer for 4 minutes, then drain. Heat chicken broth and season with soy sauce. Divide soup among bowls, add won tons to each, and garnish with scallion tops, or won tons can be added to broth for final simmering.

Tempura was not originally an Oriental preparation. The Portuguese Jesuit missionaries who lived in Japan in the 1500s ate a deep-fried, battered-shrimp dish on re-

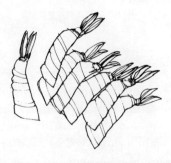

ligious days when meat was forbidden. The Japanese refined the method, using a lighter batter and including other foods.

A favorite Japanese luncheon dish is Tempura Soba in which fresh noodles are cooked in broth, drained into individual, large soup bowls and topped with a piece of tempura shrimp, chicken, or vegetable.

TEMPURA SOBA

SERVES 4 TO 6

TEMPURA BATTER:

1 egg yolk
⅔ cup ice-cold water
⅓ cup all-purpose flour
⅓ cup cornstarch
2 teaspoons sugar
2 teaspoons dry mustard
⅛ teaspoon baking soda

Cooking oil for deep-
    frying
4 to 8 cleaned and raw
    giant prawns
1 quart chicken broth,
    heated
1 pound fresh cooked soba
    (see page 33)

The trick to the tempura is to get the batter as cold as possible and the oil very hot for deep-frying (375 degrees). Mix all the batter ingredients together and refrigerate until thoroughly chilled. I prefer to make this batter several hours in advance and store it in the refrigerator until needed.

Coat one prawn at a time in the batter, deep-fry (the batter should explode as it hits the oil) until golden, remove and keep warm as you continue with the other prawns.

Add the home-made or store-bought fresh soba to the pot of hot chicken broth. Cook noodles until tender. (This should take about a minute as fresh soba is already soft.) Remove the noodles to individual soup bowls, top with one cooked tempura prawn, and carefully pour the broth into the bowls around the tempura until the noodles are barely covered.

A well-prepared Oriental dish appeals to three senses— taste, sight and smell. In this recipe, the sesame oil adds the fragrance.

VERMICELLI SOUP

SERVES 2

2 cups rich chicken broth
1 ounce vermicelli, which has been soaked in hot water to
*   soften, then drained*
1 teaspoon soy sauce
2 teaspoons chopped scallion tops
2 teaspoons sesame oil

Heat chicken broth in a soup pot. Add vermicelli and stir; add soy sauce and allow soup to simmer about two minutes. Add scallion tops; stir. Continue to simmer another minute. Remove to individual serving bowls. Garnish each one with one teaspoon of sesame oil.

The Hunan school of Chinese cooking is noted for its spiciness. This delicate Beef and Noodle Soup is sparked with dry chili peppers and pungent, fermented black beans.

HUNAN BEEF & NOODLE SOUP
SERVES 6 TO 8 AS A FIRST COURSE

MARINADE:

2 teaspoons sake

2 teaspoons cornstarch

2 teaspoons cooking oil

¾ pound top sirloin steak, sliced paper-thin across the grain

2 tablespoons cooking oil

3 tablespoons fermented black beans, rinsed and dried with paper towels

6 small dried hot chili peppers

1 tablespoon minced garlic

1½ quarts chicken broth

1 tablespoon soy sauce

2 teaspoons sugar

4 ounces bean thread noodles, soaked in warm water for 15 minutes, drained and cut into 6-inch lengths

4 scallions, cut into 2-inch lengths

1 teaspoon sesame oil

In a small bowl, combine all marinade ingredients, add meat and mix well. Heat wok over high flame. Add cooking oil, black beans, chili peppers and garlic. Stir-fry * until peppers begin to brown, about 2 minutes. Add chicken broth, soy sauce, sugar, and noodles. Bring to a boil; stir in the meat with its marinade and the scallions. Continue to cook soup, stirring occasionally, until meat is no longer pink, about 3 to 5 minutes. Ladle into serving bowls. Garnish each with a few drops of sesame oil.

* If you are not familiar with stir-frying, check page 60 for instructions.

PORK BALLS WITH WATERCRESS SOUP

SERVES 6 AS A FIRST COURSE

1 pound ground pork
1 tablespoon minced fresh
  ginger
½ teaspoon sugar
1 tablespoon cornstarch
Dash of salt
1 tablespoon sake
1 medium egg, lightly
  beaten
Four 10¾-ounce cans
  condensed chicken
  broth (A rich chicken

broth is essential. If
you wish to use 6 cups
of home-made, elimi-
nate the following
water.)
1 cup water
½ pound watercress,
  trimmed and chopped
3 ounces cellophane
  noodles, soaked in
  warm water for 30
  minutes

Place pork, ginger, sugar, cornstarch, salt, sake, and beaten egg in a large mixing bowl. Using your hands, combine all the ingredients and form into balls the size of golf balls (about 12 to 15). Arrange balls on a steamer plate above boiling water, cover and steam for 20 minutes.

In a large soup pot, pour the chicken broth and water. Bring to a boil and reduce to a simmer. Continue simmering the broth while preparing the watercress.

Place the watercress in a bowl and add enough boiling water to cover. Let sit for 3 minutes and rinse immediately in cold water to stop the cooking process. Set aside.

Add the watercress and soaked noodles to the chicken broth. Add the steamed pork balls. Continue to simmer for another three minutes to combine the flavors.

Every Oriental family has its own rendition of Chicken Soup with Noodles. This is one of my favorites.

˙CHICKEN SOUP WITH NOODLES

SERVES 4

¼ *cup memmi (packaged*
    soup base, available at
    Japanese markets)
3 cups water
2 cups boned raw chicken
    breasts, cut into bite-
    size pieces

2 scallions, shredded to
    matchstick size
4 fresh snow peas (pea
    pods)
1 pound udon (see page
    34), cooked and
    drained

Pour soup base and water into a soup pot and bring to a boil. Add the chicken, cover, and simmer until done, about 10 minutes. Add the scallions and snow peas; stir, and immediately remove from heat. Divide noodles among four soup bowls (donburi). Pour soup over noodles.

One of the cutest television commercials I've seen features a lively, cherub-like youngster slurping a whole bowl of instant Oriental noodles and soup. Neighborhood, Oriental, and specialty markets offer a great selection of packaged noodles with instant soup or seasoning mixes. You can follow the directions and serve simply as is or with a garnish of meat, eggs, seafood, vegetables, or leftovers. For a man-size luncheon dish like the following, I add a touch of seasoning.

OYSTER SAUCE NOODLE SOUP

SERVES 2 AS A LUNCHEON, 4 AS
A FIRST COURSE

One 6½-ounce package shirataki or yee fu mein noodles,
cooked according to directions, reducing boiling time by
1 to 2 minutes, drained
2 teaspoons oyster sauce
1 tablespoon cooking oil
1 to 2 teaspoons chopped scallions
Hard-boiled eggs (optional)

While noodles are cooking, prepare the instant soup according to package directions. Add oyster sauce to soup.

Heat wok over high heat, add oil and cooked noodles; stir-fry * a few seconds to coat noodles with oil. Add heated soup, continuing to stir for another 1 to 2 minutes. Ladle soup into individual bowls. Scatter chopped scallions on top. You can also garnish with sliced hard-boiled eggs.

This Egg Drop Soup made with fresh spinach is fresh tasting and lightly seasoned. The tree-ears, or cloud-ears,

* If you are not familiar with stir-frying, check page 60 for instructions.

which resemble dried mushrooms, are a dried fungus that grows on the bark of trees.

SPINACH EGG DROP SOUP

SERVES 4 TO 6

1 tablespoon dried tree-ears or cloud ears, soaked in hot water for ½ hour
1 quart chicken stock
2 cups fresh spinach, cleaned and torn into small pieces
1 tablespoon soy sauce

1½ tablespoons corn-starch, dissolved in 2 tablespoons water
1 ounce saifun (see page 33), soaked ½ hour, drained, cut into 3 to 4-inch lengths
2 eggs, lightly beaten

After tree-ears have soaked, drain and remove tough stems. In a medium size soup pot, over medium heat, bring stock to a boil. Add tree-ears, spinach, and soy sauce. Continue to cook for a few seconds, or until the spinach begins to soften. Thicken soup with cornstarch, stirring with a chopstick. When soup returns to a boil, add saifun. Remove from heat and slowly pour egg in a steady stream into the soup, stirring constantly and carefully with a chopstick. Serve as soon as eggs are set.

SALADS

Chinese chicken salad has always been one of my favorite dishes to make and to eat. The secret is in the combination of textures. And the dressing, unlike the mayonnaise-based one used in American chicken salad, is lighter and spicier.

MAIFUN WITH CHICKEN

SERVES 4

Cooking oil for deep-
* frying*
1 to 2 ounces maifun (see
* page 32)*

1 head iceberg lettuce,
* shredded*
½ pound cooked chicken,
* shredded*

SOY-VINEGAR-OIL DRESSING:

2 teaspoons soy sauce
3 tablespoons rice vinegar
1 tablespoon sesame oil

¼ cup salad oil
2 tablespoons sugar
½ teaspoon dry mustard

Pour about 3 inches of cooking oil into a large pot, and heat to 375 to 400 degrees. Break maifun into small portions, about 3 inches long. Drop a small handful into the hot oil; they will puff within seconds. Turn the noodles, using two spoons, so that they cook on all sides. Remove the maifun as soon as they stop crackling, and place them on paper towels to drain. Continue this procedure until all noodles are cooked.

Place the lettuce in a salad bowl. Top with the chicken; then add the fried noodles.

Combine all dressing ingredients in a jar. Shake well to mix.

Pour dressing over salad. Toss gently, and serve.

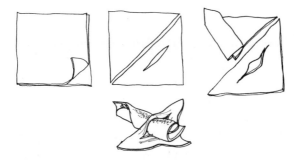

In the middle of bustling Century City, Los Angeles, is
Jade West, one of the finest Chinese restaurants in Southern California. The decor and china have been selected
with royal taste. Their chicken salad is tossed at your table
for all to enjoy its preparation.

TOSSED SHREDDED CHICKEN
SALAD JADE WEST

SERVES 4

Cooking oil for deep-
  frying
1 pound white meat of
  chicken (breasts pre-
  ferred), cut into
  chunks
2 ounces rice noodles
1 cup hoi sin sauce
  (available at specialty
  markets)

5 teaspoons fine-crushed
  almonds
Pinch of salt
1 tablespoon sesame seeds
½ head iceberg lettuce, cut
  into strips
4 sprigs cilantro (Chinese
  parsley), chopped
6 scallions (bulb and white
  stem only), chopped

Heat cooking oil in a large pot for deep-frying (about
375 degrees). Add chicken a few chunks at a time, and
deep-fry for 5 minutes. Drain the cooked chicken on paper
towels. Cut chicken into two-inch strips, lengthwise.

Add the noodles to the hot oil a handful at a time. When
they are golden and puffed, remove and drain on paper
towels.

Place chicken strips in a large wooden salad bowl. Add
mustard, hoi sin sauce, almonds, salt, and sesame seeds, and
mix well. Add lettuce, cilantro, scallions, and the fried
noodles. Toss thoroughly, but take care not to overtoss, lest
the salad become soggy.

Pancit, a rice stick noodle, puffs beautifully when deep-
fried. Besides using it as part of your salad, save some to

garnish a hot dish. If you have any extras, salt them lightly for a snack. My young son eats them by the fistful.

One evening I prepared this salad for close friends, Bob and Kitty Hilton. I first met Bob when I was a guest on his television talk show. He was a fun person to cook for then, and through the years I have continued to enjoy preparing unusual dishes for him.

This dressing is delicate and excellent to use on other salads, too.

PANCIT SALAD
SERVES 4 TO 6 AS A FIRST COURSE

1 ounce pancit, broken into smaller pieces, deep-fried in hot oil a few at a time, and drained on paper towels
1½ cups coarse-chopped watercress

1 medium cucumber, peeled, sliced thin, and quartered
6 scallions, chopped
1½ cups bean sprouts, chopped

PANCIT DRESSING:
3 tablespoons soy sauce
1 tablespoon rice wine vinegar
¼ teaspoon minced fresh ginger

2 tablespoons sesame seeds
Dash sesame oil (for flavor, very special)
Fresh-ground black pepper, to taste

In a large wooden salad bowl, mix together the noodles, watercress, cucumber, scallions, and bean sprouts. In a small bowl, combine all the salad dressing ingredients. Pour dressing over salad. Toss carefully a few times.

When Cathie Calvert, an associate editor of *Mademoiselle,* visited me from New York City for an interview, I invited her to lunch. We sat and talked for hours over a

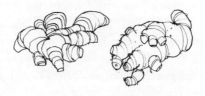

salad of fresh California vegetables, seafood, and Oriental noodles.

SEAFOOD PANCIT SALAD

SERVES 4 TO 6 AS A FIRST COURSE
OR 2 TO 3 AS A MAIN COURSE

1 ounce pancit (see pages 50–51)
Cooking oil for deep-frying
4 giant mushrooms (about ¼ pound), sliced very thin *
6 large scallions with a little of the green portion, sliced thin
½ cup chopped watercress
½ hothouse-style cucumber (with thin skin), unpeeled, sliced very

thin.* (If substituting regular cucumber, scrape off a little skin and allow to dry on paper towels to remove excess water.)
3 ounces cooked large shrimp, rinsed with salt, lemon juice, and water to freshen
1 ounce crabmeat, shredded
1 recipe for Pancit Dressing (see page 51)

Break noodles into smaller pieces. Heat cooking oil in a wok or deep pot to 375 degrees. Deep-fry a small portion of noodles at a time. They will puff up almost immediately;

---

* To slice the mushrooms and cucumber very thin, I use my food processor with slicing blade. If you do not own one, use a very sharp slicing knife.

when golden, remove with strainer onto paper towels to drain off excess oil. Set aside for a few minutes until salad is completed.

Place mushrooms, scallions, watercress, and cucumbers in a salad bowl. Toss lightly, adding the shrimp and crabmeat. Pour in dressing; toss again. Prior to serving, top with noodles and gently toss again.

To complete the luncheon, I served wedges of fresh pineapple (with the skin still on for appearance) and Japanese tea cakes.

Although won ton skins are generally stuffed, you can shred them to matchstick size and use them in a salad.

WON TON CHICKEN SALAD

SERVES 4 TO 8

Preheat oven to 375 degrees

*1 small roasting chicken
    (about 2 pounds)
1 cup teriyaki sauce (use
    your favorite or the
    following recipe *)
2 teaspoons sesame seeds
8 scallions, shredded into
    1-inch lengths*

*1 tablespoon sesame oil
1 tablespoon dry mustard
Salt and pepper
1 tablespoon hoi sin sauce
One 8-ounce package won
    ton skins, shredded
Cooking oil for deep-
    frying*

Marinate the chicken in teriyaki sauce in refrigerator for 3 to 4 hours. Remove chicken from marinade and roast it in a preheated 375 degree oven until tender (about 1½ hours), basting occasionally with the marinade. Reserve extra marinade.

---

* Teriyaki Sauce: 1 cup mirin (sweet sake), 1 cup chicken stock, and 1 cup soy sauce, all mixed together. Pour into a bottle and refrigerate. It will keep for several weeks.

Meanwhile, place sesame seeds in an unoiled heavy skillet, and toast them over high heat, shaking constantly, for 1 to 2 minutes. (Toasted sesame seeds are great for all salads!)

When chicken is cooked, shred it, including the skin, into fine pieces about 1 inch in length. Place chicken pieces in a salad bowl with scallions, toasted sesame seeds, sesame oil, mustard, salt and pepper to taste, hoi sin sauce, and a dash of the reserved teriyaki sauce. Toss to mix well.

Deep-fry shredded won ton skins, a few slices at a time, in hot cooking oil (375 degrees). Drain on paper towels. Add warm won tons to salad, and toss again.

In summer, the Japanese enjoy cold dishes, especially those made with noodles. If you want to serve this as a main dish, you may add slices of cooked, cold omelet or ham. The recipe as given is very light. The dressing adds a touch of sweetness.

CHILLED BUCKWHEAT NOODLES WITH CUCUMBERS AND MUSHROOMS
SERVES 4 TO 6 AS FIRST COURSE

½ cup rice vinegar
1 teaspoon salad oil
½ cup and 2 tablespoons
   soy sauce
½ cup beef broth
4 tablespoons sugar
4 large dried mushrooms,
   soaked 15 minutes in
   warm water, center

core cut out, shredded
½ pound buckwheat
   noodles, cooked,
   drained, rinsed and
   chilled
2 large cucumbers, peeled,
   seeded, and shredded
   into 3-inch lengths
2 scallions, chopped

Combine vinegar, oil, ½ cup soy sauce, ¼ cup of the beef broth, and 2 tablespoons of the sugar in a saucepan. Simmer for 5 minutes, cool, then chill.

Place shredded mushrooms in a sauce pan with remaining ¼ cup broth, 2 tablespoons soy sauce, and remaining 2 tablespoons sugar. Heat the liquid, stir for 3 minutes, remove mushrooms, and set aside. Add this liquid to the chilled cooked sauce. Continue to chill sauce.

Heap chilled noodles in a large serving bowl. Arrange shredded cucumbers and mushrooms decoratively. Pour sauce over noodles. Garnish the center with chopped scallions.

New Year's Day is a time of great celebration according to Japanese custom. One year, we spent the day at the Ozaki home in California. For days the mother and her daughters had been preparing foods. On the day of the feast, Mrs. Ozaki was constantly filling the buffet table with such beautiful Japanese delicacies as sushi (raw fish and rice balls), a shrimp and vegetable tempura, salads, stews and sweets. One of the cold dishes I remarked about was a combination of seafood, cucumbers and noodles. The noodles symbolize good luck and health in the new year.

MRS. OZAKI'S JAPANESE SALAD

SERVES 4 AS A FIRST COURSE
SIDE DISH, UP TO 10 AS PART
OF A BUFFET

½ to 1 ounce (a handful) of saifun (see page 33)

One #303 can abalone, cut into strips (or fresh raw squid, sliced)

1 cucumber, peeled and sliced thin

2 stalks celery, sliced on an angle (optional)

1 carrot, cut in julienne-style strips (optional, for color)

MRS. OZAKI'S DRESSING:

½ cup sugar	1 teaspoon MSG
¼ cup lemon juice	1 teaspoon grated fresh
½ cup rice vinegar	ginger
1 tablespoon salt	

Cook saifun in boiling water for 4 to 5 minutes. Drain and cut into 1½-inch lengths. Combine with abalone (or squid), cucumber, celery, and carrot.

Combine all the dressing ingredients; mix well. Toss with salad ingredients and refrigerate.

SAUCED AND STIR-FRIED NOODLES

Oriental food is very artistic and simple. Consideration is given to texture as well as taste. Use of decorative arrangements for eye appeal are stressed rather than contrasting flavors.

BASIC JAPANESE BROTH

MAKES 1 QUART

3 cups dashi (soup stock, see page 57)
4 tablespoons soy sauce
1 tablespoon sugar

The basic broth used to sauce noodles is made by simmering together the above ingredients. The broth is then poured over cooked, drained noodles. "Dashi-no-moto," soup stock, can be purchased in two forms—bags, like tea bags, or pellets, like bouillon cubes. It is a broth made of katsuobushi (dried bonito fish), yamadashi (black sea weed) or kombu (dried sea kelp) and water. It is clear and light in flavor. You can substitute fish or chicken broth, or you can make your own dashi.

DASHI

MAKES 1 QUART

1 sheet black seaweed
1 quart water
½ cup bonito flakes

Place seaweed and water in a large saucepan and bring to a boil. Reduce heat and simmer for 5 minutes. Turn off flame and remove seaweed. Add bonito flakes and let saucepan sit until flakes sink to the bottom. Strain liquid. Dashi can be stored in the refrigerator for a long period of time.

Cold noodles are often further chilled with ice cubes before serving. This sauce for dipping cold noodles is flavored with mirin, soy, dashi, and bonito flakes. The strong tasting garnishes are not added until the last minute so that they do not lose texture in the sauce.

MENRUI WITH DIPPING SAUCE

SERVES 4 TO 6

MIRIN, SOY, DASHI DIPPING SAUCE:

¼ cup mirin (sweet sake)
¼ cup soy sauce
1 cup dashi (see above)
4 to 6 ounces somen (see page 33), cooked

2 tablespoons dried bonito flakes (katsuobushi)
Pinch of salt drained, and rinsed in cold water

GARNISHES:

3 tablespoons fine-grated
    daikon (Japanese
    white radish)

1 tablespoon grated fresh
    ginger
4 scallions, shredded

Heat mirin in a saucepan over medium heat until luke-warm. Turn off heat and ignite mirin with a match, shaking pan until the flame dies out. Add soy, dashi, katsuobushi, and salt. Bring to a boil, then strain sauce through a sieve. Cool to room temperature.

Place cold noodles in a glass or plastic bowl. Serve each person an individual bowl filled with sauce and an individual plate with garnish. Each person is to garnish his own sauce to taste. Noodles are eaten community-style with chopsticks. Each person takes a small amount of noodles, dips them into his sauce, and eats them.

(Note: Canned dipping sauce, "Ten Tsuyu," is also available at most Oriental markets.)

The Japanese use a "zaru," or round, curved bamboo basket, for one of their most popular summer foods, "Zarusoba," iced buckwheat noodles. The greenish-brown noodles are piled into this basket. Each person takes a small portion of slithery noodles and dips them into a sauce made from soy sauce and dashi, garnished with scallion and bits of seaweed.

ZARUSOBA

SERVES 6

1 pound soba (see page 33)

2 sheets of nori (dried laver or seaweed), passed over a flame on one side only to toast, and then coarsely crumbled

3 scallions, including at least 3 inches of the green stems, sliced into thin rounds

2 tablespoons wasabi (horseradish powder), mixed with just enough cold water to make a thick paste. Set aside for 15 minutes to bring out flavor

1½ cups Mirin, Soy, Dashi Dipping Sauce (pages 57–58)

Cook soba in boiling water for 5 to 6 minutes. Drain, rinse, drain again. Place noodles in a bamboo basket or divide into six serving bowls. Top with crumbled nori. Serve with individual plates of scallions and wasabi and individual bowls of dipping sauce.

A spicy version of cold somen, similar to Zarusoba, features horseradish as a condiment.

DASHI-WASABI SOMEN

SERVES 4

1 pound somen (see page 57), boiled and rinsed in ice-cold water
3 cups dashi (see page 59)
3 tablespoons wasabi paste (see Zarusoba recipe, p. 00, for directions)
½ sheet nori (see page 59), toasted over flame and crushed into flakes
2 scallions, chopped fine

Place somen in a large serving bowl with 1 to 2 quarts of ice water. Pour dashi into four small serving bowls. Place little piles of wasabi, nori, and scallions on four individual small dishes. Each person should season his own dashi according to personal taste. Noodles are eaten community-style, with each person taking a small portion at a time with chopsticks, and dipping each bite into his own flavored dashi.

Stir-frying is similar to sauté-cooking, constantly stirring. It is best to use a wok because its conical shape assures proper heat distribution. If you do not own one, use a large skillet. Place your empty wok over very high temperature to heat, and then add the oil by pouring it down the sides of the utensil. In most recipes, all the ingredients for stir-frying are cut uniformly into bite-sized pieces or shredded. Add them to the hot oil and toss gently but constantly until cooked.

Noodles can be stir-fried with oil and such simple seasonings as minced garlic and/or ginger, and perhaps soy sauce,

for an easy side dish. Fresh or leftover meats and vegetables can be added for a main course.

STIR-FRIED PLAIN NOODLES

SERVES 4 TO 6

½ *pound fresh Chinese noodles, boiled*
2 tablespoons cooking oil (or more, if you prefer them
oilier)

Rinse cooked noodles in cold water and separate. Pat
them dry with paper towels and allow to air-dry for 30
minutes. This prevents oil from splattering, especially if
using extra oil. Heat oil in a hot wok; add the noodles.
Stir-fry, keeping the noodles in motion without mashing
them, for 3 to 5 minutes. Noodles should be slightly translucent but still moist.

Variation: Noodles can be crisp-fried to use as a base or
garnish for a dish. Thin, round noodles work best because
they puff up to a greater size. Boil them in salted water for
5 minutes. Rinse to rid them of surface starch. Drain,
separate and dry well. Separate strands and cut into shorter
lengths. Heat several inches of cooking oil in a large pot to
375 degrees. Add a small amount of noodles at a time, turning to separate. Fry until golden on all sides. Remove with
a slotted spoon. Drain on paper towels. Keep warm. If you

are using the very delicate rice stick noodles, they need not be parboiled before frying.

SOY STIR-FRIED NOODLES
SERVES 6 TO 8

> *2 to 4 tablespoons cooking oil*
> *½ teaspoon minced garlic*
> *1 pound fresh Chiness noodles, cooked and drained*
> *3 tablespoons soy sauce*
> *2 tablespoons chopped scallions, as garnish*

Heat wok over high flame. Add oil and stir-fry garlic for a few seconds. Add noodles to seasoned oil. Stir-fry until hot. Add soy sauce and continue stir-frying until the noodles are coated with the sauce. Place on a serving dish. Garnish with scallions. Chopped peanuts are another excellent and nutritious garnish. (Variation: A half pound of shredded roast pork can be added once noodles are hot.)

When vegetables are added to stir-fried noodles, you have a simple, meatless main dish.

SOBA WITH ZUCCHINI AND MUSHROOMS
SERVES 2 TO 4

> *1 tablespoon cooking oil*
> *2 cloves garlic, peeled and minced*
> *3 large Chinese mushrooms, soaked in warm chicken broth for 30 minutes, drained, tough center core removed, and shredded*
> *½ pound zucchini, shredded into 2-inch lengths*
> *3 ounces soba (see page 33), cooked and drained*
> *1 tablespoon soy sauce*

Heat wok over high flame; add cooking oil and garlic. Stir-fry garlic for a few seconds, then add mushrooms and zucchini and continue to fry, stirring constantly for another few seconds. Add soba, stirring for two minutes. Add soy sauce, stirring for another minute; serve immediately. If you like, cooked pork or shrimp can be added.

Hot noodles, appropriate to cold weather, are served with combinations of fish, meat, and vegetables. In Japan, you might hear the noodle vendor's horn, announcing his wares. Or, you might enter a soba shop and sit down to eat. In these restaurants, you will find lacquer bowls filled with such condiments as sliced scallions, laver, dried bonita flakes, grated sea-slug, grated daikon, and crushed nuts. A covered bowl of hot buckwheat noodles and broth is served. You then select the garnishes that you wish to add.

SOBA SHOP NOODLES

SERVES 4

*1 cup raw chicken, sliced
   thin*

M A R I N A D E :

2 teaspoons sake

*1 teaspoon minced fresh
   ginger*

1 teaspoon cornstarch

*3 cups dashi (see page
   57)*

½ cup soy sauce

2 tablespoons sugar

2 tablespoons cooking oil

3 tablespoons sake

1 teaspoon salt

*½ pound soba, boiled until
   tender, drained, rinsed
   in cold water*

C O N D I M E N T S :

*½ cup each ground wal-
   nuts, chopped scallions,*

*laver, dried bonita
   shavings*

Place chicken in a small bowl with the sake; mix with your fingers to coat. Add the ginger and cornstarch; combine well and marinate chicken for 30 minutes.

Combine dashi, soy sauce, sugar, 1 tablespoon of cooking oil, sake, and salt in a large pot. Bring to a boil and reduce heat. Simmer for five minutes.

Place wok over high heat; add remaining oil. When hot add chicken and its marinade and stir-fry for 2 minutes. Add noodles to simmering dashi broth. When noodles are heated through, pour with broth into individual serving bowls; top with chicken. Serve with small bowls of condiments.

Although meats for Oriental dishes are generally shredded or cubed, occasionally, whole thick pork chops are extravagantly served for special occasions on top of sautéed noodles.

PORK CHOPS AND NOODLES

SERVES 4

MARINADE:

2 tablespoons soy sauce

2 teaspoons sugar

1 tablespoon rice vinegar

2 teaspoons minced fresh
   ginger

4 extra-thick pork chops
   (or 8 regular ones)

1 tablespoon cooking oil

1 large onion, peeled, sliced
   into thin rings, then
   halved

8 small dried Chinese
   mushrooms, soaked in
   hot water for ½ hour,
   drained, and hard center cores cut out

2½ cups beef stock

2 tablespoons rice vinegar

4 ounces harusame (see
   page 32), boiled about
   2 minutes and drained

Combine marinade ingredients and pour into a plastic bag. Add pork chops; shake to coat meat and marinate for ½ hour. Remove pork chops from marinade; place in a large skillet with the cooking oil, over medium heat. Brown chops on one side for about 3 to 5 minutes. Then turn, add onions, and continue to brown meat for 3 to 5 minutes. Pour out any excess oil. Add mushrooms, 1 cup of stock, and the rice vinegar. Cover skillet and reduce heat to a simmer. Cook for 45 minutes, turning several times, until chops are done. (Note: Thin chops take considerably less time than extra thick.) When chops are done, remove and keep warm. Add remaining beef stock to the skillet; bring to a boil. Add cooked noodles; stir for about two minutes to flavor the noodles.

Place noodles and sauce in the bottom of a large, deep serving bowl. Top with pork chops and serve.

For a different texture, cellophane noodles which have been soaked for 30 minutes in warm water can be substituted for the harusame.

San Francisco is famous for its restaurants, especially Chinese. Cecilia Chiang, owner of The Mandarin, located in Ghiradelli Square, shared with me her favorite spicy Szechwan dish.

DAN DAN MIEN

SERVES 2 TO 4

½ pound fresh egg noodles

DAN DAN SAUCE:

½ cup each black mushrooms, bamboo shoots, and pickled Szechwan Mustard Pickle vegetables (spicy pickled Oriental vegetables), all chopped fine

¼ cup cottonseed oil (or, your favorite cooking oil)

½ pound pork butt (slightly marbled with fat), diced

1 heaping tablespoon minced red chilis

¾ cup chicken stock

Dash sherry

1 teaspoon salt

1 teaspoon sugar

1 tablespoon soy sauce

Few drops of sesame oil

1 tablespoon cornstarch mixed with 1 tablespoon water

3 tablespoons crushed peanuts (optional)

Drop noodles into a pot of boiling unsalted water; bring to a second boil, then add 2 cups of cold water. Bring to a third boil; remove noodles, drain and reserve.

To make the sauce: Place chopped vegetables together in a bowl. Heat cottonseed oil in a hot wok over high flame. Brown the pork for 1 to 2 minutes, then add the chopped vegetables and chilis. Stir to combine ingredients. Add chicken stock and cook for another 1 to 2 minutes. Sprinkle with sherry; add salt, sugar, soy sauce, sesame oil, and cornstarch solution. Cook for another 1 to 2 minutes. Sauce should be about the consistency of spaghetti sauce, not too watery.

Place the noodles in a serving bowl, cover with sauce, and garnish, if you wish, with crushed peanuts. Toss thoroughly before serving.

My Chinese Cooking teacher Susan Mozingo, who has been a great inspiration to my studies and preparations, invited my husband and me to a feast in which she included two noodle recipes. For hors d'oeuvre we had Jao-Tze (page 39–40), and for a main dish she served shredded chicken garnished with crunchy, fried bean thread noodles.

SHREDDED CHICKEN WITH OYSTER SAUCE

SERVES 4 TO 6

1 cup cooking oil
1 to 2 ounces bean thread noodles

1½ chicken breasts, boned, skinned and shredded

M A R I N A D E :
1 tablespoon sake
½ teaspoon salt
Dash white pepper

1 small egg white
1 tablespoon cornstarch
1 tablespoon finely-shredded fresh ginger

1 tablespoon oyster sauce
1 teaspoon sesame oil
1 tablespoon soy sauce
¼ teaspoon sugar
1 tablespoon cornstarch dissolved in 2 tablespoons chicken stock
1 cup bean sprouts, washed and dried

1 teaspoon minced garlic
6 Chinese dried mushrooms, soaked, tough center core removed, and shredded

Heat oil in a wok over high flame; when hot, drop in a handful of loosened bean thread noodles for 1 second; drain. Set aside. Save oil.

Marinate shredded chicken for 30 minutes in sake, salt, pepper, egg white, and cornstarch. Reheat oil and drop chicken into it, stirring constantly to keep separated. Cook until meat is firm and white, about 1 minute; drain.

Discard oil, reserving a few tablespoons for later use.

In a small bowl, combine oyster sauce, sesame oil, soy sauce, sugar and dissolved cornstarch.

Over high heat, add one tablespoon of reserved oil to your wok; drop in bean sprouts and stir-fry for about 10 seconds; remove. Add another tablespoon of oil; add ginger and garlic and stir-fry for a few seconds. Add chicken, mushrooms, bean sprouts and the sauce; mix thoroughly. Transfer to a plate and garnish with the fried noodles.

My husband's favorite Oriental sauce is this Sweet and Sour. For a beautiful entrée, I made up a batch of fried won tons, place them on a platter, and pour the heated sauce on top.

SWEET AND SOUR WON TONS
SERVES 3 TO 4

SWEET AND SOUR SAUCE

½ cup pineapple juice	1 teaspoon minced garlic
¼ cup Oriental crabapple sauce (or catsup)	1 tablespoon cornstarch dissolved in 2 table-
¼ cup cider vinegar	spoons water
3 to 4 tablespoons sugar	12 deep-fried won tons
1 tablespoon soy sauce	(See pages 36–37.)
1 tablespoon cooking oil	

In a small bowl, combine pineapple juice, crabapple sauce, vinegar, sugar and soy sauce, mixing well. Heat wok over medium flame; add oil and garlic and stir-fry for a few seconds. Add the sweet and sour sauce; bring to a boil. Continue to boil the sauce at a high temperature until the sugar has completely dissolved. Add the dissolved cornstarch to thicken. Keep sauce warm until serving time. Place won tons on a platter and pour sauce over them.

If you want to make the sweet and sour sauce a little more deluxe, you can add vegetables and fruit.

SUPER SWEET AND SOUR WON TONS
SERVES 3 TO 4

2 carrots, scraped and cut into 1-inch wedges
1 green pepper, seeded and cut into 1-inch squares
One 8-ounce can pineapple chunks, drained
1 recipe for sweet 'n'sour sauce(see page 68)
12 deep-fried won tons (see pages 36–37)

Bring a medium pot of water to boil; add carrots. When water returns to a rapid boil, continue to cook for another 2 minutes. Immediately drain carrots, rinsing them with cold water to stop the cooking process and set the color. (Note: I even add ice cubes to help reduce the heat faster.) Repeat the same blanching process for the green pepper, boiling only 1 minute before rinsing. Place carrots, peppers, and pineapple together in a mixing bowl. Add this mixture to the thickened Sweet and Sour sauce and simmer until vegetables and pineapple are warmed through. Place hot won tons on a platter and pour sauce over them.

The climate of Thailand is hot and so are the native dishes, made with chilis and curry. Traditionally, the noodles for this Thai dish are boiled, then fried with pork, shrimp, vegetables, eggs and sauce. The condiments seem to cut the fire, but beware, it's spicy!

SPICY THAI NOODLES

SERVES 6 TO 8

5 tablespoons cooking oil
½ pound ground pork
1 large onion, peeled and chopped
2 cloves garlic, peeled and minced
3 medium-size carrots, scraped and shredded
1 medium green pepper, shredded

1 pound Chinese celery cabbage, shredded fine
5 ounces harusame (see page 32), boiled for 2 minutes, drained, rinsed, iced to cool immediately, and sliced into shorter lengths
2 eggs, lightly beaten
¼ pound cooked, baby shrimp

SPICY HOT SAUCE:

¼ cup Szechwan chili sauce. (If not available, or if too spicy, substitute your favorite tomato-based chili sauce.)
2 teaspoons sugar
2 teaspoons rice vinegar

½ teaspoon salt
¼ teaspoon cayenne pepper
¼ teaspoon ground black pepper
2 tablespoons soy sauce
1 tablespoon minced cilantro

CONDIMENTS:

½ cup chopped, dry roasted peanuts
¼ pound fresh bean sprouts, chopped

1 lime, cut into wedges
4 scallions, chopped
½ cup shredded coconut

SOY-LEMON SERVING SAUCE:

½ cup soy sauce

1 tablespoon lemon juice

Heat wok over medium flame. Add 1 tablespoon of oil. When warm, add pork, stirring constantly to break up the meat, and cook for about 5 minutes, or until it is browned. Add onion, garlic, carrot, green pepper, and cabbage; continue to stir for another 2 minutes. Pour another tablespoon of oil down the sides of the wok and add the cooked noodles, continuing to stir. Make a well in the center of the wok by pushing everything to the sides. Pour the eggs into the well and allow them to begin to set, then stir them into the noodles. Add the shrimp. Mix together the Spicy Hot Sauce ingredients in a small bowl and add to the wok. Stir to blend well for another 1 to 2 minutes. Turn onto a serving dish. Serve with small bowls of condiments and Soy-Lemon Serving Sauce.

Crunchy noodles provide an exotic complement to the Thai spiciness. When a small handful of noodles are dropped into hot oil, they puff up quickly and almost explode. Minutes before serving, toss them with pork, chicken, shrimp and a rich sweet and sour sauce.

CRUNCHY THAI NOODLES

SERVES 4 TO 6

Cooking oil for deep-frying   *4 ounces rice stick noodles*

THAI TART SAUCE:
¼ cup sugar   *or hoi sin sauce*
¼ cup lime juice   *¼ cup catsup*
¼ cup yellow bean sauce   *2 tablespoons soy sauce*

2 tablespoons cooking oil   *½ pound medium-size raw*
1 small onion, peeled and   *shrimp, shelled and de-*
* chopped fine*   *veined*
4 cloves garlic, peeled and   *1 pound uncooked white*
* minced*   *meat of chicken, shred-*
½ pound lean boneless   *ded into 2-inch lengths*
* pork, shredded into*
* 2-inch lengths*

GARNISH:
½ pound bean sprouts   *4 green onions, cut into*
1 lime, cut into thin   *3-inch lengths*
* wedges*

Pour cooking oil into a deep pot for frying; heat the oil to 375 degrees, then drop in a handful of noodles at a time. Noodles will puff up and turn golden within a few seconds; remove and drain on paper towels. Continue until all noodles are deep-fried. Keep noodles warm in a 200-degree oven. If you want to fry noodles in advance, reheat before tossing them with the other ingredients by placing them in a 200 degree oven for about 10 minutes.

Mix all sauce ingredients together in a small bowl. Set

aside to allow the flavors to mingle while preparing meat. Place 2 tablespoons of oil in a warm wok over high heat. When oil is hot, add onion and garlic and stir-fry for about a minute, or until the onions soften. Add the pork, continuing to stir-fry; cook for about 3 minutes. Add the shrimp and chicken, continuing to stir constantly. Cook meats and shrimp for another 3 minutes. Pour in the Tart Sauce, stirring constantly as you add, and continue to cook for another 3 to 4 minutes. Remove from heat and carefully fold in the fried noodles, coating them with the sauce. Turn out into the center of a warmed platter. Arrange the bean sprouts around the edges and top them with the lime wedges and green onions.

Silky vermicelli clings to shredded beef when the two are stir-fried together, and both noodles and meat are enhanced by the predominating gingery flavor.

SILKY VERMICELLI GINGER BEEF
SERVES 2 TO 3

1 pound lean sirloin beef, sliced thin against the grain

MARINADE:
1½ tablespoons sake
1½ tablespoons soy sauce
½ teaspoon sugar

3 tablespoons cooking oil
1 generous tablespoon chopped fresh ginger
Dash of salt and pepper
1 tablespoon cornstarch
1 cup shredded scallions (6 to 10, depending upon size)

One 2-ounce bundle of vermicelli, soaked in warm water for ½ hour, drained
2 tablespoons chicken broth
1 tablespoon soy sauce

In a small bowl, first marinate the meat in the sake for a few seconds, then add the soy sauce, sugar, salt, pepper, and cornstarch, and continue to marinate for ½ hour. Place your wok over high heat; when hot, add 2 tablespoons of oil. When oil is hot, add the meat with its marinade and stir-fry until lightly browned, about 1 minute; remove meat. Add remaining oil to the wok along with the ginger and scallion; stir-fry for a few seconds. Return the cooked meat to the wok. Add noodles, broth and soy sauce. Mix thoroughly and serve immediately.

Chao Mein, which means fried noodles, provides the framework for an infinite variety of dishes. Among the extras you might add are raw or cooked pork, chicken, ham, beef, shrimp, duck, game and eggs with such vegetables as spinach, green onions, celery, cabbage, lettuce, cucumbers, bean sprouts, bamboo shoots, mushrooms (fresh or dry), water chestnuts and snow peas (pea pods).

I first prepared authentic Chao Mein with my Chinese cooking teacher. I was warned that once I tasted it, I would never be able to eat the Americanized version again. Although this recipe may appear complicated, it is actually quite easy if you follow the instructions slowly and carefully. It will stand alone as a handsome brunch or luncheon dish, so you don't have to make a lot of other courses. A sliced, fresh fruit platter will complete the menu. To cut down on last minute preparation, you can make the sauce earlier in the day, even the night before.

CHAO MEIN MOZINGO

SERVES 4

½ *pound fresh Chinese egg noodles*
½ *teaspoon sesame oil*
¾ *teaspoon salt*
7 *tablespoons cooking oil*

½ *pound fresh young spinach (including some of the pink stems)*
½ *pound chicken breast*

MARINADE:

½ tablespoon sake
½ tablespoon soy sauce

2 green onions, shredded
    into 2-inch lengths
4 ounces small raw shrimp,
    shelled deveined,
    rinsed in salted water,
    drained, and dried
4 large dried Chinese
    mushrooms, soaked for
¼ teaspoon sugar
1 teaspoon cornstarch
    ½ hour, drained, tough

center core removed,
    and shredded
½ cup bamboo shredded
    shoots
1½ tablespoons soy sauce
1 cup chicken broth
1 tablespoon oyster sauce
Dash pepper
1 tablespoon cornstarch,
    dissolved in 2 table-
    spoons water

In a large pot, bring 2 quarts of water to a boil over high heat. Add the noodles. When the water returns to a boil, add 1 cup of cold water. Again, return water to a boil and continue cooking at this intense heat until noodles are done. Drain noodles in a colander with cold running water to remove any excess starch and toss with sesame oil and ½ teaspoon salt. Heat 2 tablespoons of oil in a large skillet. When hot, place noodles in the pan, pancake-style. Constantly shake skillet as the noodles pan-fry so that they do not stick to the pan. When the bottom noodles are golden, after 3 to 5 minutes, use two spatulas and turn the noodles over to the other side, adding 2 tablespoons of oil. Again, shake pan constantly as the second side browns. Remove noodles to a serving platter and keep warm in a 200-degree oven.

Clean spinach leaves, retaining the sweet pink stems. Tear spinach into shreds, ¼-inch wide by 2-inches long. Set aside. Skin and bone chicken, removing any membranes. Shred chicken fillets and place them in a small bowl with marinade ingredients for ½ hour.

Place wok over high heat; add 1 tablespoon of oil. When heated, add green onions, shrimp, and chicken. Stir-fry quickly for 1 minute. Remove ingredients. Again heat the wok; pour in the remaining 2 tablespoons oil. Add spinach and ¼ teaspoon salt, stirring for a few seconds. Add the mushrooms and bamboo shoots, continuing to stir-fry for another minute. Return the green onions, shrimp, and chicken to the wok; add the soy sauce, chicken broth, oyster sauce, and dash of pepper. When the liquid comes to a boil, pour in the dissolved cornstarch to thicken. Pour the chao mein mixture over the fried noodles. Serve immediately.

Use instant seasoned noodles with soup base to prepare an easy chow (chao) mein.

SIMPLE CHICKEN CHOW MEIN
SERVES 4

Two 3-ounce packages of instant Oriental noodles with seasoned soup base
¼ cup cooking oil
2 cups cold water
2 tablespoons soy sauce
2 tablespoons cornstarch

2 tablespoons cooking oil
2 boned chicken breasts, shredded
1 medium onion, peeled and shredded
2 celery stalks, shredded
1 green pepper, shredded

Remove noodles from packages, reserving soup base. Bring 1 quart of water to a boil in a large pot. Add the noodles and boil, stirring occasionally, for a few minutes, until noodles separate. Rinse noodles in cold running water and drain. Heat the ¼ cup of oil in a large skillet. Spread one-quarter of the noodles at a time in the hot skillet and fry until golden on both sides. Place one portion of fried noodles on each of 4 individual serving plates.

Pour the 2 cups of water into a medium-size bowl; add the soup base packages and blend well. Add the soy sauce and cornstarch, mixing again.

Heat the 2 tablespoons of oil in a hot wok; add the chicken and stir-fry until lightly browned. Add the shredded vegetables and stir-fry for a few minutes, or until chicken and vegetables are cooked through. Pour the soup base mixture over the chicken and vegetables and stir until the sauce begins to thicken. Spoon chicken and vegetables with sauce over the noodles. For additional flavor, bean sprouts, Chinese greens, mushrooms, and scallions can be added.

Japanese foods cooked at the table, "nabemono," are considered winter dishes. Use a chafing dish or electric skillet to prepare this one in the traditional manner. Each diner should have a small decorative cup or bowl of steamed white rice. In a communal manner, one person at a time should reach into the skillet with chopsticks and place a small portion of cooked sukiyaki on top of his rice.

SUKIYAKI

SERVES 4

1½ cups your favorite
  bottled Sukiyaki Sauce,
  or make your own

SUKIYAKI SAUCE:
1⅓ cups chicken broth
¼ cup sugar
¼ cup mirin (sweet sake)

¼ to ½ cup beef suet or
   cooking oil
One 8-ounce can shirataki
   (see page 33), drained
½ head Chinese celery
   cabbage, shredded into
   2-inch lengths
2 bunches scallions (about
   12), cut into 2-inch
   lengths
1 large onion, peeled and
   shredded into 2-inch
   lengths
4 large fresh mushrooms,
sliced thin
¼ cup shredded bamboo
   shoots
¼ pound tofu (soybean
   curd), drained
½ pound fresh bean
   sprouts
½ pound spinach, shred-
   ded into 2-inch lengths
1 pound sukiyaki beef (or
   1 pound top sirloin
   steak, sliced thin like
   prosciutto, almost
   transparent)

If you are going to prepare this dish at the table, the
only things you have to do in advance are (1) prepare the
Sukiyaki Sauce (if making your own) by combining all
the ingredients in a mixing bowl and pouring it into a
decorative cup and (2) place all the vegetables, tofu, and
meat on a large platter.

Heat 1 tablespoon of fat or oil in the chafing dish over
high heat. Slowly add the noodles, cabbage, scallions, onion,
mushrooms, bamboo shoots, and tofu, one at a time, stirring
carefully with a pair of chopsticks. Occasionally add more
fat or oil. As the vegetables cook, pour in the sukiyaki
sauce. Let everything cook over high heat, for about 6 to
8 minutes, stirring occasionally. Add the bean sprouts,
then the spinach and meat. Reduce heat to a simmer and
continue to cook for about 5 minutes.

I tasted Shabu-Shabu for the first time at a restaurant in downtown Los Angeles's Little Tokyo district. Karen Anderson, a long time friend who is the fashion editor of L.A.'s *Herald Examiner,* and I sat and talked at the shabu-shabu bar as we dipped our foods into individual pots of simmering broth. A cross between fondue and sukiyaki, the concept of this dish is that each person uses chopsticks to dip his noodles, vegetables and meat in broth and then into the seasoned sauces before eating.

To serve at home, keep the broth simmering in one central fondue pot. Serve each person a platter of noodles, vegetables and meat and two small bowls of sauces.

SHABU-SHABU

SERVES 4

1 quart good chicken broth
4 to 6 ounces kishimen (see page 32), cooked, drained and cut into thirds
1 bunch watercress
1 bunch chrysanthemum leaves (Oriental vegetable. If not available, use other Japanese greens or spinach leaves.)
8 small dried mushrooms, soaked
4 fresh mushrooms, sliced ⅛-inch thick

1 pound Chinese celery cabbage, shredded into 1½-inch lengths
12 scallions, sliced in 2-inch lengths
¼ cup bamboo shoots
4 ounces tofu (soybean curd), cut into rectangles about ¼-inch thick and 2-inches long
1½ pounds sirloin steak, cut paper-thin, almost transparent

CITRUS-SOY SAUCE:
2 cups soy sauce
1 cup orange juice
1 cup lemon juice

Chopped scallions, to garnish

SESAME-SOY SAUCE:

½ cup sesame seeds, lightly toasted (see page 54) and ground into a paste with mortar and pestle

2 teaspoons sugar
3 tablespoons sake
2 teaspoons soy sauce
Dash fresh-ground pepper

Bring the broth to a simmer in a fondue pot. Arrange noodles, vegetables, tofu, and meat attractively on serving platters. Combine the ingredients for the sauces.

Using chopsticks, each person should dip his food into the pot of simmering broth and, once it is cooked, into one of the sauces. Accompany with individual bowls of steamed white rice.

SWEETS

Oriental desserts are light and refreshing. Usually, a fresh fruit, ice cream, sherbet or custard is served. Cookies are another favorite. Won tons can be stuffed with a sweet filling, deep-fried, and dusted with powdered sugar.

NUTTY WON TON COOKIES
MAKES 14 COOKIES

14 won ton skins (see page 35)
2 teaspoons sesame seeds, toasted (see page 54)
¼ cup chunky-style peanut butter

¼ cup dark brown sugar, packed solid
Cooking oil for deep-frying
Powdered sugar

Prepare the won ton skins.

Mix sesame seeds, peanut butter, and brown sugar together. Place one teaspoon of filling on each skin. Roll with the palms of your hands to form a cylinder, twisting the two ends. Seal folds with water. (If you wish, you can also shape into little caps like meat-filled won tons. Children may prefer this.) In a large pot, heat oil for deep-frying to 375 degrees; add a few won tons at a time. Fry until golden, drain on paper towels, and dust with powdered sugar. Serve warm or cold.

A more sophisticated, adult filling features chopped dates, nuts and oranges.

FRUIT-FILLED WON TONS
MAKES 6 TO 8 DOZEN COOKIES

6 to 8 dozen won ton skins
2 pounds pitted dates, chopped fine
2 cups fine-chopped walnuts
3 tablespoons grated orange rind

3 to 5 tablespoons orange juice (1 to 2 tablespoons may be an orange liqueur, such as Cointreau)
Cooking oil for deep frying
Powdered sugar

Prepare the won ton skins.

In a large mixing bowl, combine the dates, nuts, orange rind and 2 tablespoons of orange juice. Knead mixture with your fingers until it can be gathered into a ball, adding more juice if mixture is too dry. Roll 1 tablespoon into a small cylinder, $\frac{1}{3}$ inch in diameter by 1 inch in length. Place this filling on a won ton and roll and seal as in preceding recipe (see page 80). Deep-fry in cooking oil at 375 degrees, turning occasionally until golden, about 2 to 3 minutes. Transfer to paper towels, drain and cool. Sprinkle with powdered sugar before serving. Serve warm or cold.

Butterflies are represented in various art forms throughout Oriental culture. They are pictured for their color and spirit of life. It seems only natural that they also be portrayed as cookies in the art of Oriental cuisine.

BUTTERFLY COOKIES
MAKES 3 DOZEN COOKIES

6 dozen won ton skins
Cooking oil for deep-frying

BUTTERFLY GLAZE:
¾ cup water
1¼ cups sugar

Cut skins in half into rectangles, two layers thick. Make a small slit lengthwise in the center of half the double rectangles and insert one unslit pair into a slit pair to form butterflies. Deep-fry a few butterflies at a time in hot oil. When golden brown, remove, drain on paper towels, place on wax paper, and drizzle on all sides with glaze. To make glaze: combine the water and sugar in a heavy saucepan. Cook at high temperature to dissolve the sugar and bring to a boil, stirring constantly. Reduce heat to medium and continue to cook, stirring constantly, for about 3 minutes, or until syrupy. (I use a wooden chopstick for all the stirring.) Serve warm or cool.

(Note: You can also shape the wrappers into other designs, such as flowers.)

The Italian Noodle

T H E R E ' S a rumor going around that the streets of Italy
are paved with pasta and that all roads lead to a spaghetti
museum. I'm not too sure about the first story, but the
Agnesi Historical Museum of Spaghetti is situated on the
Ligurian Coast, near the Gulf of Genoa. Vicenzo Agnesi,
the poppa of Italy's oldest pasta manufacturer, Agnesi
and Sons, has been collecting material for this museum for
some fifty-five years. Among the antique documents and
relics, and the vast collection of cookbooks, memoirs, and
international catalogs proudly housed in the family's 17th-
century palace, is a copy of a Genoese soldier's will leaving his wife a basket of macaroni (see page 10) ; an early
Latin cookbook, *De Onesta Voluptate* (1475), which refers
to pasta tossed with butter and cheese; an original edition
of Thomas Coryate's *Coryate's Euditions Hastefully Gob-
bled Up In Five Months of Travel in France, Savoy, Italy*

(*Etc.*), (1597), in which the English author commented on the use of a strange new utensil, the fork, by pasta-eating Italians; and a note sent from Paris by the famous 19th-century composer Gioacchino Rossini—‘‘Your Rossini without macaroni’’—which tells of his craving for his native cuisine.

To an Italian, a day without pasta is like a day without sunshine. Whether eaten at home or at a restaurant, pasta once or twice a day is the staple diet. Served in small portions, tossed with seasoned oil or butter, in broth or married to a sauce, pasta is served as a first course, traditionally preceding, never accompanying, a meat, fowl, or fish course. Occasionally, it is served as an entrée, but then it is usually a light summer meal, a midday snack, or a late night supper.

The Italian pasta family can be divided into three categories—flat strips or shapes called noodles (often further defined as egg noodles when the basic dough includes eggs), solid rods called spaghetti, and hollow tubes called macaroni. As romantic as the language are the names given to the hundreds of shapes from ‘‘a’’ (acini di pepe, meaning peppercorns) to ‘‘z’’ (ziti, meaning bridegrooms).

This glossary should assist your selection of the appropriate pasta. Remember to mix and match your favorite sauces and stuffings with your favorite shapes.

Agnolotti: Crescent-shaped, meat-stuffed ravioli typical of the Piedmont region. Often look like priests' caps. Served like cappelletti and tortellini for such winter festivities as Christmas, New Year's Eve, and Twelfth Night.

Bavettine: Very narrow linguine.

Bucatini: Short, straight macaroni. Also known as perciatelli.

Cannelloni: Large tubes to be stuffed. Often grooved.

Capelli d'angelo: Angel's hair (used in soups).

Capellini: Very fine rods.

Capelvenere: Fine noodles (for soup).

Cappelletti: Little hats. Dumpling in shape of small, peaked hat. Traditionally served on Christmas day.

Cappelli di prete: Priest's hats.

Cappelli pagliaccio: Clown's hats.

Cavatelli: Long-crinkle-edged shells. Traditionally served with cheese. (Cavatiedd, small curly seashells.)

Conchiglie: Conch shells. Available ridged or smooth. Traditionally served with meat sauces (the most famous being sausage and cream or ham and pea). (Conchigliette—little conch shells.)

Coralli: Coral. Small tubes for soup.

Creste di gallo (galli): Cockscombs (coxcombs).

Ditali: Thimbles, short macaroni. (Ditalini—little thimbles.)

Farfalle: Butterflies or bows.

Farfalline: Small butterflies or bows.

Farfalloni: Big butterflies or bow ties.

Fettucce: Ribbons, widest of fettuccine family.

Fettuccine: Small ribbons. Egg noodle. In between size of Tagliarini and Tagliatelle. Most often served with cream sauce.

Fedelini (Fidelini): Little faithful ones. Very fine rod or spaghetti.

Fusilli (Fusili): Little springs, spindles, or spirals. Respond well to thick sauces. Also a spring or twisted pasta.

Lancette: Little spears. Small soup pasta.

Lasagne: Extra broad noodles, about 2″ wide, smooth or ripple-edged ribbons. Used primarily for baking.

Lingue di passeri: Sparrows' tongues. A little thicker than the average linguine.

Linguine (Linguini): Small or little tongues. Rods are slightly flattened or oval. Finest variety is Bavettine.

Lumache: Snails, shell-shaped. Lumachine and lumacone, little and big snails.

Maccheroni: Macaroni of all types. Hollow or pierced

pasta. Elbow macaroni—semi-circular tubes.

Maccheroni alla chitarra: Noodles cut with steel wires of a special guitar-like tool. The dough is placed on top of the wires and cut with a rolling pin. Often coiled when packaged. Usually served with meat sauce, traditionally with lamb. Also called Spaghetti alla chitarra.

Mafalda (Mafalde): Broad noodle, rippled on both sides. Wider than fettuccine family and narrower than lasagne family.

Maglietti: Links. Variety of types. Usually refers to slightly curved, short lengths of hollow pasta.

Maltagliato: Badly cut or irregular shapes. Corners cut on bias.

Manicotti: Muffs, giant tubes. Usually homemade. To be stuffed.

Margherita: Daisies. Narrow noodles, rippled on one side. Named after an Italian queen.

Maruzze: Seashells. Available in a variety of sizes.

Mezzani: Short, cut, curved macaroni.

Mostaccioli: Little moustaches. Also known as penne. Usually 2-inch lengths with ends cut diagonally.

Occhi di lupo: Wolf's eyes. Large tubes.

Occhi di passeri: Sparrows' eyes. Tiny circles.

Ondulati: Wavy-shaped pasta.

Orecchiette: Little ears. Shape comes from twist of fingertips. Traditionally tossed with garlic, anchovy-seasoned oil and broccoli or cauliflower.

Orzo: Barley, rice-like pasta. Usually cooked like rice.

Pappardelle: Broad noodles. Traditionally served with game sauce.

Passatelli: Very thin egg noodles.

Pasta Fresca: Fresh pasta dough. All'uovo—egg dough.

Pasta Verde: Dough including spinach (green color—verde).

Pastina: Tiny dough. Minute pasta used for soup. Called pasta grattugiata if fresh. Since children are especially fond of these shapes, many of them have been given special "charming" names, such as: Acini di pepe (peppercorns), Alfabeto (alphabet), Amorini (little cupids), Anellini or anezzi (little rings), Arancini (little oranges), Astri (stars), Avena (oats), Crocette (little crosses), Elefanti (elephants), Foratini (small pierced ones), Funghini (little mushrooms), Pulcini (little chickens), Rosemaries ("Rosa Marina," rose of the sea), Rotini (little wheels), Semi di mela or melone (apple or melon seeds), Stellini (little stars), Stivaletti (little boots), and Tubettini (little tubes).

Penne: Pens or quills. Tubes cut diagonally at both ends. Usually smooth, though some are ridged. Same as thick mostaccioli.

Perciatelli: Long, thin, macaroni. Look like spaghetti. (Perciatelloni are a larger version.)

Pizzoccheri: Thick, dark-colored noodles made of buckwheat flour.

Quadrettini (Quadrucci) : Small, flat squares.

Ravioli: Pasta squares stuffed with meat, cheese and/or vegetables.

Ricciolini: Little curls.

Rigatoni: Literally, large, fluted ones. Slightly curved, large, grooved, macaroni.

Rotelle: Small wheels.

Ruote (Rote) : Spiked wheels with hubs. (Great for children!)

Spaghetti: Literally strings. Variety of long, thin rods, including capellini (very, very fine), fedelini (very fine), spaghettini (very thin), and spaghettoni (largest).

Tagliatelle: Family of egg noodles, similar to fettuccine family, ¾-inch wide. Tagliarini—smallest, about $\frac{1}{16}$-inch wide tagliolini are wider. "Tagliare" means to cut.

Tonnarelli: Very thin noodles, also called pasta alla chitarra or maccheroni alla chitarra because of the guitar-like equipment (chitarra) used to cut them.

Tortellini: Small stuffed pasta of Roman background, similar to cappelletti (Bologna). Ring-shaped dumplings.

Trenette: Version of tagliatelle, narrower and thicker.

Tubetti: Small hollow tubes.

Tufoli: Larga pasta tubes to be stuffed. Similar to manicotti or cannelloni, but smaller.

Vermicelli: Resemble Angel's hair. (See page 84.) Thin spaghetti. Available in rods or twisted as a bird's nest. Often broken by hand for soups.

Ziti: Bridegrooms. Slightly curved, large tubes. Similar to rigatoni, but not grooved.

A list of several stores that will mail order Italian ingredients and cooking utensils can be found on pages 321–24. When writing to them, you might ask if they have a catalog and price list for future use.

Basic Noodle Dough recipes (pages 25–28) can be used for most Italian pasta. In addition to the following recipes, more specific ones will be found in the "Stuffed" section.

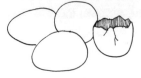

EGG NOODLES
(Pasta Fatta in Casa—Home-Made Pasta)

SERVES 4 TO 10, DEPENDING ON
COURSE

3 or more cups semolina or unbleached, all-purpose flour
1 teaspoon salt
4 extra large eggs

In a large mixing bowl (or on a large board), combine the semolina and salt. Make a well in the center and break the eggs into it. Using your fingers, begin to work the flour into the eggs until the flour is moistened and the dough begins to gather into a ball. If dough is too moist, add more flour. If it's too dry, add a few drops of warm water.

Place the ball of dough on a floured board. Knead by pulling, folding, and pressing with the heel of your hand for about 10 minutes, until the dough is smooth. Return the dough to the bowl, cover with a kitchen towel (or wrap in plastic) and let it rest for ½ hour. Divide the dough into four pieces. Roll out one at a time, as thin as possible, and cut into desired shape—width and length. (This entire process can be done with a noodle or pasta machine.) Toss the strips lightly with flour and place on a floured towel to dry.

If you plan to use fresh noodles, dry them on the towel for only an hour before cooking or freezing them. To cook, boil in salted water for a few minutes. Fresh noodles will be ready generally within 3 to 5 minutes. To freeze the unboiled, fresh noodles for later use, place the towel with noodles (after they have dried for the hour) in your freezer until the noodles are stiff. Take them off the towel and pack into plastic bags. Or, to preserve these noodles for later use, you may dry them on a towel for 12 hours.

Some Italian cooks add one tablespoon of olive oil to the dough along with the eggs when making cappelletti, ravioli, or tortellini. See pages 91–94 for shaping dough and fillings.

Spinach can be added to any pasta to make green noodles.

PASTA VERDE

SERVES 4 TO 10, DEPENDING ON
COURSE

3 cups semolina or unbleached, all-purpose flour
One 10-ounce package frozen chopped spinach, defrosted
  (or ¾ pound fresh spinach, cooked 5 minutes), drained
  and thoroughly dried
2 large eggs
1 teaspoon salt

Follow instructions for egg noodles (pages 88–89) adding
the spinach at the same time as the eggs. Also, see pages
25–28.

STUFFED NOODLES AND PASTA

"Ravioli" comes from the word "rabioli," meaning things
of little value. Originally, leftovers were used for stuffing
and then hidden in these little pillows. Fillings vary from
cheese to eggs, seafood, meat, chicken and vegetables. The
ravioli are most often boiled or simmered in water or
broth and then gently tossed with melted butter or a white
or red sauce. Any ravioli which have been boiled but not
sauced may be sprinkled with cornstarch, covered with
wax paper, and frozen in bags or boxes for later use.

To make ravioli, use the Basic Egg Noodle recipe (pages
25–28) with the addition of one tablespoon of olive oil. Roll
out the dough into rectangles. Cut into 3-inch wide strips.
Place heaping teaspoons of filling about 1½ to 2 inches

apart. Cover each strip with a second and press firmly to-gether around each spoonful of filling. Use a fluted pastry wheel, serrated roller, or ravioli stamp to cut into 3-inch squares. Check to make sure the edges are properly crimped and sealed.

If you have a metal ravioli tray, fit the pan with a sheet of dough. Place the filling into each depressed area; top with another sheet of dough, and roll with the pin to crimp and cut the squares.

Place ravioli on a rack to dry for 45 minutes to 1½ hours. To cook, place in a large pot of gently boiling water (or chicken or veal broth) and simmer for about 10 min-utes. Remove carefully with a slotted spoon and place in a heated bowl. Toss with sauce.

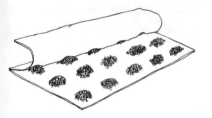

CHEESE RAVIOLI
MAKES APPROXIMATELY 4 CUPS
TO FILL 75 TO 100 RAVIOLI

¼ pound each Romano, mozzarella, and Gru-yère cheeses, grated
1 cup ricotta cheese
1 cup heavy cream
1 egg, lightly beaten
¼ cup minced fresh pars-ley

Dash fresh-grated nutmeg
Fresh-ground pepper to taste
½ cup melted butter
1 cup fresh-grated Parme-san cheese

In a large mixing bowl, combine the Romano, mozzarella, Gruyère, and ricotta cheeses. Add the cream, egg, parsley, nutmeg, and pepper. Mix well. Stuff the ravioli and allow to dry for 45 minutes. Cook according to directions on page 91. Top ravioli with melted butter and crown with Parmesan cheese. A light tomato sauce can be substituted for the butter. (See Sautéed Tomato Sauce, page 125.)

RAVIOLI GENOVESE

MAKES APPROXIMATELY 1 CUP TO
FILL 25 RAVIOLI

¼ *pound lean ground beef*	*1 tablespoon sugar*
¼ *pound sweet sausage, crumbled*	½ *teaspoon ground red pepper (or cumin)*
2 tablespoons olive oil	*1 teaspoon salt*
2 tablespoons fine-chopped onion	*2 tablespoons golden raisins*
1 clove garlic, peeled and minced	*1 tablespoon flour*
2 tablespoons lemon juice	¼ *cup crushed walnuts*

Sauté beef and sausage together in a large skillet with oil, onions, and garlic until the meat is lightly browned. Add all the remaining ingredients except the nuts; stir to combine all seasonings. Cover and simmer for ½ hour, stirring occasionally. Remove from heat; add nuts and stir. Adjust seasoning. Distribute spoonfuls of filling over dough, shape and cook as directed on page 91. Serve with a thin, fresh tomato sauce and grated Parmesan cheese as a garnish. (See Sautéed Tomato Sauce, page 125.)

The Piedmontese ravioli, agnolotti, are stuffed with meat and vegetables and served with melted butter, meat sauce, and grated cheese. Shape as for ravioli. Or, to make the authentic crescent, cut the dough into circles with a jagged edged ravioli cutter. Place filling off-center. Fold dough in half, covering the filling and crimping the top and bottom edges together to form a semi-circle.

PIEDMONTESE RAVIOLI

MAKES 2 CUPS TO FILL 50

RAVIOLI

1 cup cooked ground veal
½ cup cooked puréed
  spinach
½ cup grated Parmesan
  cheese
¼ cup soft breadcrumbs
2 eggs, lightly beaten

1 teaspoon each minced
  fresh parsley and fresh
  basil
Salt and pepper to taste
2 to 4 teaspoons heavy
  cream or chicken stock

In a large mixing bowl, combine the veal, spinach, cheese, and breadcrumbs. Moisten with the eggs. Season with herbs and salt and pepper to taste. Bind the filling together with cream or chicken stock. You can also use this filling for cannelloni, tortellini, manicotti, and seashells.

Using the same dough as for ravioli, tortellini begin as a circle and, once stuffed, are folded to look like hats or rings. Take a floured cookie cutter or tortellini cutter and cut the dough into 2-inch circles. Place a teaspoon of filling (use Cheese Ravioli, Piedmontese Ravioli or Ravioli Genovese filling; see pages 91–93) on each circle, fold in half, and press edges firmly together. Pull the two ends around to form a ring, overlap the points, and press firmly together. Dry a few minutes (up to ½ hour) before cooking..

Cappelletti, which also use ravioli dough, start as small squares (1½ to 2 inches). Place a small amount of filling near the center of each square. Fold the dough into a triangle, press the edges together and pull the ends around like a won ton (see page 37). Place cappelletti on a floured board to dry for about 30 minutes before cooking.

If you wish, both tortellini and capelletti can be prepared a few days in advance and refrigerated or frozen.

To cook cappelletti or tortellini, place in boiling chicken stock and boil gently for 5 minutes if fresh, or about 15 minutes if dry. Serve in individual soup plates along with the broth and top with fresh grated Parmesan cheese for a soup course. Or boil in salted water and toss with melted butter and cream before serving as a pasta course.

GIANT SHELLS WITH QUICK CHEESE FILLING

SERVES 6 TO 8

Preheat oven to 350 degrees

QUICK CHEESE FILLING:

2 pounds ricotta cheese
¼ pound Gruyère cheese, grated coarse
¼ pound mozzarella cheese, grated coarse
2 eggs, lightly beaten
½ cup grated Parmesan cheese
1 tablespoon minced fresh parsley
Dash sugar

Salt, pepper, freshly-grated nutmeg to taste

12 ounces giant shells, parboiled for 8 minutes and drained

1 quart favorite meatless red sauce (at room temperature) (see pages 104, 125–27.)

Lots of grated Parmesan cheese for garnish

Mix all the filling ingredients together in a large bowl. Using a teaspoon, fill each shell. Use the back of the spoon to smooth out any excess. Pour a layer of sauce into the bottom of a baking dish. Place shells on top and pour remaining sauce over them. Bake in the preheated oven for 25 to 30 minutes. Serve with Parmesan cheese.

Cannelloni, or "big rolls," are available as large, hollow tubes at most markets. Or you can make your own noodles according to instructions below. Two lovely stuffed cannelloni, a sweet butterhead lettuce and red onion salad, some fresh fruit slices garnished with chopped mint, and a glass of Chablis are all you need for a marvelous supper.

For several years, my close friend and cooking buddy Ann Osburn and I have celebrated each other's wedding anniversary by preparing a feast of good food and wine. For our fifth anniversary, the main dish was cannelloni stuffed with a delicate combination of spinach, beef, and liver, then bathed with Béchamel and Sweet Plum Tomato Sauces.

ANNIVERSARY CANNELLONI
SERVES 6 TO 8

CANNELLONI NOODLES:

1½ cups flour	1 tablespoon olive oil
1 egg	1 teaspoon salt
1 egg white	Few drops water

MEAT & SPINACH FILLING:

2 tablespoons olive oil	1 pound ground beef
⅓ cup chopped onion	round
3 large garlic cloves,	3 chicken livers
peeled and crushed	½ cup grated Parmesan
One 10-ounce package	cheese
frozen chopped spin-	2 tablespoons heavy cream
ach, defrosted and	2 eggs, lightly beaten
squeezed dry, then	½ teaspoon dried oregano
chopped again	Salt and pepper to taste
2 tablespoons butter	

RICH BÉCHAMEL SAUCE:

¼ *cup butter*	*1 teaspoon salt*
¼ *flour*	⅛ *teaspoon white pepper*
1 cup milk	*Few dashes freshly-grated*
1 cup heavy cream	*nutmeg*

SWEET PLUM TOMATO SAUCE:

¼ *cup olive oil*	*6 tablespoons tomato paste*
1 large onion, peeled and	*2 teaspoons dried basil*
chopped	*2 teaspoons sugar*
4 cups Italian plum	*1 teaspoon salt*
tomatoes, seeded and	*Fresh-ground black*
chopped (with their	*pepper*
liquid)	

TOPPING:

¼ *cup grated Parmesan*	*2 tablespoons butter*
cheese	

To make the cannelloni noodles: Put flour on a heavy pastry board. Make a well in the center and place egg, egg white, oil, and salt in it. Mix together with your fingers until the dough can be gathered into a rough ball. Use the drops of water to help you gather the bits of flour remaining on the board, pressing them into the ball. Knead the dough on the floured board until it is smooth, shiny, and quite elastic, about 10 minutes. Wrap in plastic (or wax paper) and let rest for at least 10 minutes at room temperature before rolling.

Divide the dough into four parts. Roll out the dough, one part at a time (keeping remaining dough wrapped), with a heavy, long rolling pin. Keep turning the dough and rolling it out until it is paper thin. Cut dough into rectangles, 2 inches by 3 inches.

Noodles must be precooked before stuffing. Drop the rectangles into 6 to 8 quarts of boiling, salted water and stir gently with a wooden fork or spoon so they don't stick to each other (or to the side of the pan). Continue to cook over high heat for 5 minutes, or until tender, but not soft. Drain, cool slightly and place side by side on paper towels to drain.

To make the filling: Heat the olive oil in a large skillet. Add the onion and garlic and cook over medium heat, stirring frequently, for about 5 minutes, until they are soft, but not brown. Stir in the spinach and cook, stirring constantly, until the spinach sticks lightly to the pan, about 3 minutes. Transfer the seasoned spinach to a large mixing bowl.

Melt 1 tablespoon of butter in the same skillet and sauté the beef until light brown. Now add the beef to the spinach mixture. Melt the remaining tablespoon of butter in the skillet and cook the livers, turning frequently, until they are light brown, but still pink inside. Remove from skillet and chop the livers coarse. Add the livers to the mixing bowl along with the Parmesan cheese, the cream, eggs, oregano, salt, and pepper. Mix gently, but thoroughly. Set the stuffing aside until noodles are fully drained and sauces are ready.

To make the Rich Béchamel Sauce: Melt the butter in a saucepan. Remove the pan from the heat and stir in the flour. Pour the milk and cream into the pan all at once, whisking constantly. Return the pan to high heat and cook, stirring constantly with the whisk. When the sauce comes to a boil and is smooth, reduce heat and simmer, stirring, 2 minutes longer, or until the sauce heavily coats the wires of the whisk. Season with salt, white pepper, and nutmeg.

For the Tomato Sauce: Heat the olive oil in a large saucepan and add the onions. Cook them over moderate heat for 5 minutes until they are soft, but not brown. Add all the remaining ingredients and bring to a boil. Reduce the heat to very low and simmer, partially covered, for about 40 minutes, stirring occasionally.

To assemble and complete the cannelloni: Preheat the oven to 375 degrees. Place a tablespoon of filling on the bottom third of each noodle and roll into a tube. Pour a thin film of tomato sauce into the bottom of two 10 x 14-inch shallow bake-and-serve casseroles. Lay the hilled tubes side by side in one layer on the sauce. Pour the besciamella over them and spoon the remaining tomato sauce on top. Sprinkle with Parmesan cheese and dot with the butter. Bake in the preheated oven for 20 minutes, or until sauce is bubbling. Serve directly from the baking dish.

DRESSY CHEESE-FILLED CANNELLONI

Preheat oven to 350 degrees

SERVES 4 TO 5

¾ pound ricotta cheese
¾ pound mozzarella cheese, grated coarse
¼ cup grated Parmesan cheese
3 eggs, lightly beaten
2 tablespoons sugar
2 tablespoons cinnamon
1 teaspoon sweet basil flakes, crushed by hand
¼ cup chopped walnuts
¼ cup chopped ripe black olives

¼ cup golden raisins, plumped in Marsala wine
Juice and grated rind of 1 lemon
Salt and pepper to taste

8 to 10 cannelloni
3 cups favorite tomato or spaghetti sauce
¾ cup grated mozzarella cheese
½ cup grated Parmesan cheese

In a large mixing bowl, combine the cheeses with all but the last four ingredients.

Fill the cannelloni and place in an oiled baking dish with 3 cups of your favorite tomato or spaghetti sauce.

Sprinkle with the cheeses and bake in the preheated oven for 1 hour.

For a Seafood Stuffing: Eliminate the sugar, cinnamon and raisins and substitute 1 cup of minced clams, crab, lobster, and shrimp. Add a dash of brandy instead of the Marsala to bind the mixture together.

If you have the time, prepare two different fillings. You can bake them side by side in the same sauce, and serve two cannelloni to each person, one cheese and one mushroom-chicken.

MUSHROOM-CHICKEN FILLING

MAKES APPROXIMATELY 2 CUPS
TO FILL 8–10 CANNELLONI

½ pound fresh mush-
  rooms, minced fine
1 clove garlic, peeled and
  minced
3 tablespoons olive oil
1 cup fine-minced or
  ground cooked chicken

1 hard-boiled egg
Dash each of ground
  thyme and rosemary
1 to 2 tablespoons heavy
  cream

In a large skillet, sauté the mushrooms with the garlic in the olive oil, add the chicken and coat with the mushroom oil. Remove from heat. Push the egg through a sieve into the skillet. Season with thyme and rosemary. Allow to cool. Bind mixture together with cream. Proceed as in previous cannelloni recipe.

Seasoned cheese and spinach filling combine with herb and tomato sauces for an easy, yet special manicotti.

EASY TWO-CHEESE MANICOTTI

SERVES 4

Preheat oven to 375 degrees

One 10-ounce package frozen chopped spinach, defrosted and thoroughly drained
1 pound ricotta cheese
¼ cup minced onion
½ teaspoon salt
½ teaspoon dried basil, crumbled through your fingers

¼ teaspoon fresh-grated nutmeg
⅛ teaspoon pepper
2 tablespoons lemon juice
8 manicotti, parboiled 5 minutes, drained (see pages 232–33 for home-made manicotta instructions)

HERB SAUCE:
¼ cup butter
3 tablespoons flour
1 clove garlic, peeled and minced
1 teaspoon dried basil, crumbled
1 teaspoon salt
2 cups milk
2 tablespoons minced fresh parsley

1 cup favorite tomato sauce (or your favorite 8-ounce canned tomato sauce); see pages 104, 125–29)
½ cup grated Monterey Jack cheese (for topping)

In a large mixing bowl, combine the spinach, ricotta cheese, onion, seasonings, and lemon juice; stuff the pasta tubes.

To make the Herb Sauce: Melt the butter in a medium saucepan and blend in the flour, garlic, basil, and salt. Stir in the milk. Continue to cook, stirring, over medium heat, until mixture thickens and boils. Stir in the parsley.

Pour half of the Herb Sauce into the bottom of a bake-and-serve casserole. Place the filled tubes in a single layer on the sauce. Cover completely with remaining herb sauce. Pour the tomato sauce in a lengthwise strip over the manicotti. Sprinkle with grated cheese. Cover with foil. Bake in the preheated oven for 45 minutes, or until heated through.

The following manicotti recipe was given to me by a very dear friend, Martha Jean, whom I can best describe as mother, earth, and culture combined. She is a basic, loving, royal lady. Though we are separated by many miles, I always feel that she and her family are close to me.

VEAL MANICOTTI VELOUTÉ

SERVES 4

Preheat oven to 400 degrees

8 to 10 manicotti (or cannelloni, parboiled and drained

VEAL FILLING:
2 to 4 tablespoons butter
1 cup chopped onion
1 cup thin-sliced mushrooms
1 pound ground veal
1 cup white wine
Fresh-ground nutmeg, to taste

Coarse-ground black pepper, to taste
½ cup chopped fresh parsley
2 eggs, lightly beaten
Soft breadcrumbs

VELOUTÉ SAUCE (SIMILAR TO A BÉCHAMEL):

1 tablespoon butter	*2 egg yolks*
1 tablespoon flour	*Dash salt, pepper, and*
⅔ cup milk, heated	*oregano*

TOPPING:

Dash fresh-grated nutmeg	*Few tablespoons fresh-*
¼ cup chopped fresh	*grated Parmesan*
parsley	*cheese*

To make the veal filling: Melt enough butter to cover the bottom of a medium-size skillet. Sauté the onions and mushrooms together. When the vegetables are slightly limp, add the veal; continue to sauté, stirring occasionally, until the meat is no longer pink. Add the wine, a little nutmeg, a few grindings of pepper, and the parsley. Stir gently until blended. Remove skillet from heat. Add the eggs and enough breadcrumbs to hold the mixture together.

Fill the manicotti and place in a buttered baking dish.

To make the Velouté Sauce: Melt the butter in a medium saucepan; add the flour and make a roux. Stir in the heated milk and cook, stirring constantly, until the sauce is thick and smooth. Remove from heat; stir in the egg yolks. Season to taste with salt, pepper, and oregano.

Top the manicotti with the Velouté Sauce and sprinkle with nutmeg, parsley, and Parmesan cheese. Cover and bake in the preheated oven for ½ hour.

For a slight variation in taste, alternate the veal manicotti with cheese manicotti and bake them side by side in the same dish. Mix together: I pound ricotta cheese, 1 cup breadcrumbs, ¼ teaspoon each tarragon and savory, 1 well-beaten egg, and a dash of freshly-grated nutmeg.

Lasagne, a dish of broad noodles layered with sauces, cheese, meat and/or seafood, and then baked in the oven, is a classic Italian pasta.

My mother's lasagne is one of the lightest I have ever tasted. If you have the time, double the recipe to make an extra one. Freeze it in a large, aluminum pan and reheat it for a company feast.

BOATS'S EASY FLUFFY LASAGNE
SERVES 4 AS A MAIN DISH

Preheat oven to 350 degrees

8 ounces very broad lasagne, parboiled, drained, and rinsed under warm water so they will handle easily
2 tablespoons cooking oil
1 medium onion, peeled and diced
1 clove garlic, peeled and minced fine
1 pound ground beef

Two 15-ounce cans spaghetti sauce (or 1 quart of your favorite sauce)
1 pound ricotta cheese
½ pound mozzarella cheese, shredded
¼ cup grated Parmesan cheese
¼ cup grated Romano cheese
4 eggs

Pour oil into a large skillet and sauté the onion and garlic. Crumble the ground beef and sauté it until light brown in the skillet. Add the spaghetti sauce and simmer for 5 minutes.

In a mixing bowl, combine all four cheeses and the eggs.

Spoon a little of the spaghetti-meat sauce from the skillet into the bottom of a large, oblong, glass baking dish or metal pan. Add a single layer of noodles, a layer of the cheese mixture, another single layer of the noodles, a layer of the spaghetti-meat sauce, a layer of noodles, etc., ending with sauce.

Bake, uncovered, in the preheated oven for 50 minutes.

Sausages and a dash of hot pepper sauce stand out in this lasagne.

SAUSAGE LASAGNE

SERVES 6 TO 8

Preheat oven to 375 degrees

*1 pound lasagne, parboiled
    and drained*

*½ pound mild Italian sau-
    sages, sliced*

TOMATO SAUCE:

2 tablespoons olive oil
*1 clove garlic, peeled and
    crushed*
½ cup chopped celery
*One 6-ounce can tomato
    paste*
¾ cup hot water
*One 28-ounce can peeled
    plum tomatoes (with
    their liquid)*

1½ teaspoons salt
*¾ teaspoon bottled hot
    pepper sauce*
*¾ cup grated Parmesan
    cheese*
*½ pound mozzarella
    cheese, diced*
1 cup ricotta cheese

Cook sausages in a large skillet over medium heat, turning, until well browned. Remove and set aside.

To make the sauce: Heat the olive oil in the skillet, add the garlic and cook one minute. Add the celery and tomato paste; cook over high heat, stirring constantly, for 2 to 3 minutes. Add the hot water to the skillet along with the canned tomatoes and their liquid, salt, and hot pepper sauce. Bring to a boil; reduce heat, cover and simmer for 30 minutes. Set aside one cup of sauce to serve with the lasagne.

To assemble the lasagne, pour ½ cup sauce into the bottom of a shallow 2-quart casserole. Add a layer of noodles; sprinkle with Parmesan cheese, add another layer of sauce, a few pieces of mozzarella cheese, slices of sausage and spoonfuls of ricotta. Repeat the layers, ending with sauce and Parmesan cheese. Bake in the preheated oven for 25 minutes or until well heated. Cut into serving portions and serve with the reserved sauce and additional Parmesan cheese.

Canned tuna fish is a marvelous lasagne ingredient for an inexpensive family meal.

GREEN TUNA LASAGNE

SERVES 8

Preheat oven to 375 degrees

1 pound spinach lasagne, parboiled and drained (see page 90 for Pasta Verde)
½ cup butter
½ cup flour
3 cups chicken broth
Two 7-ounce cans tuna, packed in vegetable oil, drained, and flaked
⅓ cup chopped fresh parsley

½ teaspoon dried leaf basil
1 egg, lightly beaten
1 pound ricotta cheese
One 10-ounce package frozen chopped spinach, thawed and drained
1 pound mozzarella cheese, sliced thin
1 cup grated Parmesan cheese

Melt the butter in a medium-size saucepan; blend in flour. Gradually stir in the chicken broth and cook, stirring constantly, over medium heat until sauce thickens and comes to a boil. Remove from heat and stir in the tuna, parsley and basil.

In a small bowl, mix together the eggs and ricotta cheese.

Layer the bottom of a lightly greased 3-quart casserole with one third of the tuna sauce, half of the noodles, half of the cheese mixture, half of the spinach, and half of the mozzarella cheese. Repeat the layers, then add the last third of tuna sauce. Sprinkle with Parmesan cheese and bake in the preheated oven for 45 minutes.

One afternoon while preparing the food for a buffet-style dinner party, I was trying to create individual pasta without using a lot of casserole dishes. Thinking that lasagne would be ideal, I tried rolling up the noodles, jelly-roll style, with the filling inside. The resulting flowerets were ideal. Everyone, especially the children, enjoyed serving themselves mini stuffed lasagne.

LASAGNE FLOWERETS

SERVES 8

Preheat oven to 350 degrees

*8 green (spinach) lasagne,
    parboiled and drained*

TUNA-CHEESE FILLING:

One 7-ounce can tuna, drained	*2 tablespoons chopped fresh parsley*
1 pound ricotta cheese	*¼ teaspoon salt*
1 medium onion, peeled	

TOMATO-HERB SAUCE:

One 29-ounce can tomato sauce	*dried celery flakes, sweet basil*
1 teaspoon each ground oregano, garlic powder, sugar, dried parsley,	*¼ teaspoon each salt and pepper*

To make the filling: Place the tuna in a large mixing bowl; flake with a fork. Add cheese and continue to flake with a fork. Grate the onion directly into the bowl; add the parsley and salt. Continue mixing with a fork until you have a paste.

Place about 4 tablespoons of tuna-cheese mixture on each flat noodle. Carefully smooth out the filling with a spatula, leaving the curly part of the noodle uncovered. Carefully roll up the noodle jelly-roll style.

To make the sauce: Pour the canned sauce into a large saucepan. Add all the seasonings and herbs, crumbling the parsley, celery and sweet basil through your fingers and palms directly into the sauce. Bring the sauce to a boil; reduce to a simmer and continue to cook over very low heat for one half hour, stirring occasionally.

Pour half the sauce into a glass baking dish. Place lasagne rolls, standing on end, close to each other in the dish. Spoon the remaining sauce over each flower.

This dish may be assembled ahead of time and refrigerated until dinner. If refrigerating first, increase baking time by 14 to 20 minutes. Let flowerets stand about five minutes before serving. To vary the color: use regular egg noodles, frozen chopped spinach, and ricotta cheese with or without the tuna.

I call this recipe "Noodles Baked Like a Cake" because that's exactly how I prepare them. The baking dish is buttered and coated with breadcrumbs, cheese and egg. When you turn the pasta out, you'll have a handsome crusted "cake."

NOODLES BAKED LIKE A CAKE

SERVES 6 TO 10

Preheat oven to 350 degrees

*1 pound ziti (or rigatoni),
    cooked and drained*
*3 tablespoons sweet butter,
    cut up*

*3 heaping tablespoons
    grated Parmesan
    cheese*

C R U S T :

*2 tablespoons sweet butter,
    softened*
¼ cup breadcrumbs

*¼ cup Parmesan cheese,
    grated*
1 large egg, lightly beaten

F I L L I N G :

*8 ounces mozzarella cheese,
    grated coarse*

*¼ pound Italian ham,
    sliced thin*

Return the cooked ziti to the pot; add butter and Parmesan cheese and toss a few times to coat the pasta well. Set aside.

Butter a round baking dish or 3-quart soufflé. Combine the breadcrumbs and Parmesan cheese in a measuring cup. Add about ¼ cup of the breadcrumbs-cheese mixture to the dish and shake to coat it evenly. Shake excess crumbs back into the cup. Pour beaten egg into the dish. Again tilt to coat evenly with the egg. Now, again add about ¼ cup of the breadcrumbs-cheese mixture; shake again to coat evenly and pour excess back into the cup.

Layer about one third of the pasta into the prepared dish; sprinkle with one third of the mozzarella, one half of the ham strips, one third of the remaining breadcrumbs-cheese mixture. Again layer with one third of the pasta, one third of the mozzarella, one half of the ham, and one third of the breadcrumbs-cheese. Last, layer remaining pasta, mozzarella, and top with breadcrumbs-cheese. The dish can be made early in the day to this point and refrigerated until baking time.

Bake in the preheated oven, for 20 to 30 minutes if freshly made, or for 30 to 45 minutes if refrigerated. Allow to cool about 10 minutes, then insert a sharp knife around the edges to loosen slightly. Carefully turn out like a cake onto a serving platter. If you wish, you can top with a dollop of sour cream as a garnish. Cut into slices.

Who said pizza has to be made with bread dough? Tiny rice-like noodles can be worked into a marvelous "crust" for a deep dish pizza pie. A wedge or two of pie, a marinated vegetable salad, and some fresh fruit make a simple, yet unique, family dinner. Use whatever ingredients you have on hand in your pantry for the garnishes.

PIZZA NOODLE PIE

SERVES 4

Preheat oven to 400 degrees

8 ounces rosemaries, (or other rice-like pasta), cooked and drained
1 tablespoon butter
5 tablespoons grated Parmesan cheese
1 egg, lightly beaten
One 15-ounce can spaghetti sauce (or your favorite recipe), heated

One 4-ounce can mushroom pieces, drained
2 tablespoons pitted ripe black olives, sliced
3 ounces grated mozzarella cheese
4 strips of bacon, cooked and crumbled

Place hot cooked noodles in a large mixing bowl and immediately toss with butter. Add 4 tablespoons Parmesan cheese and the egg and toss lightly to mix. Spoon this mixture into a well-buttered 9- or 10-inch pie pan and press with your fingers to form a perfect "crust." Prebake the crust in the preheated oven for about 20 to 30 minutes, or until it is lightly browned. Remove from the oven and place on a rack to cool. If you are not going to fill immediately, cover lightly with foil to keep warm, then pop it back in the oven to reheat for a few minutes before filling.

Fill the crust with the spaghetti sauce. Arrange mushrooms and olives on top. Sprinkle with mozzarella cheese and the remaining Parmesan. Bake in the preheated oven for 5 to 10 minutes. Put under broiler for a few seconds to brown. Garnish with bacon before serving.

Just like a pizza restaurant, you can vary the toppings with your own favorites. My family also likes pepperoni, sausage, sautéed onions and green pepper. Or, the deep dish pie can be filled with an entirely different recipe, such as creamed chicken, shrimp and vegetables, or spicy chili with Cheddar cheese.

Somehow, we always think of tomatoes saucing our noodles. For an interesting switch, small rice-like noodles star in stuffed tomatoes.

STUFFED TOMATOES

SERVES 6

Preheat oven to 350 degrees

1 cup small stars (or other pastina), cooked and drained
6 large tomatoes
¼ cup pine nuts
¼ cup chopped fresh parsley
½ cup sour cream (or plain yogurt)
1 clove garlic, peeled and pressed

1 teaspoon dried sweet basil
½ teaspoon salt
¼ cup grated Parmesan cheese
¼ cup breadcrumbs
¼ cup water (or tomato juice or white wine)
2 tablespoons butter

Cut a thin slice off the top of each tomato so that you can hollow it out. Using a grapefruit knife, carefully remove as much pulp as possible without cutting any of the skin. Place the pulp in a large mixing bowl with the noodles, nuts, parsley, sour cream, garlic, sweet basil, and salt. Combine all the ingredients and carefully stuff the tomatoes. Sprinkle tops of the tomatoes with Parmesan cheese and breadcrumbs. Tomatoes may be stuffed in advance and refrigerated until cooking time.

Pour water into the bottom of a baking dish and place the tomatoes in the dish. Dot with the butter. Bake in the preheated oven for about 20 minutes, basting occasionally with pan juices. Green peppers, eggplant, or zucchini can also be prepared in this manner.

SALADS

Hot pasta is usually tossed immediately with butter (some-times, oil) and then sauced, but when it's to be served cold, a seasoned oil dressing is tastier. Medium tubes or macaroni are excellent with a garnish of Italian parsley, raisins and pine nuts. Or, on a hot summery day, egg noodles are most refreshing when tossed with an herb dressing and served with a chilled tomato sauce.

SUMMER SUPPER TAGLIOLINI

SERVES 6 TO 8

1 pound tagliolini, cooked
1 teaspoon minced garlic
½ cup chopped fresh
  Italian parsley

1 teaspoon fine-chopped
  fresh basil
1 cup olive oil

CHILLED LIGHT TOMATO PURÉE:

3 cups canned plum toma-
  toes, drained, seeded,
  chopped fine
1 clove garlic, peeled and
  mashed

1 teaspoon salt
¼ teaspoon fresh-ground
  black pepper
¼ teaspoon ground sage
2 tablespoons sweet butter

As soon as the noodles are cooked, drain and place on a serving platter. In a small bowl, mix the garlic, 5 table-spoons of the parsley, the basil and olive oil; add immedi-ately to the noodles. Toss gently, but thoroughly and set aside to cool completely. Do not refrigerate.

To make the sauce: Place the tomatoes, garlic and sea-soning in the top of a double boiler. Cook for about 30 minutes. Slowly add the butter. Remove from heat. Pour into a blender and purée. Chill. (Note: Since this sauce should be served cold, it is best to make it earlier in the day.)

Make a well in the center of the cooled noodles; pour in the chilled tomato sauce. Garnish with the remaining 3 tablespoons of chopped parsley. Serve and toss at the table. If you wish to dress this up even more, add capers and/or minced ripe black olives to the parsley when garnishing.

Fresh tomatoes, marinated artichoke hearts and herbs make an imaginative salad dressing for linguine.

HOT LINGUINE SALAD
SERVES 6 TO 8

1 clove garlic, peeled
4 large tomatoes, seeded and chopped coarse
¼ cup chopped marinated artichoke hearts
2 tablespoons chopped fresh basil
1 tablespoon fine-chopped fresh parsley
1 cup salad oil

Juice of 1 lemon
1 teaspoon fresh-ground black pepper
½ teaspoon salt
1 red chili pepper, chopped fine (optional)
1½ pounds linguine, cooked and drained
2 to 4 tablespoons pine nuts (optional garnish)

Bruise the garlic and rub the bottom and sides of a wooden salad bowl with it. Discard garlic.

Place the tomatoes, artichoke hearts, basil, and parsley in the bowl. Season with the oil, lemon juice, pepper, salt and chili pepper. Marinate vegetables for two hours. Meanwhile, prepare the linguine.

To serve, add the cooked linguine to the bowl and toss. If you like, sprinkle pine nuts on top as a garnish.

SOUPS

Pastas served in soup are classified as "pasta in brodo." The simplest soups consist of milk, chicken or beef broth. They can be homemade, canned, or prepared from bouillon cubes. Small shapes such as shells, bows, and tubes, pastina (small soup pasta shapes and flakes), or, in a pinch, broken pieces of spaghetti can be used.

When my young son is sick, I boil alphabets in chicken broth to settle his upset stomach. He calls it "crunchy soup." To every two cups of boiling broth, I add 3 table-spoons of pastina and continue to let the soup boil for a few minutes until done. If you like, sprinkle soup with grated Parmesan cheese at the table. The choice of pastina is yours. (If you prefer, you can add it precooked to the soup.)

A mixture of fresh and dried vegetables with pasta is considered a "zuppa." It can be sophisticated as well as countryfied.

COUNTRY-STYLE TOMATO SPLIT PEA SOUP
SERVES 4 TO 6

*1 large onion, peeled and
    chopped*
*2 strips bacon, cut into
    1-inch lengths*
1 cup dried split peas
2 stalks celery, chopped
*2 carrots, scraped and
    chopped*
*One 28-ounce can peeled
    tomatoes (with their
    liquid), mashed with
    wooden spoon*
*1½ tablespoons chopped
    fresh parsley*

*1 small green pepper,
    seeded and chopped*
*2 small yellow chilis,
    seeded and chopped*
*¼ teaspoon each dried
    thyme, black pepper,
    garlic powder, and
    sweet basil*
½ teaspoon salt
Dash cumin
1 bay leaf
3 cups good chicken broth
2 cups water
*3 to 4 ounces small sea-
    shells, parboiled*

In a large soup pot, sauté the onion with the bacon over
low heat, for 10 minutes, or until onion is soft. Add the
vegetables, one at a time, stirring. Add the spices and seasonings, stirring to blend the flavors. Add the chicken
broth and water; stir to mix well. Bring soup to a boil;
cover and reduce heat to the lowest possible. Simmer for
3 hours. Remove the bay leaf and force soup through a
sieve (or purée in a blender). Mash the vegetables as much
as possible through the sieve and add to the stock. Check
seasonings, especially for salt, pepper, and garlic. Simmer
soup (uncovered) for another couple of hours. About 5
minutes before serving, add the seashells to the pot.

Accompany soup with avocado slices topped with a tomato sauce and onion dressing, melted Swiss cheese on
toasted English muffins and a gooey chocolate cake for
dessert.

One of the most popular Northern Italian winter soups is minestrone, a thick soup made with vegetables, beans, and macaroni.

HEARTY MINESTRONE

SERVES 6

1 teaspoon olive oil
2 strips bacon, chopped
1 clove garlic, peeled and
*   minced*
1 small onion, peeled and
*   chopped*
1 teaspoon chopped fresh
*   parsley*
½ teaspoon salt
Dash pepper
1 tablespoon tomato paste,
*   diluted in 1 cup white*
*   wine*

2 cups canned navy beans
2 potatoes, peeled and
*   chopped*
2 stalks celery, chopped
2 carrots, scraped and
*   sliced into thin discs*
1½ cups beef stock
1 cup macaroni tubes, par-
*   boiled*
¼ cup grated Parmesan
*   cheese for garnish*

In a large soup pot, pour in the olive oil and add the bacon, garlic, onion and parsley; sauté over medium heat for a few minutes. Season with salt and pepper. Add the diluted tomato paste; stir to combine and cook for 10 minutes. Add the remaining vegetables and the beef stock. Bring to a boil, then reduce to a gentle simmer and cook for about an hour. Ten minutes before serving add the macaroni tubes. Ladle soup into individual bowls and pass grated Parmesan cheese separately.

Another version of the popular minestrone is a minestra di verdura featuring fresh, seasonal vegetables. To serve Genovese style, top the soup at the last moment with pesto, a rich sauce of basil, garlic, Parmesan cheese, olive oil and pine nuts (see pages 134–37). On hot summer days, this soup can be served chilled.

MINESTRA DI VERDURA
(Vegetable Soup)

SERVES 6

1 medium yellow onion, peeled and chopped
1 leek, diced
1 clove garlic, peeled and minced
½ cup olive oil
½ cup chopped carrots
½ cup chopped celery
1 cup chopped zucchini
1 cup chopped green beans
One 8-ounce can peeled Italian plum tomatoes, chopped (with their liquid)
1 cup shredded Savoy cabbage
1 teaspoon salt
2 quarts boiling beef stock
1 cup lumachine (or other macaroni), cooked and drained
⅓ cup grated Parmesan cheese for garnish

In a large soup pot, over medium heat, sauté the onion, leek, and garlic in the olive oil until they are soft and golden. Add the carrots; sauté 2 minutes, stirring occasionally. Add the other vegetables, one at a time, sautéeing each for a few minutes before adding the next. Sprinkle with salt and add the boiling stock, stirring to mix well. Cover the pot and continue to cook at a slow boil for 2 to 3 hours, to allow ingredients to mingle. Add the macaroni about 10 minutes before serving. Serve with grated Parmesan cheese.

Dried beans or lentils can also be added to the soup. Soak them until tender, then sauté them in a bit of olive oil and salt pork before adding with the vegetables.

Macaroni and bean soup is a classic Italian dish. It is quite thick, almost dry. Traditionally, the pasta was "rimanenze," the left over cuts—long and short—all mixed together. This is a good way to use up the little bits of various pastas you have in the kitchen and at the same time give the soup a variety of textures.

MACARONI AND BEAN SOUP

SERVES 6 TO 8

1 medium onion, peeled
2 large cloves garlic, peeled
1 stalk celery
2 carrots, scraped
¼ cup chopped fresh parsley
⅓ cup olive oil
One 8-ounce can peeled tomatoes, chopped (with their liquid)
Salt and pepper to taste
1 teaspoon rosemary

One 20-ounce can cannellini (white kidney beans) with their liquid
2 quarts beef stock, brought to a boil, then simmered
8 ounces assorted macaroni (I use 4 ounces each ditalini and soya rice shells)
1 quart boiling water
Grated Parmesan cheese for garnish

Mince the onion, garlic, celery, carrots and parsley together to make a "battuto." Put the minced mixture into a large soup pot with the oil and sauté over medium heat for about 5 minutes. Add the chopped tomatoes with their liquid, salt and pepper, and rosemary; lower the heat and continue to cook another 20 minutes. Add the beans with their liquid; stir to mix thoroughly and continue to cook another 5 minutes. Add the heated broth and boiling water. Bring soup to a boil. Taste for seasoning. Add the macaroni to the boiling soup, stirring constantly, and continue to cook until they are almost tender, but still firm. Turn off heat and allow soup to set and cool slightly for about 5 to 10 minutes before serving. Serve with plenty of grated Parmesan cheese.

The basic soup can be made in advance, adding the pasta just before serving. To reheat the soup, add enough boiling water to achieve the proper consistency and simmer to warm thoroughly.

If you have any leftover meat bones in your refrigerator, you can add these to the soup for extra flavor. (Note: The vegetable sauté or "battuto" is a beautiful assortment of colors—greens, oranges, and reds. It is an excellent base for any soup, meat, fowl, or vegetable dish.)

With the harvest of sweet summer corn, I make a huge pot of corn soup and freeze it in boilable bags for the winter months. This recipe can easily be cut in half. The choice of pasta is yours, though it should be small, about the size of a corn kernel.

CORN AND MACARONI SOUP

SERVES 16 TO 18

5 tablespoons butter
5 tablespoons olive oil
1 cup chopped onion
1 tablespoon minced garlic
1¼ cups fine-chopped carrots
1 cup fine-chopped celery (including some leaves)
1½ cups diced, peeled tomatoes (with their liquid)

18 ears fresh-picked corn, kernels scraped off
4 teaspoons chopped fresh parsley
1 tablespoon salt
1 teaspoon black pepper
1 teaspoon marjoram
6 quarts chicken broth, heated
1 pound tubettini

In a large soup pot, melt 4 tablespoons of the butter; add 4 tablespoons of the oil. Sauté the onion with the garlic over medium heat until the onion softens. Add the carrots with the remaining 1 tablespoon each of butter and oil; lower the heat. Stir, and continue to cook until the carrots soften, for about 15 minutes. Add the celery and tomatoes, stirring to mix well, and continue to cook about 5 minutes. Add the corn and parsley; stir to mix well. Season with salt, pepper, and marjoram; add one quart of the chicken broth. Place cover on the pot slightly askew, allowing some liquid to evaporate. Continue to cook at a very low simmer for about an hour, stirring occasionally.

If you have a food processor, use the steel blade and pour 2 cups of corn mixture into the body, jogging it for a few seconds, then pour the mixture into a large bowl. If you don't have a food processor, use an electric blender or a sieve, but be sure to check for proper texture. You want to jog the corn only enough to open the kernels and release the natural ''milk.'' You do not want to make a paste or purée. Return the processed corn to the soup pot. Add the remaining chicken stock and continue to cook at a low simmer for 1 hour, stirring occasionally. Taste for seasoning.

A few minutes before serving, bring soup to a boil, add the macaroni and watch carefully as they will soften quickly. Serve soup immediately in heated individual bowls. If you wish, as a delicious extra, swirl a bit of heavy cream into each soup bowl seconds before serving.

SAUCED AND SAUTÉED NOODLES (Including Casseroles)

Many sauces for pasta take hours to cook; others are ready within minutes. Some are chopped or pounded, never simmered. But, no matter the preparation, a proper Italian sauce should be "married" immediately to the fresh-cooked pasta. The pasta should never be smothered or drowned; instead, it should be lightly coated and tossed.

Use fresh herbs whenever possible—particularly parsley and basil. Fresh-ground black pepper, fresh-grated nutmeg and fresh-pressed or minced garlic are the most common seasonings. A good olive oil, of which the first pressing (or virgin) is superb and, occasionally, sweet butter, are best for sautéeing.

Fresh-grated cheeses for tossing and topping are considerably more flavorful than pregrated, packaged varieties. Most markets carry cheese in wedges. Otherwise, take a trip to your local Italian market to stock up on ingredients.

American Asiago cheese can be substituted for Italian Parmesan (Parmigiano); Romano (Pecorino Romano) is much sharper than Parmesan. Keep cheeses wrapped and in the refrigerator. Do not grate more than needed for each recipe.

Other cheeses popular with Italian recipes include mozzarella (a light, whitish yellow cheese which melts and strings), Gorgonzola (blue cheese), and ricotta (similar to cottage cheese in appearance). Italian ricotta, made from unpasteurized ewe's milk, is sweeter to the taste and has a looser texture than the American version which is made from pasteurized cow's milk.

Fresh garlic sautéed in olive oil, "aglio e olio," is a basic Italian dressing for spaghetti. Like the proverbial simple, black dress it can be dressed up to go anywhere.

SPAGHETTI WITH GARLIC, OIL, AND ANCHOVIES

SERVES 4 TO 6

1 pound spaghetti
3 whole garlic cloves, peeled
½ cup olive oil (¾ cup if you prefer your pasta wetter)
One 2-ounce tin anchovy fillets, minced
1 tablespoon chopped fresh parsley

Since this is a quick, last-minute dish, it is best to prepare the sauce at the very last minute, while the spaghetti is boiling.

In a small skillet over low heat, brown the garlic in warm olive oil. Once the oil is flavored, discard the garlic. Stir in the anchovies and crush them with the back of a wooden spoon as you are stirring. Add the parsley, stir, and remove skillet from heat. Drain the cooked spaghetti and toss it with the sauce. (Note: If you are not fond of anchovies, spaghetti tossed with garlic, oil, and a touch of parsley is also a lovely dish. You can also add a dried red chili pepper to the oil along with the garlic.)

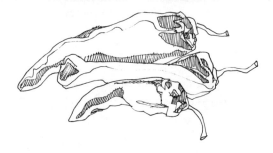

Warm melted butter dresses practically any pasta exquisitely.

SPAGHETTI WITH BUTTER-CHEESE SAUCE
SERVES 5 TO 6

1 pound spaghetti, cooked and drained
½ cup melted butter
½ cup fresh-grated Parmesan cheese
Fresh-grated ground black pepper

Return drained pasta to the pot in which it was cooked. Toss with melted butter; add cheese and continue to toss. Serve sprinkled with black pepper. *Variations:* for a Garlic Butter Sauce, add 4 to 6 minced garlic cloves to the butter and sauté them until golden before pouring over the spaghetti—this is my husband's favorite. For a Butter Herb Sauce, add 1 tablespoon chopped chives and 2 tablespoons chopped parsley to the melted butter before tossing with the pasta.

Tomatoes and herbs, perked with some fresh lemon juice, combine to create a luscious raw tomato sauce.

ZITI WITH RAW TOMATO SAUCE
SERVES 4 TO 6

2 pounds ripe tomatoes,
peeled, seeded, and
chopped
¼ cup chopped fresh
parsley
¼ cup chopped fresh basil
Juice of 1 large lemon

3 tablespoons olive oil
1 large clove garlic, peeled
and minced
Salt and pepper to taste
1 pound ziti, cooked and
drained

Combine all the ingredients (except ziti) in a large mixing bowl. Pour over hot ziti. Toss and serve immediately.

Italian cooking is known for its variety of tomato sauces. Every sauce I've ever tasted has had its own twist, perhaps in the addition of a little different seasoning or vegetable. When using fresh tomatoes, select only the sweet, ripe ones. Otherwise, canned, peeled Italian plum tomatoes are the best for sauces. Most sauces should not be cooked all day. Often, too long a period of cooking produces a bitter taste.

To peel fresh tomatoes, dip them in boiling water, one at a time, for one minute. Rinse the tomatoes immediately in ice-cold water. The skin should slip off easily. To seed, cut peeled tomatoes in half and scoop out the seeds with a spoon.

When the harvest of tomatoes is excellent, you can make a rich, sweet sauce in your blender without cooking. The hot pasta will warm the sauce. Before preparing this sauce, all vegetables should be brought to room temperature.

PASTA WITH HARVEST TOMATO SAUCE
SERVES 4

3 cups chopped fresh to-matoes, peeled
2 cloves garlic, peeled
¼ cup chopped fresh parsley

1 tablespoon chopped fresh mint
¼ cup olive oil
Salt and pepper to taste
1 pound pasta of your choice

Place all ingredients except the pasta in a food processor or electric blender, and purée. Prepare the pasta and toss immediately with the sauce.

The simplest of cooked tomato sauces is a quick sauté done in olive oil with some crushed garlic.

FETTUCCINE WITH
SAUTÉED TOMATO SAUCE
SERVES 3 TO 4

¼ *cup olive oil*
2 *cloves garlic, peeled and*
     crushed
1 *pound ripe tomatoes,*
     peeled, seeded, and
     chopped

¾ *pound cooked fettuccine*
1 *tablespoon butter*
1 *tablespoon minced fresh*
     parsley, to garnish

In a large skillet, heat the oil and add the garlic, stirring to flavor the oil, for 1 minute. Add the tomatoes and continue to cook over medium heat for another 5 minutes. Toss the hot fettuccine with the butter, then cover with the tomato sauce and toss again. Garnish with minced parsley and serve.

Variation: A gorgeous salmon-colored sauce which responds quite well to delicately stuffed tortellini can be made by mixing the Sautéed Tomato Sauce (substitute a small, chopped, yellow onion for the garlic and add a dash of sugar) with the Béchamel Sauce (pages 96–97).

One wintry evening we were invited to a casual dinner with friends. The hostess, Beverly Klages, served a lovely last-minute spaghetti dish. Practically everything had been prepared earlier in the day, arranged in small bowls, and refrigerated until a few minutes before dinner.

LAST-MINUTE TOMATO SAUCE

SERVES 6 TO 8

½ pound butter
1 onion, peeled and
chopped fine
2 cloves garlic, peeled and
minced fine
One 28-ounce can peeled
plum tomatoes
(drained), mashed
with wooden spoon

One 2-ounce can anchovy
fillets (optional)
⅔ cup capers
One 6-ounce can black
olives, minced
½ cup minced fresh
parsley
1½ pounds spaghetti

Melt butter in a large skillet; add remaining sauce ingredients one at a time, and simmer over low heat while
pasta is cooking, approximately 10 minutes. Toss sauce
with spaghetti.

A smooth, creamed tomato sauce is excellent with stuffed
noodles as well as plain spaghetti. Try it with ravioli,
tortellini or cappelletti.

PASTA WITH CREAMED TOMATO SAUCE

SERVES 6 TO 8

¼ pound butter
1 small yellow onion,
peeled and chopped
fine
¼ cup fine-chopped
carrots
¼ cup fine-chopped celery
One 20-ounce can Italian

plum tomatoes (with
their liquid)
1 teaspoon sugar
Salt to taste
½ cup heavy cream
1½ pounds pasta of your
choice, cooked and
drained

Melt the butter in a large skillet and sauté the onion, carrot and celery until soft. Add the canned tomatoes with their liquid, the sugar and salt. Stir to combine all ingredients and continue to cook over very low heat for 1 hour, stirring occasionally. Pour the sauce into a food processor or electric blender and purée. Sauce may be made ahead of time to this point and reheated just before serving. Slowly add the cream to the warm sauce, stirring constantly; simmer for 1 minute. Toss with the prepared pasta and serve.

Some of the best Italian cooks I know have taught me the secrets of a creamy, rich ragù sauce. Lean meat should be sautéed in a combination of butter and olive oil only until it loses its raw quality, not until it is too brown and dries out. The milk (or cream) should be added to the meat and vegetables just before the tomatoes. This is one of the few

sauces that, authentically, should be cooked at a slow simmer for hours and hours.

BOLOGNESE MEAT SAUCE
MAKES APPROXIMATELY 5 CUPS

4 tablespoons chopped
    yellow onion
1 large clove garlic, peeled
    and pressed
2 tablespoons butter
2 tablespoons olive oil
3 tablespoons fine-chopped
    celery
4 tablespoons fine-chopped
    carrot
1/4 pound lean ground pork
1/2 pound lean ground beef

1/2 cup milk
Two 16-ounce cans Italian
    plum tomatoes,
    chopped (with their
    liquid)
1 cup dry red wine
    (Burgundy)
Salt and pepper to taste
1/4 teaspoon dried sweet
    basil, rubbed through
    your hands
1 to 1 1/2 quarts water

In a large soup pot over medium heat, sauté the onion and garlic in the melted butter until onion is soft. Add the olive oil, celery, and carrots, continuing to cook over medium heat for about 5 minutes. Add the ground meats, crumbling by hand, and more olive oil if necessary. When the meat is no longer raw, stir in the milk, then the tomatoes with their liquid. Stir to mix well and simmer for a few minutes. Add the wine and seasonings. This sauce is best when simmered for 3 to 4 hours, stirring occasionally. As the liquid evaporates and the sauce begins to thicken too much, slowly add one cup of heated water at a time, as needed. The resulting sauce should be very thick.

Another superb meat sauce for spaghetti uses whiskey instead of wine. The best and most enjoyable way to test this sauce for seasoning is to dip a small chunk of Italian bread into the pot and taste.

WHISKEY MARINARA SAUCE
MAKES 3 TO 4 CUPS

1 pound lean ground sir-
loin
2 ounces rye whiskey
2 pounds peeled tomatoes,
seeded and chopped
2 to 3 tablespoons olive oil

1 clove garlic, peeled and
minced
⅓ cup chopped fresh
parsley
Dash oregano, thyme, and
basil
Salt and pepper to taste

Sauté the ground sirloin in a skillet until slightly brown. (Add a touch of oil if meat is too lean.) Add whiskey and set skillet aside. In a saucepan, cook the tomatoes with the olive oil, garlic, parsley, herbs, salt, and pepper over high heat, for 15 minutes. Reheat the meat and slowly add the tomato sauce.

Meatless sauces, garnished with plenty of cheese, are high in protein and excellent for a change-of-pace menu.

EGGPLANT SAUCE

MAKES APPROXIMATELY
2 QUARTS

1 ounce dried Italian mushrooms, soaked in hot water or broth for 20 minutes
½ cup olive oil
3 garlic cloves, peeled and minced
1 medium eggplant (about 1 pound), unpeeled, chopped into ¾-inch cubes
2 green peppers, seeded and diced
3 cups peeled and chopped tomatoes
¼ cup sliced ripe black olives
¼ cup chopped fresh parsley
1 teaspoon crushed oregano
½ teaspoon dried sweet basil, crushed
Salt and pepper to taste
One 10-ounce can tomato purée
1 cup dry red wine

Drain and chop mushrooms coarse; set aside.

In a large skillet over low flame, heat the oil and add the garlic. When the garlic is light brown add the eggplant, peppers, tomatoes, black olives, and parsley. Stir well and add all remaining ingredients. Stir again and cover skillet. Simmer over very low heat for 1 hour, stirring occasionally. If more liquid is needed, add more red wine.

Clam sauces, both white and red, are traditionally served with linguine. Basil, oregano, and thyme blend best with the tomatoes, while parsley and marjoram are most compatible with a subtle white sauce.

LINGUINE WITH RED CLAM SAUCE
SERVES 6

RED CLAM SAUCE:

¼ cup butter
2 cloves garlic, peeled and minced
½ cup fine-chopped onion
½ cup chopped celery
1 teaspoon salt
½ teaspoon dried leaf basil
¼ teaspoon each dried leaf thyme and dried leaf oregano

One 28-ounce can peeled whole tomatoes, chopped and seeded
Two 10 ½-ounce cans minced clams, drained (with their liquid reserved)
¼ cup good brandy, (optional)
⅓ cup chopped fresh parsley

1 pound linguine, cooked and drained
Hot pepper sauce, optional

In a large saucepan, melt the butter; add the garlic, onion, and celery. Cook over medium heat for 5 minutes, until onion and celery are tender. Add seasonings, tomatoes, clam liquid, and brandy. Simmer sauce for 30 minutes. Stir in the clams and parsley; heat thoroughly and pour over prepared linguine. If you like a zip of spiciness, top with a few drops of hot pepper sauce.

A touch of chopped pimiento adds color and flavor to a white clam sauce. The trick to this is a quickly made sauce which "marinates" the linguine for some time before serving.

LAUDY'S LINGUINE WITH
WHITE CLAM SAUCE

SERVES 6

WHITE CLAM SAUCE:

*Four 8-ounce cans chopped
    clams (with their
    liquid)*
*One 4-ounce can mush-
    rooms, drained*
*1 tablespoon chopped
    pimiento*
1 tablespoon olive oil

*1 clove garlic, peeled and
    minced*
*2 tablespoons chopped
    fresh parsley*
Pinch oregano

*1 pound linguine, par-
    boiled and drained*

In a medium saucepan, combine the clams and their liquid with the mushrooms, pimiento, olive oil, garlic, parsley, and oregano. Simmer the sauce for 5 minutes.

Return drained linguine to the pot in which it was cooked. Pour the sauce over the linguine and let it "marinate" for 20 minutes. Reheat and serve.

If fresh clams in their shells are available, the time you spend cleaning and steaming them will be repaid many times when you taste this dish.

SPAGHETTI WITH CLAMS AND TOMATOES
SERVES 4 TO 6

2 pounds cherrystone
*   clams*
¾ cup olive oil
1 tablespoon fine-chopped
*   fresh parsley*
3 large cloves garlic,
*   peeled and minced*

One 35-ounce can peeled
*   plum tomatoes, drained*
*   and chopped*
1 pound spaghetti, cooked
*   and drained*

Scrub clams very well and rinse in cold water. Place them in a heavy covered pot over medium heat, and cook until the clams open. When the clams open, their liquid will run into the bottom of the pot. Remove the clams, and strain the liquid through a sieve into a cup and reserve. Remove clams from their shells and place in a bowl. Toss with 2 tablespoons of the olive oil and the parsley.

In a large saucepan, heat the remaining oil and sauté the garlic. Reduce the heat, add the tomatoes, and cook for 10 minutes. Add the strained clam liquid and increase heat, stirring occasionally, for another 5 minutes. Add the clams and continue to cook for a few minutes. Place spaghetti on a large platter, pour sauce on top and toss.

Clams are just one of the fresh seafoods that are remarkably good with pasta. Lobster, shrimp, and mussels are also superb in a tomato sauce seasoned lightly with garlic, oregano, parsley and white wine.

At the National Macaroni Institute's 10th Annual

Family Reunion, this was one of the pasta dishes presented by Tiro A Segno's Manager, Anthony Narida.

LINGUINE WITH MARECHIARE SAUCE
SERVES 8

One 35-ounce can plum tomatoes (with their liquid)
⅓ cup olive oil
2 or 3 whole cloves garlic, peeled
¼ cup white wine
½ cup chopped fresh parsley
1 teaspoon salt
Dash pepper
½ teaspoon oregano leaves, crushed

2 raw lobster tails (4 ounces each), shelled and diced
½ pound shrimp, shelled, cleaned, and quartered
1 dozen small clams, shelled and diced
6 mussels, shelled
1 pound linguine, cooked and drained
⅓ cup fresh-grated Parmesan cheese

In a medium saucepan, combine the tomatoes with their liquid, the oil, garlic, wine, parsley, salt, pepper, and oregano. Bring to a boil; simmer for 20 minutes, stirring occasionally. Remove garlic and add seafood. Simmer the sauce another 3 minutes, or until seafood is cooked through.

Return drained linguine to the pot in which it cooked, adding 1½ cups of the sauce and 2 tablespoons of the cheese. Toss lightly, heat and place in a serving dish. Pour remaining sauce on top and sprinkle with remaining cheese.

Pesto is said to have been created in Genoa where the warm sun encourages the growth of basil, which, for me, combines all the good things found in fresh parsley, water-

cress, and mint. "Al pesto" means "by pounding." Originally, pesto was made with a mortar and pestle by
pounding the basil, garlic, pine nuts, cheese and olive oil
together. A food processor or electric blender will cut the
preparation time considerably. The resulting sauce should
be the consistency of creamed butter. It is a beautiful, deep,
green and smells aromatically of basil and garlic. If you
want to make a batch of sauce during the prime basil
season, you can freeze it. Some people suggest blending all
the ingredients except the Parmesan cheese when freezing.
However, I've completed the recipe, spooned it into containers, and frozen small amounts successfully for several
months. The finished recipe will also keep in the refrigerator for many days.

Pesto can also be added to soup (see page 117) or salad
dressings, and is delicious when used to coat a firm, light
fish fillet, such as halibut, and then broiled.

LINGUINE WITH PESTO
SERVES 6 TO 8

¼ *pound Parmesan
    cheese, cut into small
    pieces*
4 cloves garlic, peeled
¼ *teaspoon pepper*
*2 cups loosely packed fresh
    basil leaves, carefully
    torn by hand, without
    bruising*

½ *cup pine nuts*
1 teaspoon salt
¼ *teaspoon white pepper*
¾ *to 1 cup olive oil*
1½ *pounds linguine,
    cooked and drained
    (reserve some liquid)*

To make the sauce using the steel blade of a food
processor, add one ingredient at a time and process for
about 2 to 3 minutes at each step. Set sauce aside until
ready to use.

If using a mortar and pestle, it is best to grate the

Parmesan cheese instead of cutting it into small pieces. Garlic should be chopped. Then, pound and grind the basil and garlic together. Add the remaining ingredients, one at a time, until each is fully absorbed in the paste.

If fresh basil is not available, you can use the dried leaves and soak them in olive oil. Although this is a tasty sauce, it really doesn't compare to the fresh, but it's better than no pesto.

Note: To serve, place linguine on individual serving dishes. Thin 3 generous tablespoons of pesto paste with about 1½ tablespoons of the liquid in which the pasta was cooked for each 3-ounce portion of noodles. It is very important to serve this alone as an appetizer or first course as it is deliciously rich and no other flavors should interfere.

PESTO SAUCE II

MAKES APPROXIMATELY 2 CUPS
SERVES 6 TO 8 (SEE NOTE ABOVE)

2 cups chopped fresh
    parsley
2 tablespoons dried basil
    leaves, soaked in ¼ cup
    olive oil for 30 minutes
2 cloves garlic, peeled

½ cup olive oil
¼ cup pine nuts
½ cup fresh-grated
    Parmesan cheese
1 teaspoon salt
¼ teaspoon pepper

Place all the ingredients in a food processor or blender (as in above recipe) and make a paste.

Pesto Sauce is often referred to as Green Sauce, and sometimes walnuts are used instead of pine nuts. This unusual version also suggests replacing the basil with spinach leaves.

GREEN SAUCE

MAKES APPROXIMATELY 2 CUPS
SERVES 6 TO 8 (SEE NOTE PAGE
136)

2 cups firmly packed
  spinach leaves
½ cup firmly packed
  chopped fresh parsley
2 cloves garlic, peeled
¼ cup chopped walnuts

½ cup olive oil
2 tablespoons butter
½ cup fresh-grated Parmesan cheese
1 teaspoon salt
¼ teaspoon pepper

Combine the ingredients in a food processor or electric blender (as in preceding pesto recipes).

Note: The preceding Simple Pesto Sauce and Green Sauce recipes are sufficient to cover 1¼ to 1½ pounds of pasta. Cook and drain your choice of pasta, reserving some liquid to thin the sauce slightly if you find it too thick for individual tastes. See instructions for Pesto Sauce, pages 134–36.

The tales spun around fettuccine are like a spider's web. A man known as Zeffirino is reputed to have invented the noodles in 15th-century Bologna, having been inspired by the golden curls of Lucrezia Borgia. But the restaurant credited with making fettuccine famous is Alfredo all' Au-

gusteo on Piazza Augusto Imperatore, Rome, known as Alfredo l' Originale. Stories tell that Alfredo received a golden spoon and fork from Mary Pickford and Douglas Fairbanks, Sr., engraved "to Alfredo, The King of the Noodles." He is also famous for tossing his noodles for actress Elizabeth Taylor and for Richard Nixon when he was U.S. Vice President. Alfredo always attributed his superior sauce to the farm-fresh dairy products he used. The trick is to use plenty of butter, cream and fresh-grated Parmesan cheese, with a dash of fresh-cracked black pepper added at the last minute. The creamy sauce can be made separately and then mixed with hot noodles.

FETTUCCINE ALFREDO

SERVES 4 TO 6

¼ pound sweet butter,
   softened
1 cup heavy cream
1 cup grated Parmesan
   cheese

1 pound fettuccine, cooked
   and drained
½ teaspoon salt
Fresh-cracked black pepper
Touch of grated nutmeg,
   (optional)

In a large skillet over medium heat, melt half the butter. Stir in the cream and, as it begins to thicken, add ⅓ cup grated cheese. Add the hot noodles to the sauce and toss gently with a fork and spoon. Add all remaining ingredients, mixing and blending until the noodles are well coated and creamy. Serve very hot with additional grated cheese and fresh-cracked black pepper. For an added delight, toss in at the last minute, one ounce of Italian truffles sliced very thin.

Melinda Wehrle, daughter of Ralph Sarli, the President of American Beauty Macaroni Company, developed her own family favorite. Her recipe is similar to Alfredo's but she uses a thin, angular noodle instead of the usual flat fettuccine.

FETTUCCINE MELINDA

SERVES 4 TO 6 AS A FIRST
COURSE

10 ounces fettuccine, cooked and drained
¼ pound butter, cut into small pieces
½ cup milk or cream
*½ cup grated Romano or Parmesan cheese, or ¼ cup of
    each*
Chopped parsley and black pepper to taste

Pour fettuccine into a heated serving bowl. Add butter, milk and cheese and toss gently with two forks until the pasta is well coated. If the noodles seem too dry, add a bit more milk. Mix in parsley and black pepper for color and taste. Serve at once. Pass additional cheese separately.

If you start with the basic Alfredo Sauce and add spinach and bacon, you'll have a Florentine dish.

FETTUCCINE FLORENTINE

SERVES 6 TO 8

½ cup butter
One 10-ounce package
  frozen chopped spin-
  ach, thawed and
  drained
1 pound bacon, lightly
  browned, drained, and
  crumbled

1 pound fettucine, cooked
  and drained
1½ cups heavy cream
1 egg, lightly beaten
2 cups grated Parmesan
  cheese
2 teaspoons salt

Melt butter in a large skillet. (Or, if you like, prepare this table-side in a chafing dish.) Add the spinach and bacon; cook until heated through. Add the cooked noodles and toss lightly. Combine the cream and eggs and add to the noodles along with the grated cheese and salt. Toss to mix well. Cover and cook for 5 minutes.

Similar to Fettuccine Alfredo in appearance, this Gorgonzola Sauce gets its extra-tangy taste from the Italian blue cheese.

MOSTACCIOLI WITH GORGONZOLA SAUCE

SERVES 4

½ pint whipping cream
6 ounces Gorgonzola
  cheese, crumbled
Salt and white pepper to
  taste
12 ounces mostaccioli,
  cooked and drained

4 teaspoons butter
⅓ cup fresh-grated Par-
  mesan cheese
Dash fresh-grated nutmeg

With the use of a food processor, this sauce can be made within seconds. Pour the whipping cream into the container with the plastic blade. Slowly feed the crumbled Gorgonzola cheese into it to combine the two into a very smooth paste. Season with salt and pepper. Scrape all of the mixture into a saucepan to heat.

If you do not have a processor or electric blender, the sauce can be made in the saucepan from scratch. Gradually heat the cream; as it warms, slowly add the crumbled Gorgonzola, making sure the cheese is completely melted and the mixture is smooth before the next addition. Use a wooden spoon or wire whisk to break up any lumps. Season with salt and pepper.

Return drained noodles to the pot in which they were cooked and toss with butter over low heat to coat evenly. Pour heated cheese sauce over noodles and continue to toss. Add the Parmesan cheese, continuing to toss carefully. Turn noodles onto individual platters, if serving as a first course, or onto a serving platter if serving as a side course. Grate fresh nutmeg directly on top. (Note: Although the choice of noodles is yours, this recipe needs a good thick variety as a contrast to the smooth sauce.)

If you toss an abundance of fresh mushrooms, sautéed in oil, with some pasta, you'll have a marvelous side dish for poached fish or broiled meat.

MOSTACCIOLI AND MUSHROOMS

SERVES 6 TO 8 AS A FIRST
COURSE, 8 TO 10 AS A SIDE
DISH

1½ *pounds fresh mush-*
  rooms, sliced thick
10 *tablespoons olive oil*
1 *large clove garlic, peeled*
  and minced
¼ *teaspoon each salt and*
  pepper

6 *tablespoons fine-chopped*
  fresh parsley
1 *pound mostaccioli (or*
  rigatoni), cooked and
  drained
6 *tablespoons fresh-grated*
  Parmesan cheese

Sauté the mushrooms in the oil with the garlic over medium heat. After 5 minutes, reduce the heat to low. Simmer for 10 to 15 minutes longer. Season with salt and pepper and add the parsley. Stir to blend well and simmer another 5 minutes.

Place cooked mostaccioli in a large, warm serving bowl. Pour the mushroom sauce over them and toss. Serve immediately, passing the cheese separately.

Instead of bacon, my friend Josie Vella, whose Italian cooking is a tribute to her heritage, uses prosciutto for her linguine carbonara.

LINGUINE CARBONARA

SERVES 4

¼ pound prosciutto (or 3 slices bacon)
2 eggs, lightly beaten
¼ cup grated Parmesan cheese
1 pound linguine, cooked and drained

Cut prosciutto or bacon into small pieces, cook in a skillet until golden, not crisp; remove. Combine eggs and cheese in a small bowl. Return hot linguine to the pot in which they were cooked and mix with meat and eggs, stirring constantly.

Broccoli is one of the most popular vegetables to be tossed with pasta. One of my mother's dearest friends, Evy Darren, prepares mostaccioli with fresh broccoli for her entertainer husband James Darren.

EVY'S BROCCOLI AND NOODLES

SERVES 4 TO 5 AS A MAIN
COURSE

1½ pounds fresh broccoli, cut into large chunks
½ cup olive oil
1 large clove garlic, peeled and crushed
Salt and pepper

1 pound mostaccioli (or rigatoni), cooked and drained
½ cup grated Parmesan cheese

Cook broccoli in boiling salted water until tender; drain thoroughly. Set cooked broccoli aside in a covered pan in the oven to keep warm. While the broccoli is cooking, heat ¼ cup of the olive oil in a skillet and in it sauté the garlic until golden. Remove the garlic and add salt, pepper, and the remaining olive oil, turning heat just low enough to keep the oil warm.

Place cooked noodles in a large serving dish; toss with the cooked broccoli and the hot olive oil. When thoroughly mixed, sprinkle with Parmesan cheese and serve immediately.

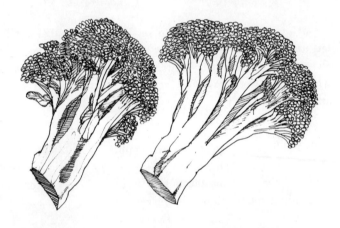

Frozen, chopped broccoli tossed with medium-wide noodles makes an excellent supper dish or substitute spinach for the broccoli.

FETTUCINE WITH BROCCOLI
SERVES 3 TO 4

8 ounces medium-wide fettuccine, cooked and drained
3 tablespoons butter
2 large cloves garlic, peeled and pressed
One 10-ounce package frozen chopped broccoli, defrosted
¼ cup grated Parmesan cheese

Return hot noodles to the pot in which they were cooked and place over low heat. Toss with butter, garlic and broccoli, adding Parmesan cheese as you toss. Continue to cook and toss until broccoli is warm and cheese and butter have melted.

Other vegetables that are heavenly with pasta are fresh fennel or cooked artichoke hearts (fresh, canned, or even the jarred, marinated ones). Lightly sauté some chopped onion with minced garlic in ¼ cup of olive oil. Add 1½ cups of the vegetable of your choice and season with salt and pepper. Spoon the sauce over a wide noodle and crown with lots of grated cheese.

In the home of Joseph Pellegrino, Chairman of the Board of Prince Macaroni Manufacturing Company, they often prepare a mixture of assorted pasta, using as many as a half dozen different shapes (even breaking up spaghetti to use with small shapes like pasfina or small shells).

PASTA PISELLI
(Pasta with Sweet Peas)

SERVES 3 TO 4

¼ *cup olive oil*
1 *tablespoon butter or*
 margarine
1 *cup fine-chopped onion*
2 chicken bouillon cubes,
 crumbled
One 10-ounce package
 frozen peas cooked as
 directed (reserve liq-
 uid), or, one 8-ounce

can of sweet peas
 with their liquid
8 ounces small shells,
 medium shells, elbow,
 and/or rotini, cooked
 and drained
Salt and pepper to taste
Grated cheese, for garnish
Chopped fresh parsley, for
 garnish

Combine the olive oil and butter in a pan (combining the butter and oil prevents the oil from splashing when it is hot), add the onion and sauté until it is coated with butter and oil. Add the chicken bouillon cubes and cook until onion is soft—add water if onion gets too dry before it is soft. Add peas (and their liquid) and cook for 5 minutes over low heat.

Add macaroni to mixture and carefully toss until everything is well combined. Add salt and pepper, sprinkle with cheese and parsley before serving.

Green noodles tossed with tuna, parsley, and capers make a beautiful dish. I always have these ingredients on hand in case company drops by around dinner time and seems to stay.

GREEN FETTUCCINE WITH TUNA AND CAPERS

SERVES 4 TO 6

½ cup olive oil, or more, if needed

½ cup chopped fresh parsley

2 large cloves garlic, peeled and minced

½ cup fresh-grated Parmesan cheese

¼ teaspoon salt

⅛ teaspoon pepper

⅓ cup lemon juice

2 teaspoons dried basil leaves

One 2½-ounce can minced black olives, drained

Two 7-ounce cans tuna, drained (If packed in oil you can add this to the olive oil)

¾ pound spinach fettuccine, cooked and drained

Combine the olive oil, parsley, garlic, cheese, salt, pepper, lemon juice, basil and olives in a large mixing bowl and marinate for 30 minutes. Break up tuna into small chunks and add to mixture.

Pour into a large skillet and heat over medium temperature until everything is thoroughly warmed. Add drained hot noodles to skillet and toss to coat well with tuna sauce. Serve immediately.

Variation: Sauté some anchovies in a little olive oil with black pepper and fresh parsley. When they begin to melt, add chunks of tuna. Continue to sauté another few minutes, add capers (or pitted black olives) and continue cooking another minute. This is delicious tossed with linguine and crowned with grated cheese.

The saltiness of anchovies combines in a gentle way with the sweetness of pine nuts and raisins. Cooking expert James Beard discovered this dish in Sicily.

SAUCE WITH PINE NUTS, RAISINS, AND ANCHOVIES

MAKES APPROXIMATELY $2\frac{1}{2}$ CUPS
SERVES 6 TO 10

1 cup olive oil
4 to 6 garlic cloves, peeled and chopped fine
1 cup pine nuts
$\frac{2}{3}$ cup seedless raisins, plumped in Madeira and drained

2 cans anchovies, drained and chopped coarse
$\frac{1}{2}$ cup chopped fresh parsley
Fresh-ground black pepper to taste

Heat the oil, add the garlic and let it soften in the oil. Then stir in the pine nuts, raisins, anchovies, parsley, and pepper. Heat through. Spoon over spaghetti or linguine.

"Paglia e Fieno," meaning straw and hay, is famous for its teaming of green and white noodles. To preserve their distinct taste, you should boil the noodles in separate pots. If you wish to impress your guests, this is an ideal choice to prepare last minute in a chafing dish at the table.

STRAW AND HAY

SERVES 6 AS A FIRST COURSE

¼ cup butter
¾ cup heavy cream
3 ounces prosciutto, sliced thin and cut into ½-inch strips
8 ounces medium fettuccine (or egg noodles), cooked and drained

8 ounces medium spinach fettuccine, cooked and drained
One 10-ounce package frozen petite peas, cooked and drained
1 teaspoon salt
½ cup grated Parmesan cheese

Melt the butter in a large skillet or chafing dish over medium heat. Stir in the cream; add prosciutto, noodles, peas and salt. Toss with forks to mix until thoroughly heated. Sprinkle with 2 tablespoons of grated Parmesan cheese; toss again and serve. Pass remaining cheese separately.

Variation: Try substituting crabmeat for the Italian ham.

Singer Enrico Caruso enjoyed hosting dinner parties at restaurants, where he would add the finishing touches to the sauce. Mushrooms, chicken livers, and Madeira combine for an elaborate Caruso.

MOSTACCIOLI CARUSO

SERVES 4

10 tablespoons butter
½ pound chicken livers, halved
½ pound mushrooms, sliced
1 clove garlic, peeled and minced

4 ounces black olives, minced
½ cup sweet Madeira
8 ounces mostaccioli, cooked and drained
Grated Parmesan cheese

In a large skillet over medium heat, melt 4 tablespoons of the butter and sauté the chicken livers for about 8 minutes, or until done. Remove and chop them coarse. Sauté the mushrooms with the garlic and olives in 4 more tablespoons of butter. When the mushrooms are tender, return the livers to the pan. Quickly pour in the Madeira and stir to deglaze the pan. Add a little water, if necessary.

Return the noodles to the pot in which they were cooked and toss with the remaining 2 tablespoons of butter. Add the chicken liver sauce and toss again. Serve with Parmesan cheese.

A rich tomato sauce with chicken livers is the family specialty for Lou Arena, vice president of Angelus Macaroni Manufacturing Company.

LINGUINE ARENA

SERVES 4

1 pound chicken livers
6 tablespoons butter
1 cup sliced mushrooms
  (fresh or canned)
½ cup chopped onion
½ cup diced green pepper
2 cloves garlic, peeled and
  minced
One 28-ounce can plum
  tomatoes, drained,
  chopped, and seeded
One 15-ounce can tomato
  purée

2 teaspoons dried basil,
  crushed
2 teaspoons oregano,
  crushed
½ teaspoon salt
½ teaspoon pepper
12 ounces linguine, cooked
  and drained
2 tablespoons chopped
  fresh parsley, to
  garnish

In a large skillet, sauté the chicken livers in 4 tablespoons of butter until brown; set aside. In the same skillet, sauté the mushrooms, onion, green pepper, and garlic in the remaining butter until onions are tender. Add tomatoes and purée; stir in basil, oregano, salt and pepper. Add sautéed chicken livers to tomato mixture and simmer 5 minutes. Place hot linguine on a large platter. Spoon the livers and tomato sauce over the pasta and sprinkle with parsley.

Italian dried mushrooms remind me of small rosebuds. The water used to reconstitute them is flavorsome and should be added to the sauce.

LIVER BOLOGNESE

4 strips bacon, diced
1 pound calves liver,
   chopped into 1″ pieces
½ cup chopped onions
Salt and pepper to taste
1½ cups your favorite
   tomato sauce

1 ounce dried Italian
   mushrooms, soaked for
   30 minutes in 1 cup
   warm water
¼ cup heavy cream
1 pound spaghetti, cooked
   and drained

In a large skillet, sauté the bacon until crisp; remove, drain on paper towels and set aside; reserve the drippings. Sauté the calves liver in the bacon drippings with the onions for about 5 minutes, or until browned. Season with salt and pepper. Add the tomato sauce to the skillet with the mushrooms and their liquid. Simmer for 15 minutes, or until sauce is nicely thickened. Remove from heat. Stir in the cream. Place spaghetti on a large platter; top with the sauce and garnish with bacon.

I have shared many great hunting and fishing tales with John R. William, of Globe "Al" macaroni. One of his father's favorite recipes calls for tossing rigatoni with sausages and then popping the combination in the oven.

To make Rigatoni Roberto: Boil, drain, and butter 6 ounces of rigatoni. Sprinkle with seasoned salt; mix in ¼-inch chunks of Italian sausage; turn into a bake-and-serve casserole. Place casserole in a 400-degree oven for 5 minutes. Garnish with chopped chives. Serve with a dash of Parmesan cheese. Serves 2 to 3.

Sweet sausages and peppers combined with spaghetti and tomato sauce, are a great choice for a hearty meal on a cold evening. If you like meatballs, ribs or chicken breasts, simmer any or all of them along with the sausages. Serve with a bottle of robust Zinfandel, and you've got a party.

SAUSAGE AND PEPPERS WITH SPAGHETTI
SERVES 5 TO 8

SAUSAGE & PEPPERS:

1 large clove garlic, peeled and mashed
¼ cup olive oil
12 sweet Italian sausages
3 large green peppers, seeded and cut into large chunks
4 large onions, peeled and cut into large chunks

¼ cup chopped fresh parsley
Two 15-ounce cans stewed tomatoes
Seasonings to taste: salt, pepper, garlic powder, and sweet basil leaves

SPAGHETTI SAUCE:

2 medium onions, peeled and chopped
1 large clove garlic, peeled and crushed
¼ cup olive oil
One 6-ounce can tomato paste
One 15½-ounce can spaghetti sauce
One 15½-ounce can tomato sauce
One 32-ounce can peeled whole tomatoes (with liquid)

½ cup dry red wine (preferably Burgundy)
¼ cup chopped fresh parsley
2 tablespoons sugar
Seasonings to taste: salt, pepper, dried sweet basil leaves, and oregano

1 pound spaghetti (penne are great, too), cooked and drained
Fresh-grated Parmesan cheese (optional)

For the Sausage and Peppers: In a large skillet over high heat, sauté the garlic to flavor the oil. When the garlic is very brown, remove and discard; lower the heat to medium. Add the sausages and sauté for 10 to 15 minutes, browning all sides. Add the green peppers, onions, parsley, stewed tomatoes, and seasonings to taste; continue to cook, stirring, for 5 to 10 minutes. Cover, reduce heat and simmer for another 15 to 20 minutes.

For the Spaghetti Sauce: Sauté the onions and garlic in the olive oil in a large saucepan. Add the remaining ingredients one at a time, stirring with each new addition. Allow the sauce to simmer for about two hours, stirring occasionally.

To serve: Place cooked spaghetti on a very large platter; top with a generous helping of sauce. Arrange sausage and peppers attractively around the spaghetti. Pour remaining sauce into a bowl to pass separately, and, if you like, serve with a cup of fresh-grated Parmesan cheese.

Joseph P. Viviano, the president of San Giorgio Macaroni, shared with me one of the most enticing recipe booklets I have ever seen, based on the idea that the way to a man's heart is through his pasta. His rigatoni baked with meats in a pie crust is unusual and very delicious.

According to his instructions, to enjoy this dish properly, you need a secluded gazebo or other private place to spend a long, rainy afternoon. The music would be gentle rain on the roof; the lighting, daylight filtered through tall trees and light mist; the wine, sangria filled with fruit slices; and to complete the menu, watercress salad, tomatoes with chopped scallions, and zabaglione, an Italian wine custard, for dessert.

RIGATONI FOR A RAINY DAY
SERVES 8 TO 10

Preheat oven to 400 degrees

½ pound Italian sausages, broken up into small bits

2 slices bacon, diced

1 medium onion, peeled and chopped fine

1 cup meatless tomato sauce

2 chicken breasts, skinned, boned, and diced

¼ pound lean ground pork

¼ pound lean ground veal

⅓ cup heavy cream

5 eggs, lightly beaten

One 4-ounce can button mushrooms, chopped coarse

2 teaspoons salt

⅛ teaspoon freshly grated pepper

⅛ teaspoon powdered nutmeg

12 ounces rigatoni, par-boiled, drained, rinsed in cold water, drained again

Two 10-ounce packages pie crust mix

Sauté sausage meat and bacon until lightly browned, then remove from the pan with a slotted spoon and reserve. Slowly sauté the onion in the pan drippings until transparent. Add the tomato sauce and simmer slowly for 5 minutes. Add the chicken, meats, reserved sausage and bacon, and simmer for another 15 minutes. Add the cream, beaten eggs, mushrooms, salt, pepper, and nutmeg, and simmer very slowly for 10 minutes. Remove pan from heat, taste for seasoning, and cool. Add the rigatoni and carefully toss to cover pasta with mixture; chill while you prepare the pie crust.

Prepare pie crust dough according to package instructions. Roll out ¾ of the dough and fit into a 3-quart buttered ring mold. Spoon the rigatoni mixture into the mold, pressing down well. Roll out remaining dough and cover filling, sealing the edges as you go. Bake in the preheated oven for 40 minutes. Cool for 15 minutes and turn out onto a serving platter. May be served hot or cold.

This simple yet elegant casserole was created by my cooking buddy's artist-aunt, Anna Hoffman. She uses fresh, homemade tagliarini purchased from a little market on the Monterey peninsula. But if you are not fortunate to have this fresh pasta in your area, substitute medium-wide egg noodles.

TAGLIARINI CASSEROLE

SERVES 3 TO 5

Preheat oven to 350 degrees

10 ounces fresh tagliarini, cooked and drained
1 cup fresh-grated Parmesan cheese
1 cup pitted, ripe black olives
2 tablespoons capers, drained

2 cloves garlic, peeled and minced
3 tablespoons butter
Salt and fresh-ground pepper to taste
Chopped fresh parsley for garnish

Pour the hot noodles back into the pot in which they were cooked and add all the remaining ingredients, except ½ cup of the grated cheese and the parsley. Toss gently and turn into a large buttered casserole. Sprinkle remaining cheese on top and bake in the preheated oven for 25 minutes. Garnish with parsley and serve.

My husband has a handful of dishes which he has created and excels in. His spaghetti sauce is outstanding—the trick is that he simmers it for a short time then allows it to sit off the heat for a while to allow the flavors to blend. Bill uses this sauce with spaghetti or, when he's in the mood to cook up a special dinner, it's part of his steak bake.

SPAGHETTI STEAK BAKE

SERVES 4 TO 6

BILL'S SWEET SPAGHETTI SAUCE:

1 medium white onion, peeled and chopped

5 tablespoons butter

Two 15-ounce cans tomato sauce

3½ teaspoons garlic powder

½ teaspoon powdered oregano

½ pound fresh mushrooms, sliced thick

2 tablespoons sugar

2 pounds boneless top sirloin steak, cut into cubes

Salt to taste

1 tablespoon butter

4 ounces mostaccioli (or rigatoni), cooked and drained

5 ounces Monterey Jack cheese, grated

To make the sauce: Sauté the onions in a medium skillet with 2 tablespoons of butter until they are browned, about 3 to 5 minutes. Meanwhile, pour the tomato sauce, 1 tablespoon of the garlic powder, and the oregano into a large saucepan. Cook, stirring, over medium heat for about 2 minutes; add the sautéed onions. In the first skillet, sauté the mushrooms in the remaining 3 tablespoons of butter for about 2 minutes. Add remaining ½ teaspoon of garlic powder, stirring to combine. Let the mushrooms cook until they begin to shrink a little, about 5 minutes. Spoon the mushrooms into the sauce and mix well. Add sugar to the sauce. If you prefer a thinner sauce, you can add some water. Allow the sauce to simmer for about 10 minutes, stirring constantly so it doesn't burn. Turn off the heat and let the pot sit for at least an hour for seasonings to blend. (Note: If you're in a hurry you can use it immediately without the "sitting" period, but it really isn't as good.)

Preheat the broiler. Place the meat on a broiler tray, season with salt and dot with the butter. Broil a short time, about 3 minutes on each side, so that the meat is still rare. Remove meat from broiler and set oven at 375 degrees.

To assemble: Pour a thin layer of sauce on the bottom of a large casserole or soufflé dish. Place all the cooked noodles on the sauce to form a bed. Pour half the remaining sauce on top of the noodles. Place the meat on top of this sauce; add remaining sauce and top with grated cheese.

Place in the preheated oven for 10 to 15 minutes, or until cheese is completely melted, then pop it under the broiler for a few seconds to brown the top.

SWEETS

Rich pastries, custards, ice creams, and fruit ices are served most frequently after an Italian meal. But noodles do turn up in a few desserts. I like to toss cooked noodles with butter, nuts, and grated orange and lemon rind. Then I complete the dish with wine and sugar.

SWEET NOODLES MARSALA

SERVES 3 TO 5

10 ounces narrow fettuccine or farfalle, cooked and drained

½ cup sweet butter

½ cup blanched slivered almonds

2 tablespoons grated orange rind

2 tablespoons grated lemon rind

1 to 3 tablespoons sweet Marsala

2 to 4 tablespoons confectioners' sugar

Toss noodles with 6 tablespoons of butter. Cover with a dish towel to keep warm for a few minutes while browning the nuts.

Melt the remaining 2 tablespoons of butter in a skillet over medium heat; add the almonds, stirring constantly with a wooden spoon, and cook for about 3 minutes, or until the nuts begin to turn golden. Spoon the almonds over the noodles, add the orange and lemon rind, and toss to combine thoroughly. Spoon noodles onto individual dessert plates. Sprinkle each serving with 1 to 2 teaspoons of Marsala and dust with confectioners' sugar. Serve immediately.

For a simple sweet to complete an Italian feast, gelati (ice cream) and cookies would be my choice.

NOODLE COOKIES

Cooking oil for deep-frying
Cooked farfalloni (or other favorite shape)
Confectioners' sugar or cinnamon and granulated, sugar mixed

Heat oil in a large, deep pot to 375 degrees; deep-fry the "bow-ties" a few at a time, until they are lightly browned on all sides. Drain on paper towels and dust with sugar. Hint: To coat cookies easily, pour sugar into a plastic bag and gently shake fried "bow-ties" a few at a time in the bag.

The Jewish Noodle

I w a s born in Philadelphia and remained there until my teens when my parents moved to Southern California. As a child, I always visited my mother's parents on weekends and holidays. These were happy times, filled with much laughter and eating.

My grandmother, whom I called "Buba," was an excellent cook. I grew up on such delicacies as gefilte fish (chilled fish balls), cold borsch (beet soup), kreplach (stuffed noodles), knaidlach (matzo balls), kasha varnishkas (groats and noodles), and luckshen kugel (noodle pudding).

Although my family did not keep a strict kosher kitchen, I was aware of the religious, dietary customs from school friends and reading. Dairy foods were not to be served with meat. Oil was used in recipes that required fat to cook or accompany meat. Butter was to be used with dairy dishes.

Noodles hold an important position in the Jewish cuisine —they appear in soups, as a substitute for rice or potatoes, as a main or side course, even as a dessert. Traditionally, sweet dishes were reserved for holidays and celebrations. Simple or hearty ones preceded periods of fasting.

Bowties: Noodles in the shape of bowties.

Egg Barley: Small, grainlike noodles. Most often used in soup or as a side dish. Same as farfel.

Egg Noodles: Flat noodles with egg in the dough. Available fine, medium, wide, and extra wide.

Farfel: Same as egg noodles.

Kreplach: Noodle squares. Stuffed like Chinese won tons. Sometimes called Jewish ravioli.

Luckshen: Yiddish name for egg noodles. Thin are most often used for soups; medium and wide for puddings.

Plaetchen: Noodle squares (usually ½ inch), used in soups.

Spaetzel: Pencil-thin dough (1-inch lengths).

Verenikas: Similar to Kreplach. Dough is cut into 3-inch circles, stuffed with a sweet filling, folded in half like a crescent or moon, cooked, and served as a dessert.

Many markets now carry an assortment of packaged Jewish foods, or, Italian egg noodles can be used in their place. If you need to locate other ingredients, check pages 321–24.

BASIC EGG NOODLE (LUCKSHEN)

SERVES 2 TO 6

1½ to 2 cups all-purpose flour
½ teaspoon salt
2 eggs, lightly beaten

Combine all ingredients in a large bowl, using just enough flour to make a stiff dough. Place dough on a lightly floured board, and knead it until smooth. Roll the dough out to ⅛-inch thick, and place it on a kitchen towel to dry for 20 to 30 minutes. Do not allow dough to become brittle.

Roll up dough, and cut it into desired widths with a sharp knife. For fine soup noodles, cut dough ⅛ to ¼-inch wide; for medium noodles, ½-inch wide; for wide, ¾-inch. (A noodle or pasta machine can be used for kneading, rolling, and cutting.) To cook, boil in salted water or soup for 8 to 10 minutes. Or store dried noodles in a covered container for later use.

To make fried noodles for soups, roll out dough as thin as possible, and allow to dry for about 15 minutes. Cut dough into small circles with a melon-ball cutter. Heat cooking oil to 375 degrees for deep-frying. Add about ¼ cup of the dough circles at a time, fry until golden brown, and drain.

EGG-BARLEY (FARFEL)

SERVES 8 TO 10

4 cups flour
1 teaspoon salt
4 eggs, lightly beaten
Water, if necessary (a few tablespoons)

Combine all ingredients in a large bowl, blending and kneading with your hands until dough is stiff, about 5 minutes. Divide dough into small balls (about the size of a golf ball), flattening them a little with the heel of your hand. Allow to dry for about an hour. Using the coarse side of a cheese grater, rub dough against it to make pea-size particles. Spread out on a board and dry thoroughly.

STUFFED NOODLES

Kreplach are stuffed noodles similar to Chinese won ton or Italian cappelletti. Traditionally, a cheese filling is used for Shavuoth (Festival of the Torah), honoring the laws of the Torah; meat for Succoth (Festival of the Tabernacles), celebrating the harvest. I have also eaten kreplach filled with cheese and potato, kasha, chicken, and chicken liver. I enjoy them most in a simple chicken broth. They can also be served as a main dish with sauce, gravy, or sour cream.

CHICKEN LIVER KREPLACH
MAKES 2 TO 4 DOZEN

1 Basic Egg Noodle recipe
   (See pages 160–61)

CHICKEN LIVER FILLING:

½ pound chicken livers,	*½ cup minced onions*
cut in half	*2 hard-cooked egg yolks*
2 tablespoons rendered	*1 teaspoon salt*
chicken fat (See Note)	*Dash white pepper*

Prepare the kreplach squares: On a lightly floured board, roll out the dough until it is ⅛ to ¼-inch thick. Cut into 3-inch squares.

For the filling: In a medium skillet, sauté the chicken livers in the rendered chicken fat for 8 minutes, stirring occasionally. Add the onions, cooking until softened. Spoon this mixture into a meat grinder (or food processor), and grind lightly, adding the egg yolks to bind the stuffing together. Add the salt and pepper. Cool the mixture.

Place a heaping spoonful of filling in the center of each

kreplach square. Moisten edges of dough lightly with water, and fold in half diagonally to form triangles. Crimp edges with a fork.

Kreplach can be made in advance, covered with a damp cloth, and refrigerated for several hours. Or they can be wrapped for freezing.

To cook, simmer the kreplach in a large pot of boiling, salted water for 8 to 12 minutes. Drain, and serve.

Variation: For a meat filling, substitute ground beef and cooking oil for the chicken livers and fat, and follow the rest of the recipe. Because the meat is already ground, you will not have to combine the mixture in a meat grinder. (Check Oriental, Italian, and Continental chapters for other suitable fillings.)

Note: Rendered chicken fat can be purchased in jars at some markets and specialty stores, but it is expensive. Instead, I make my own and store it in the refrigerator for weeks. It solidifies when chilled, and you can melt as much as you need. To render, remove all fat from the chicken (especially breasts), wash, drain, and cut into small pieces. For 1 cup of chicken fat, I chop 1 small onion (about ¼ cup). Cook the chicken fat in a small saucepan over low heat until completely melted. Season with 1 teaspoon salt. Add the chopped onion, and cook, stirring, until it is brown. Set aside to cool; then strain the rendered fat into a jar. Save the browned onions and any cracklings from excess skin (called *grebenes*) to season another dish. (They are outstanding tossed with noodles and baked as a kugel.)

My "adopted" Aunt Rose has always been like a second mother. When I was a child, I loved to stay at her home while my parents traveled. A basic cook, her noodle stuffing was—and is—one of my favorites. She used it in roast chicken or turkey.

NOODLE STUFFING PITCHON

MAKES APPROXIMATELY 3 CUPS

*1 tablespoon rendered
    chicken fat (see Note,
    page 163)*
6 whole chicken livers
*2 stalks celery, chopped
    fine*
*1 large onion, peeled and
    chopped fine*

*8 ounces fine egg noodles,
    cooked and drained*
4 eggs, lightly beaten
1 teaspoon salt
1 teaspoon white pepper
*1 cup matzo meal (or plain
    breadcrumbs)*

Melt the chicken fat in a skillet, and sauté the chicken livers, celery, and onion until slightly browned. Spoon mixture into a bowl. Add the noodles, eggs, salt, and pepper. Toss to blend well. Add the matzo meal to bind the stuffing, and mix thoroughly. Stuff a chicken or turkey, and roast according to your favorite recipe.

SOUPS

The simplest of soups consist of heated milk or chicken or beef broth with a handful of thin egg noodles. To dress up a basic broth, add some minced parsley.

CHICKEN EGG DROP SOUP

SERVES 4

1 quart chicken or beef broth
6 ounces fine egg noodles
2 tablespoons minced fresh parsley
2 eggs, lightly beaten

Bring chicken or beef broth to a boil in a soup pot. Add the noodles, and boil, stirring occasionally, until noodles begin to soften, about 5 minutes. Add parsley. Pour eggs into soup in a stream, stirring as you pour. Reduce heat, and simmer for a few minutes, or until egg drops are fully set.

As a small child, I looked forward fondly to Friday nights at my grandmother's home. That was when she prepared her chicken soup. Usually, she also made knaidlach, matzo balls, to enhance the golden broth. But on special occasions, when she had some leftover cooked chicken, she would make her special Chicken Noodle Balls.

CHICKEN NOODLE BALLS

MAKES 12 TO 18 BALLS

½ cup thin egg noodles, broken into small, ricelike pieces, cooked, and drained
2 cups cooked chicken, cut into small pieces, then
put through a meat grinder
½ teaspoon onion powder
½ teaspoon salt
¼ teaspoon white pepper
1 egg, well beaten

In a large mixing bowl, combine the noodles, ground chicken, and seasonings. (If you like, add more salt to taste.) Add the egg and some water (if necessary) to bind the mixture. Shape into small balls, about the size of walnuts. Add the noodle balls to the simmering chicken soup about 5 to 10 minutes before serving.

If you're following dietary laws strictly, you shouldn't add noodles to chicken matzo ball soup, especially during the eight days of Passover (Festival of Deliverance), when leavened breads are forbidden. But I can't imagine my grandmother's soup without both the noodles and matzo balls.

BUBA'S CHICKEN NOODLE MATZO BALL SOUP

SERVES 4 TO 8

BUBA'S CHICKEN SOUP:

1 whole pullet or soup chicken, cut up (or 3 chicken breasts)

2 stalks celery with leaves

3 carrots, scraped and cut into large chunks

2 or 3 sprigs fresh parsley

½ medium onion, peeled and cut in half

1 small sweet potato, peeled and cut into small chunks

Small handful soup greens (if available)

BUBA'S MATZO BALLS (KNAIDLACH):

2 extra-large (or 3 large eggs)

2 tablespoons rendered chicken fat, melted

½ cup matzo meal (see Note)

1 teaspoon salt

¼ cup water

8 ounces fine egg noodles, cooked, drained, and returned to the pot to keep warm

Place all soup ingredients in a large (8 to 10 quarts) pot, and add water to cover. Bring to a boil; then lower heat to a simmer. Skim off the scum ("shum" or foamy skin) as it rises. Check seasoning, adding salt if necessary. Cover, and simmer for about 2 hours. Again, add salt to taste. If the chicken flavoring isn't strong enough, add 1 or 2 chicken bouillon cubes.

Start making matzo balls several hours before dinner. In a porcelain or glass mixing bowl, beat the eggs and fat together. Add the matzo meal and salt, and mix. Add the water. Cover, and refrigerate at least 1 hour.

Bring a large pot of salted water to a boil. Shape the matzo mixture into small balls, about the size of walnuts (they expand!) with your hands. (This will be easier to do if you wet your hands first.) Carefully lower balls into the boiling water, cover, and boil for 30 minutes.

My grandmother would assemble the soup in individual bowls. First, she would use a fork to place a thin layer of noodles on the bottom of the soup bowl. Then she would ladle about 1 cup of broth, with a few pieces of vegetables, into the bowl. Finally, using a slotted spoon, she would carefully place one or two matzo balls into the soup. After all the soup bowls had been filled, she would place the boiled chicken and the remaining vegetables on a large platter and serve these separately. I always preferred to add a few small pieces of chicken to my soup bowl. This is one of those heavenly family dishes that make you want to go back for seconds and thirds.

Leftover matzo balls can be refrigerated or frozen in the leftover soup or in water.

Note: This amount of matzo meal will give you soft, fluffy matzo balls. If you prefer harder matzo balls, simply add more matzo meal to the batter.

SAUTÉED AND SAUCED NOODLES (Including Casseroles)

Because the Jewish people have lived all over the world, their foods offer a variety of seasonings and ingredients gathered from many different cuisines. You can serve a simple dish of Basic Buttered Noodles or dress the noodles up with one of many garnishes.

BASIC BUTTERED NOODLES

SERVES 3 TO 5

*10 ounces bow-shaped, medium or wide noodles, cooked and
    drained*
¼ cup melted butter
1 teaspoon salt
Dash of white pepper

Place noodles in a serving bowl, and toss them lightly but thoroughly with melted butter, salt, and white pepper to taste.

Variations: Add 2 teaspoons caraway seeds (Hungary), 2 teaspoons poppy seeds (Czechoslovakia), or 2 tablespoons toasted, slivered almonds (France).

Instead of rice or mashed potatoes, try farfel as a side dish.

BOILED FARFEL

SERVES 4

1 cup farfel
2 cups rapidly boiling water (or scalded milk), (see Note)
¼ cup rendered chicken fat (see page 163)
Salt and pepper to taste

Stir farfel into a pot with water (or milk), and cook over medium heat, stirring constantly, until farfel is soft, about 10 minutes. Add chicken fat, salt, and pepper.

Note: Farfel can also be boiled in salted water or soup.

Honey-sweetened noodles combined with poppy seeds make an interesting dish.

NOODLES WITH HONEY AND POPPY SEEDS

SERVES 6

1 cup half-and-half (or ½ cup each heavy cream and milk)
½ cup honey
3 tablespoons poppy seeds
1 pound medium egg noodles, cooked and drained

Pour the half-and-half into a saucepan, and heat over low flame, adding the honey and stirring until it is fully dissolved, about 3 to 5 minutes. Add the poppy seeds, stir, and cook for another 3 minutes. Place noodles in a serving dish, pour the sauce over them, and toss lightly but thoroughly.

My father tells childhood stories of seven growing children always looking for something to eat, and he fondly remembers his mother's noodle and cheese dish.

BUBA SCHWARTZ'S NOODLES
AND CHEESE

SERVES 9 TO 12

1½ pounds medium noodles, cooked and drained
¾ cup melted butter
2 teaspoons salt
2 pints pot cheese (similar to cottage cheese)

Return noodles to the pot in which they were cooked, and toss with butter and salt until well coated. Add the cheese, and mix well.

Cabbage, whether used for coleslaw, in soups, stuffed with meats and sauced, or cooked with noodles, is a popular Jewish vegetable.

NOODLES AND CABBAGE

SERVES 6 TO 8

½ cup butter
4 cups fine-shredded
  cabbage
1 teaspoon sugar

½ teaspoon salt
¼ teaspoon pepper
10 ounces broad noodles,
  cooked and drained

In a very large skillet, melt the butter, and add the cabbage. Season with sugar, salt, and pepper, and cook over very low heat, stirring very often, until the cabbage is browned, about 30 minutes. Add the noodles, and toss to mix thoroughly.

Friday night dinner at my grandmother's house always included, in addition to chicken soup, a big bowl of kasha and bowties. It naturally accompanied her tender, roasted brisket of beef. I'd top a big helping with several spoonfuls of the beef gravy.

Kasha is roasted brown buckwheat groats, somewhat resembling brown rice. The kasha and the bowties are cooked separately, then combined and seasoned with chicken fat before serving.

KASHA AND BOWTIES VARNISHKAS

SERVES 8 AS A
SIDE DISH

8 ounces bowties, cooked and drained
4 to 5 tablespoons melted rendered chicken fat (see page 163), or butter
1 cup kasha

1 large egg, lightly beaten
2 cups actively boiling water
Salt to taste
2 cups favorite beef gravy, as accompaniment

Toss cooked bowties with 2 to 3 tablespoons of melted chicken fat and set aside.

Pour kasha into a small bowl, and stir in the egg. Over a very high flame, heat a large, dry skillet, add the kasha, and stir constantly until each grain is separate and dry. (This scorches the kasha, preventing it from becoming mushy later on.) Heat a pot, and pour the kasha into it, immediately add the boiling water, and cover quickly, as the kasha will "talk back to you." Reduce the heat, to a simmer and allow kasha to steam over low heat for 30 minutes.

Spoon cooked noodles and kasha into a large, heated serving bowl. Season with remaining melted chicken fat and salt. Serve with that favorite gravy.

When reminiscing, I can still hear my elderly aunt saying "no tzimmes" when she would help me set the dinner table. "Tzimmes" means a fuss or excitement. Tzimmes recipes, in contrast, are usually easily prepared.

FARFEL TZIMMES

SERVES 6

Preheat oven to 375 degrees

1 pound mixed dried fruits	*1 teaspoon salt*
(prunes, apricots,	*3 tablespoons orange juice*
pears, apples, peaches)	*⅓ cup honey*
1 quart water	*¼ cup butter*
1 cup farfel	*Cinnamon*

Place dried fruit in a large pot with the water, and soak for 1 hour. Bring to a boil and stir in farfel, salt, orange juice, honey, and butter. Transfer the mixture to a baking dish and sprinkle cinnamon over the top. Cover and bake in the preheated oven for 30 minutes. Remove the cover, and bake for an additional 15 minutes. Serve with the main course in place of a vegetable or potatoes.

Although I was an only child, I had a friend, also an only child, who was so very close that we always considered ourselves sisters. Our grandmothers were close friends, as were our mothers. Now grown and living across the continent, I visited her on a recent business trip. One of the dishes she served was this tasty cottage cheese and noodle casserole.

MAXINE GORDON'S CREAMY COTTAGE CHEESE AND NOODLES

SERVES 4 TO 6

8 ounces medium noodles,
    cooked and drained
1 cup creamed cottage
    cheese
¼ cup sour cream

2 scallions, chopped fine
½ cup chopped fresh
    parsley
Salt and pepper to taste

Return drained noodles to pot in which they were cooked, and add the cottage cheese, sour cream, scallions, and parsley. Cook over low heat, stirring gently to combine all ingredients. Season with salt and pepper.

An entire chapter could be written on luckshen kugels, noodle puddings. They can be served as a separate course; as an accompaniment to poultry, meat, or fish; or as a dessert.

Every Jewish household has several family recipes for their favorite kugels, simple ones for every day, more complicated ones for occasions.

They are usually allowed to sit in their baking dishes to cool for a few minutes before slicing and transferring to serving platters. Occasionally, they are topped with a sauce or sour cream. They can be eaten either warm or cold. I am known by my family as a "refrigerator robber" of kugel leftovers.

Memories of my early years often center on my grandmother's kugels. Hers were always so light that they must have been cooked with love. She would serve them as a side dish, garnished with sour cream. The fruit version was so delicious it could be eaten as a dessert—but I could never wait.

BUBA'S KUGEL

SERVES 6 TO 8 AS A SIDE DISH

Preheat oven to 350 degrees

1 tablespoon cooking oil	*1 tablespoon sugar*
8 ounces medium egg	*3 eggs, separated*
noodles, cooked and	*Dry mustard*
drained	*1 pint sour cream*
2 tablespoons butter	*Salt to taste*

Put the cooking oil into a casserole (8½-inches square and 2-inches deep) and heat the casserole in the preheated oven.

Place the noodles in a large mixing bowl, add butter and mix thoroughly. Add sugar, and mix again. Lightly beat the egg yolks, stir into the noodles along with a dash of dry mustard. Add the sour cream and salt, mix thoroughly. Beat the egg whites until stiff, and fold them into the noodle mixture.

Remove the oiled, heated casserole from the oven. Add the noodle mixture to it, tilt the dish to allow the oil to rise around the sides and dribble it over the top of the noodle mixture. Bake, uncovered, in the preheated oven 1 to 1½ hours, or until golden brown.

Succoth, a week-long holiday, commemorates the Jews' freedom in Israel after forty years of wandering through the desert to escape Egyptian slavery. Because it occurs after the fall harvest, usually in October, a dish containing fruits is quite appropriate for the celebration.

BUBA'S FRUIT KUGEL

SERVES 6 TO 8 AS A SIDE DISH

OR DESSERT

Preheat oven to 350 degrees

¼ *pound mixed dried*
  fruits
Boiling water
1 large apple
1 tablespoon sugar
½ *teaspoon cinnamon*
2 tablespoons cooking oil

8 ounces medium egg
  noodles, cooked and
  drained
2 tablespoons butter
3 eggs, separated
3 tablespoons apricot-
  pineapple jam
½ *teaspoon salt*

Cut the dried fruits into medium-size pieces, place the pieces in a small pot, and scald them with the boiling water. Let the fruit stand in the water for a few minutes to soften. Peel and core the apple; dice it into medium-sized chunks. Combine the sugar and cinnamon in a bowl, and toss the apple chunks with this mixture. Drain the dried fruits and combine them with the apple mixture.

Put the oil in an oven-proof casserole (8½-inches square and 2-inches deep), and place casserole in the preheated oven.

Place noodles in a large mixing bowl, add the butter, and toss thoroughly. Allow the noodles to cool. Beat the egg yolks, add them to the cooled noodles, and toss to mix thoroughly. Add the fruits, jam, and salt, and toss again. Beat the egg whites until stiff, and fold them into the noodle mixture.

Remove heated casserole from the oven and add the

noodle mixture to it, making sure that all the fruits are covered by the noodles. Tilt the casserole so that the oil in the bottom rises around the sides, and dribble it over the top of the noodle mixture. Bake the kugel in the preheated oven for 1 to 1½ hours, or until the top is golden brown.

This super-creamy kugel adds both cottage cheese and cream cheese to the noodles.

GUSSIE CHUDNOFF'S KUGEL
SERVES 6 TO 8

Preheat oven to 350 degrees

1 pound dry cottage cheese
  (flake style is best)
½ pound cream cheese
¼ pound butter
5 eggs, lightly beaten
1 cup milk
½ cup sugar

1 teaspoon vanilla
4 ounces medium noodles,
  cooked and drained
2 apples, peeled and grated
  (optional)
Sour cream or canned pie
  cherries

In a large bowl, mix together the cottage cheese, cream cheese, and butter. Add the eggs, milk, sugar, and vanilla. Spoon in the noodles, and coat them with the cheese mixture. Apples can be added to the noodles or reserved to place on top of the pudding. Grease a 3-quart casserole. Turn noodle mixture into it and bake in the preheated oven for 1 hour. Garnish kugel slices with sour cream or canned cherry pie filling.

My racquetball challenger Sara "Lee" Burstein adds crushed pineapple to her kugel.

PINEAPPLE NOODLE RING

SERVES 6

Preheat oven to 325 degrees

> ½ *cup dark brown sugar*
> *One 16-ounce can crushed pineapple, drained*
> *8 ounces medium egg noodles, cooked and drained*
> *4 eggs, lightly beaten*
> ½ *cup melted butter*

Combine 2 tablespoons of the brown sugar and ¼ cup of the crushed pineapple, and spread the mixture on the bottom of a greased ring mold. Place noodles in a mixing bowl, add the remaining sugar, pineapple, eggs, and butter, and combine thoroughly. Spoon the noodle mixture into the pan, and bake in the preheated oven for 1 hour. Turn out on a serving platter, and serve hot.

My grandmother always used a lot of eggs, sour cream, and cream cheese, sweetened with some sugar and vanilla, to make her cheese kugel.

CHEESE KUGEL DELUXE

SERVES 4 TO 6

Preheat oven to 350 degrees

8 ounces fine egg noodles,   *1 pint sour cream*
   cooked and drained   ½ *pound cream cheese*
8 eggs   *1 cup sugar*
1 cup butter   *2 teaspoons vanilla*

Spray a casserole (8½ inches square and 2 inches deep) with a low-calorie spray. Spread noodles on the bottom of the casserole. Place remaining ingredients in a blender (or food processor), and blend until liquified. (You should end up with a soupy consistency. Pour over noodles. If you want, you can add raisins and/or top the casserole with cinnamon. Bake in the preheated oven for 45 minutes.

If the center of this kugel sinks, don't fret. Use it as a well for the pie filling.

KUGEL LIKE A CHERRY CHEESE PIE
SERVES 6 TO 8

Preheat oven to 350 degrees

8 ounces fine noodles,	*1 pint sour cream*
cooked and drained	*2 teaspoons vanilla*
8 eggs, lightly beaten	*1 cup sugar*
1 cup butter, at room tem-	*One 21-ounce can cherry*
perature	*(or blueberry) pie*
½ pound cream cheese	*filling, heated*

Butter a 12-inch round cake pan or large, round glass dish, and line it with noodles. Blend together the eggs, butter, cream cheese, sour cream, vanilla, and sugar, and pour this mixture over noodles. Bake in the preheated oven for 1 hour.

Turn the kugel out on a serving platter. When it sets, the center will sink slightly, forming a well. Pour the warm pie filling into the well. If the center doesn't sink, pour the filling attractively over the entire top.

The High Holidays, or High Holy Days, observed for 10 days in early fall, begin with Rosh Hashonah (Day of

Judgment) and end up with Yom Kippur (Day of Atonement). Much consideration is given to planning festive menus during this period. Fruits and honey are used widely to symbolize wishes for sweetness in the New Year.

SWEET NOODLE KUGEL

SERVES 4 TO 6

Preheat oven to 350 degrees

5 eggs, separated
1 Golden Delicious apple,
*   peeled and grated*
½ cup strawberry (or
*   apricot-pineapple)*
*   preserves*
One 8-ounce can crushed
*   pineapple*

3 tablespoons honey
8 ounces medium noodles,
*   cooked and drained*
3 tablespoons butter
Cinnamon sugar, for gar-
*   nish*

In a large mixing bowl, beat the egg yolks, and add the apple, preserves, pineapple, and honey. Add the noodles and toss gently to coat. In another bowl, beat the egg whites until they form soft peaks; carefully fold them into the noodle mixture.

Grease a 1-quart baking dish, and pour the noodle mixture into it. Dot the top with butter, and sprinkle with cinnamon-sugar. Bake in the preheated oven for 45 minutes, or until golden. Cool the kugel for 5 minutes before turning it out on a platter.

When entertaining, I like to do as much as possible in advance of my company's arrival. Long-time family friend Ida Lustman completes the first half of her creamy kugel the night before, then finishes the last few steps just before baking it for dinner.

CREAMY CHEESE KUGEL

SERVES 6

Preheat oven to 350 degrees

½ *pint sour cream*
¼ *cup heavy cream*
1 *pound, plus 2 table-*
   spoons, cottage cheese
¼ *cup melted butter*
½ *cup sugar*

8 *ounces medium noodles,*
   cooked and drained
4 *eggs*
1 *teaspoon vanilla*
1 *cup crushed cornflakes*

In a large mixing bowl, combine the sour cream, heavy cream, cottage cheese, butter, and 5 tablespoons sugar. Add the noodles, mix thoroughly. Butter an 8-inch square pan and pour the noodle mixture into it. Cover with foil or plastic wrap while you prepare the rest of the ingredients, or overnight if you wish.

The following day, beat the eggs in a small bowl until light; then stir in the vanilla. Pour this over the noodle mixture. Sprinkle with the crushed cornflakes and remaining 3 tablespoons of sugar. Let stand for 2 hours or more at room temperature.

Bake at 350 degrees for 50 minutes. Turn off heat and leave the kugel in the oven with the oven door open for 10 more minutes.

Dairy dinners are a light change of pace. Salads, spaghetti with meatless sauce, and macaroni and cheese are staples. For a creative *milchig* dinner, bake these noodles in a ring mold, and fill the center with creamed vegetables.

DAIRY RING

SERVES 6

Preheat oven to 325 degrees

8 ounces medium noodles,
    cooked and drained
2 tablespoons butter
3 eggs, separated
½ cup hot milk

1 teaspoon salt
¼ teaspoon white pepper
⅛ teaspoon freshly grated
    nutmeg

Return the hot noodles to the pot in which they were cooked, toss with butter. Add egg yolks, milk, and seasonings. Beat egg whites until they are stiff, and fold them into noodle mixture. Pour noodles into a buttered 1½-quart ring mold. Set mold in a pan of hot water, and place in the preheated oven for 30 minutes. Allow to cool for 5 minutes. Then loosen edges of the mold with a sharp knife, and turn it out onto a serving platter. If you wish, you can fill the center with creamed vegetables or seafood.

SWEETS

My grandmother's house was a child's dream. There were bowls of sugar-candy balls and salted nuts everywhere; the bread box was always crammed with coffee cakes and "danish"; the freezer was so packed with ice cream that the door was difficult to shut; the cupboards were filled with wrapped boxes of candy waiting to be opened; and in case she should run out, there was another refrigerator in the basement keeping chilled extra bottles of soda pop. With all these sweets on hand, my grandmother was always ready for family and friends to drop by unexpectedly. And they usually did because they knew they were always welcome. Hers was a house filled with great love.

Her kreplach became verenikas when she filled them with something sweet, usually jam or preserves.

VERENIKAS

SERVES 6 TO 8

1 Basic Egg Noodle recipe (see pages 160–61)
1½ cups your favorite jam or preserves (Or use your
    favorite canned fruit pie filling and reserve the liquid)
1 cup confectioners' sugar
1 cup sour cream

Follow kreplach noodle instructions on pages 162–63.

Roll out dough; do not let it dry. With a cookie cutter or a juice glass and paring knife, cut into 3-inch circles. Place a tablespoon of filling on each. Fold in half and press edges together with a little water Cook rapidly in boiling, salted water for about 10 minutes, or until the "dumplings" are done. Drain and serve dusted with sugar and a dollop of sour cream. If you use pie filling, heat the reserve liquid and serve it separately. Enough filling for approximately 2 dozen verenikas. (See Sweet Vareniki recipes, pages 226–27.)

This charlotte is similar to a kugel. Rather than mixing the fruits with the noodles, this recipe from the Kosher Kitchen of The B. Manischewitz Company suggests that you layer everything and serve the charlotte with a warm Hard Sauce.

NOODLE CHARLOTTE

SERVES 6

Preheat oven to 375 degrees

8 ounces medium or broad egg noodles, parboiled and drained
3 large apples, peeled and grated
2 teaspoons lemon juice
½ cup chopped almonds (or walnuts)

2 to 3 tablespoons dark brown sugar
½ teaspoon cinnamon
½ teaspoon vanilla extract
Matzo meal or bread-crumbs
2 to 3 tablespoons butter

HARD SAUCE:
½ cup sweet butter
1 cup confectioners' sugar

Favorite fruit-flavored liqueur, to taste

Grease a 2-quart baking dish. Line the bottom with a layer of noodles. Place apples in a mixing bowl; sprinkle with lemon juice. Add the nuts, sugar, cinnamon, and vanilla. Arrange a layer of the apple mixture in the dish alternately with a layer of noodles. Continue alternating layers, finishing with a layer of noodles. Sprinkle the top with matzo meal; dot with butter. Bake in the preheated oven for 45 minutes. Serve with Hard Sauce. To make sauce: Cream together the butter and sugar in a mixing bowl; flavor with your favorite fruit wine.

The Continental Noodle

T H E C U I S I N E S of Europe and Asia, including those of the countries along the Mediterranean Sea and in the Middle East, all share a love of noodles. For centuries, cooks of all descriptions, from mother to master chef and from peasant to aristocrat, have made dough out of a simple paste to use as a case for stuffing, in soups, with sauces, or as a bed for a simmered main dish.

In this chapter, you will find a continental potpourri of noodles. The following glossary will define them.

A: Armenia
E: England
Gy: Germany
G: Greece
H: Hungary
ME: Middle East (Egypt, Iran, Israel, Lebanon, North Africa, Syria, Turkey)

P: Poland
R: Russia
S: Switzerland
Sp: Spain
C: Czechoslovakia
F: France

Calsones (ME): Sephardic stuffed noodles, similar to cheese raviolis.

Csipetke (H): Cross between a noodle and a dumpling. Also called pinced or torn noodle.

Fide (Fidelo, Fidilini) (G): Very fine egg noodle.

Fideos (Sp): Thin noodles, like vermicelli. Usually coiled when packaged.

Galuska (H): Fresh, very soft noodles. Usually served with the main course.

Hornli (S) : Little horns.

Holushki (C): Noodles.

Knopfli (S) : Little button-shaped noodles.

Kolduny (P): Stuffed noodles in the shape of circles.

Kritharaki (G): Rice-like pasta. Also called orzo. Same as Manestra.

Lapscha (Lapschoi) (R): Noodles.

Macaronami (R): Macaroni.

Macaronia (G): Macaroni.

Macarrón (S): Macaroni.

Makaron (P): Egg noodle.

Manestra (G): Ricelike pasta. Also called orzo.

Meteltek (H): Fresh noodles for soup, main course, or dessert.

Monti (A): Stuffed noodle, similar to Italian ravioli or Russian pelemeni.

Noodles (E): Fettuccine-style noodles.

Nouilles (F): Fettuccine-style noodles.

Nudeln (Gy): Fettucine-style noodles.

Orzo (G): Rice-like pasta.

Pelemeni (R): Stuffed noodles, similar to ravioli.

Pierogi (P) : Stuffed noodles similar to ravioli, won ton, or
   kreplach.

Rishta (Reshteh) (ME) : Noodle threads.

Spaetzle (Gy) : Little sparrows. Tiny noodles or egg dumplings.

Spagheto (G) : Spaghetti.

Spatzli (S) : Little sparrows. Tiny noodles or egg dumplings.

Tarhonya (H) : Egg barley.

Trahana (G) : Ricelike noodles made with sour dough.
   Used in soups and stews.

Uszka (P) : Little ears. Similar to tortellini.

Vareniki (R) : Stuffed noodle. Often the filling is sweet for
   dessert dishes.

Many markets now carry an assortment of these packaged
noodles. If you need other ingredients or are unable to
locate a specific variety of noodle, check pages 321–24.

In addition to those described in the Basic Noodle instructions on pages 25–29, the following are popular
Continental Noodles.

Spaetzle, "little sparrows," are often considered the
missing link between the noodle and the egg dumpling. In
the German cuisine, these tiny noodles traditionally accompany sauerbraten or stewed meats.

GERMAN SPAETZLE

SERVES 4 TO 8

> *2 cups flour*
> *1 teaspoon salt*
> *4 eggs, lightly beaten*
> *Milk*

Sift flour and salt together into a large mixing bowl. Beat in the eggs. Slowly add a little milk to make a heavy dough. Press the dough through a colander, a spaetzle maker, or a grater with large holes, directly into a large kettle of rapidly boiling salted water. Boil for about 6 minutes, or until the noodles come to the surface and are done. Remove with a strainer and drain in a colander.

The unusual feature of these Greek egg noodles is the additional egg yolks.

GREEK EGG NOODLES
SERVES 4 TO 8

2 cups flour
1 teaspoon salt
2 eggs, lightly beaten
2 to 4 additional egg yolks

In a large mixing bowl or on a board, sift together the flour and salt. Make a well in the center and add the 2 beaten eggs. Mix them into the flour with your fingers. Add the extra egg yolks, kneading until the dough is stiff. Divide the dough into two balls. Cover one with a kitchen towel so it won't dry out (or wrap in wax paper) while working with the other.

Roll out one ball of dough at a time on a floured board until it is paper thin. Cover both with kitchen towels and let rest for 30 minutes. Roll up each piece of dough jelly-roll style and cut into strips of desired width. To cook: Boil in salted water about 10 to 12 minutes.

The Hungarian people are renowned for their hearty dishes which very often include noodles. Their repertoire of noodles is fairly extensive. They always include eggs but differ in the quantity of water used.

Csipetke belong to both the noodle and the dumpling families. They are made with a simple flour and egg dough which is pinched into noodles for hearty soups or guyas (also known as gulyas or goulash).

CSIPETKE (Pinched Noodle)

SERVES 3 TO 6

1 cup sifted, all-purpose flour
½ teaspoon salt
1 large egg

Sift together the flour and salt. Make a well in the center and add the egg. Mix with your fingers to make a stiff dough; knead until smooth. Cover with a kitchen towel (or wrap in wax paper) and let rest for about 30 minutes. Roll out on a floured board, ⅛- to ¼-inch thick. Pinch off small, nut-size pieces with your thumb and forefinger, and drop noodles directly into boiling, salted water. Cook for about 12 to 15 minutes. Drain and stir into stew or soup. If you do not plan to use them immediately, place in a bowl, coat with a tablespoon of cooking oil and keep warm.

GALUSKA (Soft Egg Noodles)

SERVES 3 TO 6

2 cups sifted, all-purpose flour
1 teaspoon salt
1 egg, lightly beaten
¾ cup water

Sift the flour and salt into a mixing bowl; add the egg and water, mixing with your fingers. Divide the dough into three balls. Keep two balls covered and, working with one ball at a time, roll out and cut into strips 1-inch wide. Add to boiling water. Within a few minutes, noodles will rise to the surface. Remove with a skimmer and serve.

To make regular egg noodles (Meteltek), reduce the water in the previous recipe to 1½ tablespoons. Dough should rest for about 30 minutes before it is rolled out.

Tarhonya resemble barley grains.

TARHONYA (Egg Barley)

SERVES 4 TO 8

2 cups sifted, all-purpose flour
½ teaspoon salt
2 medium eggs

Mix and knead all ingredients together into a firm ball of dough. Roll out on a floured board and cut into ⅛-inch wide strips. Chop dough into fine pieces. Or divide dough in half and grate balls on the coarse side of a grater. Spread particles out on a lightly floured board to dry.

From the Middle East comes the fresh noodle, rishta. Meaning "thread" in Persian, it is of Oriental origin. Historically, these noodles have been considered a special food throughout the ancient and medieval periods.

RISHTA

SERVES 6 TO 12

3½ cups flour
1 teaspoon salt
2 large eggs, lightly beaten
5 to 6 tablespoons water

In a large mixing bowl, sift the flour and salt together into a mound. Make a well in the center and break the eggs into it; add water. Mix and knead all ingredients together and divide the dough into two balls. Roll out one ball at a time, keeping the other covered with a kitchen towel, until very thin. Allow rolled dough to rest for 30 minutes. Then roll each sheet in jelly-roll style and cut into very thin ribbons or threads. Spread on a floured board to dry slightly. To cook: Boil in salted water for about 5 minutes.

Noodles are very popular in Polish soups and stews, both of which are considered basic dishes.

LIGHT SOUP NOODLES

SERVES 2 TO 4

4 eggs, separated
½ teaspoon salt
¼ cup flour

In a large measuring cup or bowl, beat the egg whites with the salt until they form soft peaks. In a small bowl, beat the egg yolks and fold into the whites. Fold in the flour. Carefully pour the "batter" into a pot of boiling soup. Cover and cook for 2 minutes, uncover, and flip the batter to make certain it is cooked on both sides. Break up the batter with a spoon to form bite-size noodles. Serve noodles with soup.

POLISH EGG NOODLES

SERVES 3 TO 5

> 1 cup all-purpose flour
> ¼ teaspoon salt
> 1 large egg, lightly beaten
> 1 tablespoon water

Sift the flour and salt together onto a board in a mound. Make a well in the center and pour the egg and water into it. Mix and knead with your fingers to form a smooth dough. Dust board with flour and roll out dough until it is very thin. Cover dough with a kitchen towel (or wax paper) and let dry for 20 minutes. Dust dough with flour. Roll up in jelly-roll style and cut into thin strands. (Note: Many of these steps can be done with a noodle machine. See pages 24–29.) Toss strands onto a board to separate. Let dry for an hour. To cook: Boil in salted water until they rise to the surface. Drain. This dough can also be used for the Polish stuffed noodles.

Three popular noodles from Switzerland are Hornli (little horns), Knopfli (little buttons), and Spatzli (little sparrows). They are all made from the same basic flour and egg dough.

BASIC SWISS NOODLE DOUGH

SERVES 4 TO 8

> 2½ to 3 cups flour
> ¼ teaspoon salt
> 2 eggs, lightly beaten
> 1 cup cold water

For hornli and knopfli use the full 3 cups of flour. In a large mixing bowl, sift the flour and salt together. Mix the eggs with the water and gradually stir into the flour; beating until smooth. Let dough rest, covered, for 30 minutes. Dampen a cutting board with water. Divide the dough in half, place one ball of dough on the cutting board and roll out until very thin. Use a sharp, wet knife and cut into little strips. Repeat with the remaining dough. Drop noodles into boiling, salted water. For spatzli use 2½ cups of flour and prepare the dough as above. After it has rested, press through the holes of a collander or spaetzle maker into boiling, salted water. Let noodles cook for about 3 minutes, or until they rise to the surface. Remove with a slotted spoon and drain. (Also see German spaetzle, pages 186–87.)

STUFFED NOODLES

The stuffed noodles of Russia are called ''pelemeni.'' They are descendants of the dim sum pastries of China. In the Far East, including Siberia, they are shaped into half moons and eaten with soy sauce, butter, mustard, and vinegar. In Central Russia, the half moons are curled and pinched to resemble a shell, and are eaten with broth, sour cream, butter, and/or mustard.

Pelemeni are extremely popular with the hunters of Siberia who take them along on their trips. They are made and frozen at home, packed, often for several weeks, and tossed in boiling water for a few minutes before eating.

PELEMENI

SERVES 4 TO 6

PELEMENI DOUGH:

3 eggs   *1½ pounds flour*
2 cups milk
1 teaspoon salt

BEEF FILLING:

1½ pounds fine-ground   *1 cup water*
*   beef*   *1½ teaspoons salt*
1 medium onion, peeled   *¾ teaspoon pepper*
*   and chopped fine*

FOR BOILING:

2 quarts salted water,
*   chicken broth, or beef*
*   broth*

To make the dough: In a large mixing bowl, beat the
eggs with the milk and salt. Add the flour and mix well.
Turn dough onto a lightly floured board and knead until
it is very elastic. Break off one piece at a time and roll out
to ⅛-inch thick. Dust lightly with flour and cut with a
cookie cutter into circles, about 1½ inches in diameter.

For the filling: Combine all filling ingredients in a bowl.
Mix with your fingers to blend.

Place 1 teaspoon of filling in the center of each circle;
fold dough in half, pinching the edges firmly together.
Bring the two ends of the half-circle together, pinching
them closed.

At this point, you can quick-freeze the dumplings for
later use. Place them on a lightly floured cookie sheet in
your freezer for a few hours. When completely frozen, you

can transfer them to plastic bags without their sticking together.

To cook: Bring water or broth to a boil in a large pot. Add about 50 pelemeni at a time. Stir gently with a wooden spoon. Bring broth back to a boil and continue to cook pelemeni for another 3 to 4 minutes, longer if they were frozen. Remove pelemeni with a slotted spoon and serve on heated plates. Pelemeni can also be sautéed in a skillet with a few tablespoons of butter or deep-fried in a pot filled with hot cooking oil. Boil pelemeni for only 2 to 3 minutes, then sauté or deep-fry until golden. Drain if they were deep-fried. These make tasty little hors d'oeuvre to serve with Chinese hot mustard.

When serving pelemeni as a main dish, allow 30 to 40 per person. This recipe yields approximately 150 pelemeni.

Pelemeni dough or a simple egg noodle dough can be used for Russian vareniki (also see page 191). You can stuff them with mashed potatoes and garnish with crumbled bacon or chicken liver to serve as a main course. Or, filled with preserves or a sweetened cheese, they make an interesting dessert. (See page 226.)

VARENIKI

SERVES 4 TO 6

MASHED POTATO FILLING:

2 tablespoons butter
1 large onion, peeled and
  chopped fine
2 cups mashed potatoes

½ teaspoon salt
Dash of white pepper

1 Pelemeni Dough recipe
  (see page 193.)

FOR BOILING:
1 quart salted water,
*   chicken stock, or beef*
*   stock*

BACON TOPPING:
¾ pound bacon, chopped   *2 large onions, peeled and*
*   chopped*

CHICKEN LIVER TOPPING:
¾ pound chicken livers   *2 to 4 tablespoons butter*
2 large onions, peeled and
*   chopped*

In a large skillet, melt the butter and sauté the onion until golden. (Note: Rendered chicken fat and a little grebenes would be a marvelous substitute for butter. See page 163.) Remove from heat and add mashed potatoes, salt, and pepper, mixing well.

Make the dough and cut into circles. Place 1 teaspoon of filling in the center of each. Fold in half, pinching edges together to seal.

Bring the salted water or stock (preferably) to a boil in a large pot; drop in a few vareniki at a time. Boil for about 3 to 4 minutes, or until they rise to the surface. Remove with a slotted spoon to a warmed serving platter.

For the toppings: Sauté bacon with onions, or chicken livers with onions and butter, until they are lightly browned. Pour off any excess fat. Arrange over vareniki.

Several kinds of stuffed noodles are popular in the Polish cuisine.

KOLDUNY, PIEROGI, AND USZKA

1 Basic Noodle recipe (See pages 25–28)

OR

2 Polish Egg Noodle recipes (See page 191)

MAKES APPROXIMATELY 3 CUPS
TO FILL 75

SAUSAGE FILLING:

1 pound Polish sausage, skinned and chopped
¾ cup chopped mushrooms

1 tablespoon cooking oil
2 egg yolks
⅓ to ½ cup fine breadcrumbs

Sauté sausage and mushrooms with the oil in a skillet over medium heat. Remove from heat; add egg yolks and enough breadcrumbs to bind mixture.

MAKES APPROXIMATELY 3 CUPS
TO FILL 75

SAUERKRAUT FILLING:

1 medium onion, peeled and chopped fine
2 tablespoons cooking oil or bacon fat
3 cups sauerkraut, rinsed and drained several times, chopped fine
½ teaspoon caraway seeds
¼ cup sour cream

In a large skillet, sauté the onion in the oil over medium heat until soft, about 4 minutes. Add sauerkraut and caraway seeds; stir to mix and cook a few minutes longer. Remove from heat. Spoon sour cream into sauerkraut and stir through.

MAKES APPROXIMATELY 3 CUPS

TO FILL 75

CHEESE AND POTATO FILLING:

1 small onion, peeled and   *2 cups mashed potatoes*
*   chopped fine*   *1 cup pot cheese (or cot-*
2 tablespoons butter   *   tage cheese)*
½ teaspoon salt   *1 egg yolk*

In a large skillet, sauté the onion in butter over medium heat until soft. (Note: Rendered chicken fat with grebenes can be substituted for the butter for a most remarkable taste. See page 163.) Add salt and the mashed potatoes with more butter if necessary. When potatoes are fully coated, remove skillet from heat and allow mixture to cool. Add the cheese and egg yolk and blend until the mixture is bound together.

MAKES APPROXIMATELY 3 CUPS

To make kolduny: Roll out dough on a floured board to ⅛-inch thick. With a cookie cutter, cut out circles, 1 to 1½-inches diameter. Place a teaspoon of filling in the center; top with another circle. Seal edges by crimping with a fork. Traditionally, kolduny are filled with meat, boiled in broth or soup until they float, about 3 minutes, and served in the soup.

To make pierogi: Roll out dough on a floured board ¼ to ⅛-inch thick. With a cookie cutter, cut out circles, 4-inches in diameter. Place a tablespoon of filling a little off center on each circle. Fold circles in half into a crescent, enclosing the filling. Seal edges by crimping with a fork. Traditionally, pierogi are filled with meat, vegetables, po-

water, until they rise to the surface, about 5 minutes. Drizzle with melted butter if you like, or eat plain.

To make uszka: Roll out dough on a floured board to ⅛-inch thick. Cut into 2-inch squares. Place a small spoonful of filling in the center of each square. Moisten the edges with cold water and fold in half diagonally, making a triangle. Press edges together to seal. Take the two points at the base and bring around, pinching them together (like tortellini, see page 93). Traditionally, uszka are filled with meat and mushrooms. Cook a small amount at a time in boiling, salted water, until they float to the surface about 5 minutes. Remove with a slotted spoon and serve in broth or soup.

This is a Sephardic stuffed noodle similar to cheese ravioli.

MIDDLE EASTERN CALSONES
SERVES 8 TO 12

1 Rishta dough recipe (See pages 189–90.)
MAKES APPROXIMATELY 2 CUPS,
TO FILL 50

GRUYÈRE FILLING:

¾ *pound Gruyère cheese, grated*

¼ *pound grated Parmesan cheese*

3 egg yolks, lightly beaten
Salt and white pepper to taste

MAKES APPROXIMATELY 2 CUPS,
TO FILL 50

RICOTTA FILLING:

¾ *pound ricotta cheese*
¼ *pound grated Parmesan*
  cheese
3 tablespoons cold milk

2 tablespoons minced fresh
  parsley
Dash sugar

Roll out rishta dough on a lightly floured board into long, thin sheets. (This can be done with a noodle machine. See pages 24–29.) Make your choice of Gruyère or Ricotta Filling, and combine the ingredients. Place spoonfuls of filling about 1 inch apart on half the sheet of dough. When half the dough is covered, fold the empty half over on top of the filling.

Press dough gently with your fingers between each mound of filling to seal. Cut out squares with a sharp knife or use a ravioli making tray.

Gently lower the stuffed noodles into boiling, salted water. Boil for about 10 to 15 minutes, or until done. Remove with a slotted spoon or strainer, drain, and serve with plenty of melted butter. Or place drained calsones in a baking dish, drizzle with melted butter and sprinkle with grated Parmesan cheese. Bake at 350 degrees for 15 to 20 minutes, or until golden.

Armenians prepare boat-shaped stuffed noodles which are baked to a crusty brown or simmered in a spicy broth and served with a refreshing yogurt sauce.

ARMENIAN MONTI

SERVES 12 TO 16

Preheat oven to 375 degrees

MONTI DOUGH:

1 egg
1 cup water
3 to 3½ cups flour

¼ *teaspoon salt*
¼ *cup melted butter*

LAMB FILLING:

1 pound ground lamb
1 large onion, peeled and
   chopped fine

½ cup minced fresh
   parsley
Salt and pepper to taste

SPICY BROTH:

2½ quarts beef broth
¼ cup ketchup

Dash of bottled hot pepper
   sauce (or as much as
   you like)

YOGURT SAUCE:

2 cups plain yogurt
½ cup minced fresh
   parsley
1 tablespoon lemon juice

1 large clove garlic, peeled
   and minced
Salt to taste

To make the dough: In a large mixing bowl, beat the egg with the water. Add 3 cups of flour, the salt, and the melted butter; stir until well blended. Turn the dough out on a lightly floured board. Knead until smooth and elastic, adding flour as needed to eliminate stickiness. Divide into two parts; cover and allow to rest for 30 minutes. Roll out on floured board into thin sheets. Cut into 1½-inch squares. (Note: Many of these steps can be done with a noodle machine. See pages 24–29.)

To make the filling: Mix together all filling ingredients in a bowl.

Place a small spoonful of filling in the center of each square. Fold up sides of square into a tube-like shape and pinch ends together.

To butter-bake: Pour ½ cup melted butter into a large casserole and arrange stuffed monti on top. Bake in the preheated oven for about 40 minutes, or until browned. Serve immediately, or wrap and refrigerate for a few days. Cooked monti can also be frozen. To reheat, bring monti to room temperature. Preheat oven to 375 degrees.

Place in a buttered casserole, dot with additional butter, and bake in the preheated oven for 5 minutes.

For Broth and Sauce method: Heat broth, ketchup, and pepper sauce in a saucepan; bring to a boil. Place monti in a baking dish and pour hot broth over them. Bake in the preheated oven for 5 to 10 minutes, or until monti are fully warmed. Serve in soup bowls with yogurt sauce.

To make the sauce: Spoon yogurt, parsley, lemon juice, garlic, and salt into a large mixing bowl; blend well. Cover and refrigerate for at least 1 hour to allow flavors to mellow. Sauce can even be made a day in advance and refrigerated until serving time.

When serving, pour sauce into a serving bowl and pass at the table.

SOUPS

Simple soups of broth and noodles are found in every continental cuisine. For a Greek touch, you might add a bit of fresh lemon juice and float a lovely wafer-thin slice of fruit on top.

LEMON NOODLE SOUP

SERVES 4

1½ quarts chicken broth
Salt to taste
3 ounces broken fides (see page 185)
3 tablespoons lemon juice
Wafer-thin lemon slices, for garnish

Bring chicken broth to a boil in a soup pot; add salt to taste. Add the noodles and simmer about 15 minutes. Add the lemon juice, stirring to blend the flavors. Serve in wide soup bowls, garnished with a few slices of lemon.

Another Greek soup features trahana.

VEGETABLE BROTH WITH TRAHANA
SERVES 6

*One 16-ounce can whole
tomatoes, seeded and
chopped fine (with
their liquid)*
*1 onion, peeled and
chopped*
*2 stalks celery, chopped
fine*
*2 carrots, scraped and
chopped*

2 cups chicken broth
1 bay leaf
Salt and pepper to taste
*1 cup trahana (see
page 186)*
1 cup dry white wine
*1 cup fresh-grated Kefalo-
tyri cheese (This is a
Greek cheese similar to
Parmesan.)*

In a large soup pot, combine the tomatoes, onion, celery, carrots, and chicken broth. Bring to a boil; add the bay leaf and season with salt and pepper. Reduce heat to a simmer for 20 minutes. Remove and discard the bay leaf. Pour soup into a food processor (or blender) and purée until it is velvety smooth. Return soup to the pot and heat again to a boil. Add the noodles and simmer about 20 minutes. Add the wine, stirring to blend well. Simmer soup for another 2 minutes. Serve accompanied with the grated cheese.

A very dear woman and fellow cookbook author, Birdina Lewin told me of this marvelously light potato noodle. It is a family recipe which she learned from her grandmother who lived in Strasbourg, Germany.

OLD WORLD CHICKEN SOUP WITH POTATO FLOUR NOODLES

SERVES 6

POTATO FLOUR NOODLES:

3 eggs

1½ cups water

6 tablespoons potato flour (or potato starch)

½ teaspoon salt

3 tablespoons light salad oil (such as corn oil)

Additional oil for frying

2 to 3 quarts rich chicken broth, heated

Combine all noodle ingredients except the oil for frying in a large mixing bowl. Beat thoroughly until well-blended and smooth. Prepare a 5- or 6-inch skillet with a non-fat vegetable spray. Let pan sit for a few minutes. Place skillet over medium heat; sprinkle with a little oil (or brush oil on pan) and tilt to coat evenly. Use only enough oil to make pan shine.

Add about 2 tablespoons of batter and fry as when making crêpes. When batter in skillet turns golden on the first side, either turn and fry on the other side for a few seconds or turn out on a kitchen towel. (Cooking on one side is really sufficient.) Continue making crêpes until all the batter is used.

Roll each crêpe into a cylinder and with a very sharp knife, cut into ⅛-inch strips. The strips can be held for a few hours in a bowl tightly covered with plastic wrap. However, they are better when used immediately.

Divide noodles into 6 soup bowls and pour the hot chicken soup over them.

During the Tsar Peter's reign, Russia flourished with creative ideas from other countries, and Italian architects introduced macaroni to the Russian cuisine. This hearty meat and vegetable soup with macaroni is similar to the Italian minestrone. (See pages 116–17.)

RUSSIAN MINESTRONE

SERVES 4 TO 6

2 pounds soup bones
1½ quarts beef stock
1 tablespoon salt
1 teaspoon peppercorns
1 bay leaf
2 whole cloves garlic,
   peeled
2 carrots, scraped and
   chopped

1 medium onion, peeled
   and chopped
1 stalk celery, chopped
2 boiling potatoes, peeled
   and diced
3 tomatoes, peeled, seeded,
   and chopped
1 cup shredded cabbage
1 cup elbow macaroni

Place the bones, stock, salt, peppercorns, bay leaf, and garlic in a large soup pot; bring to a boil. Cover, reduce heat to a simmer, and cook for 45 minutes. Check soup occasionally and skim off any fat. Strain soup, returning the stock to the pot. Add the carrots, onion, and celery. Cook soup at a low boil for 30 minutes. Add the potatoes; cook for another 15 minutes. Add the tomatoes and cabbage; lower the heat and continue to simmer another 10 minutes before adding macaroni. As soon as macaroni are tender, remove from heat and serve.

From along the Mediterranean coast comes this Spanish garlic soup.

GARLIC SOUP

SERVES 4

4 whole large cloves garlic,
 peeled
3 tablespoons cooking oil
2 quarts hot water
2 cups chicken broth,
 heated

Salt and pepper to taste
4 ounces macarrón (see
 page 185) or other
 soup noodles, cooked
 and drained

In a large soup pot, sauté the garlic in the oil until it is a light gold. Add the hot water. Boil water, uncovered, for 10 minutes. Remove the garlic and grind in a food processor or with a mortar and pestle. Add the chicken broth to the soup pot. Return the ground garlic to the soup and season with salt and pepper. Cook at a steady simmer for another 10 minutes. Add the noodles and serve.

SAUCED AND SAUTÉED NOODLES (Including Casseroles)

All you need for a quick Continental side dish are your favorite noodles tossed with butter and seasoned with some herbs and spices. You can sauté cooked German spaetzle (see pages 186–87) in butter until golden, and then sprinkle it with a generous helping of toasted breadcrumbs. A basic Greek noodle dish suggests tossing cooked orzo (see page 185) with a handful of pine nuts (pignoli). The Russians toss their cooked noodles with butter and cottage cheese for an easy dish.

RUSSIAN NOODLES WITH COTTAGE CHEESE

SERVES 4

> ½ *pound broad noodles, cooked and drained*
> 2 *tablespoons butter*
> 1 *cup pot cheese or cottage cheese*

Return noodles to the pot in which they were cooked and toss them with butter until they are well-coated. Add the cottage cheese and toss. Serve immediately.

Green noodles, tossed with seasoned oil, watercress, and a splash of brandy are like a French melody.

FETTUCCINE WITH A SPLASH

SERVES 6

1 cup olive oil
¼ pound shallots, chopped fine
1 clove garlic, peeled and chopped fine
Salt and pepper to taste

⅓ cup chopped watercress
2 tablespoons good brandy
12 ounces green fettuccine, cooked and drained
2 ounces freshly-grated Parmesan cheese

Put oil in a large skillet and heat over medium flame. Add the shallots and garlic and season with salt and pepper. When shallots begin to turn gold, add the watercress and brandy and remove from heat. Within a few seconds, watercress will be wilted. Place noodles in a large, warmed, serving bowl; pour seasoned sauce on top and toss. Serve with a small bowl of grated Parmesan cheese.

Spinach noodles, tossed with garlic, seasoned butter, and cheeses are beautiful to see as well as to smell. Ah, the aroma!

FRENCH NOODLES WITH GARLIC AND CHEESES

SERVES 4

½ *pound spinach noodles, cooked and drained*
¼ *cup butter*
1 *clove garlic, peeled and minced fine*
¼ *cup fresh-grated Parmesan cheese*

¼ *cup fresh-grated Gruyère cheese*
Fresh-ground black pepper
Fresh-grated nutmeg, (optional)

Return noodles to the pot in which they were cooked. In a small saucepan, melt the butter and cook the garlic until light brown. Pour the garlic butter over the noodles and toss quickly to coat. Add the cheeses, again tossing quickly. Place noodles on individual serving dishes. Sprinkle at the table with pepper and nutmeg.

Save your bacon drippings for this German specialty.

GERMAN FRIED NOODLES

SERVES 3 TO 4

8 ounces medium noodles, cooked and drained
¼ cup bacon drippings (or butter), heated
½ teaspoon salt
⅛ teaspoon celery seeds (or try some marjoram instead)

Sauté noodles in a large skillet in the hot drippings; stir gently with a fork to coat them on all sides. Sprinkle with salt and celery seeds.

The people of Hungary, Czechoslovakia, and Germany are especially fond of noodles tossed with cabbage. Originally a peasant dish, this is a grand way to serve noodles.

HUNGARIAN NOODLES WITH CABBAGE

SERVES 4

1 medium head cabbage, grated coarse
2 teaspoons salt
2 tablespoons bacon drippings
¼ teaspoon each salt and pepper
½ pound egg noodles, cooked and drained

To prepare the cabbage, toss with salt in a large bowl and let stand at room temperature for 30 minutes. Squeeze out any juice. Cook the cabbage in the bacon drippings in a large skillet over very low heat for about 30 minutes, stirring occasionally. Season with salt and pepper and add the cooked noodles. Heat through and serve.

NOODLES WITH CABBAGE AND SAUSAGE
SERVES 4

1 pound sausage, casing re-
moved (I prefer the
spicy variety.)
½ cup beer (or water)
1 medium head cabbage,
shredded

1 teaspoon caraway seeds
Salt and pepper to taste
8 ounces medium egg
noodles, cooked and
drained

Place sausage in a skillet over medium heat and cook, breaking up the meat with the back of a wooden spoon. Remove to a saucepan and add beer and cabbage. Add the caraway seeds and season with salt and pepper. Cook over low heat for about 15 minutes, or until cabbage is tender.

Return noodles to pot in which they were cooked. Drain off any excess liquid from the sausage and cabbage and toss with the noodles.

Potato and noodle lovers will welcome this hearty, family dish. Paprika colors everything a beautiful shade of red. It's best as an accompaniment to roasted meat.

You'll need a large skillet so you can toss everything together without mashing the potatoes. I found it best to cook this in my Oriental wok so I'm able to scoop underneath and turn easily.

HUNGARIAN NOODLES AND POTATOES PAPRIKA

SERVES 8

7 to 8 new potatoes (Red Rose are excellent), boiled in their jackets until done, then drained (The potatoes can be boiled in advance and refrigerated until final cooking.)
¼ pound butter
1 medium onion, peeled and chopped fine

1 heaping teaspoon paprika
1 teaspoon salt
Pinch fresh-ground black pepper
8 ounces square noodles (I break the extra-wide flat noodles into 1-inch squares), cooked and drained

Peel and dice potatoes; set aside. Melt 2 tablespoons of the butter in a very large skillet over medium heat. Add the onions and sauté until they are soft. Add the potatoes along with the remaining butter and the seasonings. Continue cooking until potatoes are golden-red, turning them often. Add the cooked noodles; toss until well mixed.

This Renaissance recipe is French with Italian influence. Originally, the sauce was made with a mortar and pestle. Now, with the convenience of a food processor or electric blender, you can make a super-smooth sauce within minutes. Serve this as a first course. The sweet seasonings and delicate flavor should stand alone.

FRENCH NOODLES WITH ALMOND AND CHEESE SAUCE

SERVES 6 TO 8

ALMOND AND CHEESE SAUCE:

¾ cup peeled, slivered almonds

½ cup ricotta cheese

¼ cup fresh-grated Parmesan cheese

½ cup light cream

2 tablespoons olive oil

Dash of cinnamon and fresh-grated nutmeg

Salt to taste

1 pound medium flat noodles, cooked and drained (retain ½ cup liquid)

2 to 3 tablespoons butter

To make the sauce: Using the metal blade of a food processor, chop the almonds fine. Change the blade to the plastic blender and add the remaining sauce ingredients, one at a time. Process the sauce until you have a smooth paste. If using a mortar and pestle, pound the almonds first, slowly adding remaining ingredients. (Note: Sauce can be made in advance to this point and refrigerated until needed.)

Place cooked noodles in a warmed serving dish; toss with the butter. Add the ½ cup of reserved noodle liquid to the sauce to thin it slightly. Stir with a wooden stick or a whisk to smooth out the sauce. Pour sauce over the noodles. Serve immediately.

This very light French sauce is based on homemade "Crème Fraîche." Since the sauce is fairly thin and transparent, I like to use a colored noodle.

CRÈME FRAÎCHE SAUCE

SERVES 6 TO 8

CRÈME FRAÎCHE SAUCE:

½ cup sour cream
1 tablespoon confectioners' sugar
2 tablespoons milk
¼ teaspoon vanilla
1 teaspoon sweet Madeira

12 ounces coiled spinach noodles (fideos, for example), cooked and drained, with ⅓ cup liquid reserved
2 to 4 tablespoons butter

In a medium-size mixing bowl, combine the sauce ingredients. The sauce can be made in advance and refrigerated until serving time. If so, bring to room temperature before serving.

Place cooked noodles in a serving bowl; toss with butter. Pour enough of the reserved hot noodle liquid into the sauce to thin it to desired consistency; whisk sauce and pour over noodles. Toss to coat well and serve immediately as a side course. (Note: Use any leftovers as the base for a delicious casserole!)

The Greek tomato sauce, though not as rich as the Spanish, takes a lot of its lovely flavor from cinnamon.

GREEK TOMATO SAUCE
SERVES 4 TO 6

¼ *cup butter*
1 medium onion, peeled
    and chopped
2 pounds ripe tomatoes,
    peeled, seeded, and
    chopped

1 large cinnamon stick
Salt and pepper to taste
1 pound spaghetti, cooked
    and drained

Melt the butter in a skillet and sauté the onion until soft. Add the tomatoes, cinnamon, salt, and pepper. Bring sauce to a boil; lower heat and simmer, uncovered, for 20 to 30 minutes, or until sauce is well thickened. Remove cinnamon, toss with spaghetti and serve.

Variation: You may sauté 3 cloves of garlic (chopped) with the onion. When onion is soft, add 1 cup of broth and season with 1 stalk of celery and a sprig of parsley, instead of the cinnamon. Remove the celery and parsley before serving. Place spaghetti on a warmed platter, top with sauce, and toss.

Add some ground beef to Greek Tomato Sauce and the result will be this excellent sauce, ideal for a thick macaroni.

MACARONI AND MEAT SAUCE
SERVES 8 TO 10

2 pounds ground beef
1 medium onion, peeled and chopped
¼ cup butter
2 cups peeled, strained tomatoes
Salt and pepper to taste
1 large cinnamon stick

4 whole cloves
1 tablespoon minced fresh parsley
2 pounds thick macaroni, cooked and drained
Grated Parmesan cheese, for topping

In a medium-size pot, sauté the meat and onion together in the butter. When meat is no longer pink, add the tomatoes and seasonings. Break up the tomatoes with the back of a wooden spoon. Cook sauce over very low heat for 1 hour to thicken properly. Remove and discard cinnamon and cloves. Place macaroni on a warmed platter. Top with sauce and cheese. Toss at the table.

When my French beautician, Jacqueline, serves noodles, she tosses fettuccine with butter and generous quantities of Parmesan and Emmenthal cheeses, until threads form. I've taken her idea and tossed my noodles with butter, a little cream or béchamel sauce, and plenty of luscious cheese.

MACARONI WITH CHEESES
SERVES 4 TO 6

FRENCH CHEESE SAUCE:

¼ *cup butter*

1 cup light cream (or milk)

6 ounces Gruyère cheese, grated

1 pound ziti, cooked and drained

6 ounces Fontina cheese, grated

1¾ cups grated Parmesan cheese

1 tablespoon dry mustard

Fresh-ground black pepper, (optional)

In a large saucepan, heat the butter with the cream. When the butter has melted, slowly stir in the cheeses with a wooden spoon. Add the mustard. Stir until the sauce is very smooth.

Place noodles in warm serving bowl. Pour cheese sauce over and toss to combine. Bring to the table. Sprinkle with pepper.

These unusual French croquettes are used to top green noodles.

NOODLES WITH CROQUETTES

SERVES 4 TO 6

½ *pound green noodles,*
   cooked and drained
⅓ *cup butter*
½ *pound Gruyère cheese,*
   cut into strips (2 x 1 x
   ¼ inch thick)
1 *egg, lightly beaten*
Fine dry breadcrumbs

¾ *cup olive oil*
½ *cup grated Romano*
   cheese
2 tablespoons chopped
   fresh parsley
Pine nuts and paprika, for
   garnish

Return noodles to the pot in which they were cooked and toss with the butter. Dip strips of Gruyère cheese into egg and roll in bread crumbs. Heat the oil in a skillet and brown the cheese strips.

Place noodles in a serving dish. Sprinkle with Romano cheese and parsley. Arrange the croquettes on top and garnish decoratively with pine nuts and paprika.

Some linguists who have studied the colorful names given to noodles and pasta in various countries have given serious consideration to macaroni's having originated in Greece. The Greek word "makarios" means blessed when referring to the dead; "makaria" means food eaten in honor of the dead.

MACARONIA WITH FETA CHEESE

SERVES 6

1 pound macaroni, cooked and drained
¾ cup melted butter
3 eggs
⅓ cup evaporated milk
½ pound feta cheese (cheese made of goat's milk), cut
    into small pieces

Place macaroni in a serving bowl and toss with melted butter. In the top of a double boiler, beat together the eggs, milk, and cheese; pour over macaroni and serve.

Pilaf dishes are popular all over the world, especially in countries near the Mediterranean Sea. This one is a marvelous blend of fine noodles, rice, stock and seasonings. Prepare it for an outstanding accompaniment to roasted game, fish, fowl, or meats.

GREEK PILAF

SERVES 4

½ cup butter
1 cup crushed fides (see page 185) or vermicelli
1 cup rice
2 cups hot chicken broth
Salt and pepper to taste

In a large pot, melt the butter and add the fides, stirring constantly until browned. Add the rice and stir. Next add the hot broth and salt and pepper. Stir all the ingredients, cover, lower heat, and simmer for 20 minutes. Do not uncover! Set aside for 10 minutes. Remove lid and fluff with a fork.

This pilaf reminds me of a couscous we once enjoyed at a Moroccan restaurant. The pine nuts and raisins add the special quality.

MARRAKESH PILAF

SERVES 6 TO 8

1 cup rice-like pasta
¼ cup long-grain rice
3 tablespoons pine nuts
¼ cup butter

¼ cup seedless golden
raisins
One 10½-ounce can condensed beef broth
⅔ cup water

In a medium-size pot, lightly brown the pasta, rice, and nuts in butter. Add the raisins and continue to cook for a few seconds over medium heat, making sure the raisins are well coated with butter. Pour in the broth and water; stir. Cover, reduce heat, and simmer for 1 hour. If you need the stove-top space, you can bake this pilaf, covered, in a 350-degree oven for 1 hour.

ISRAELI PILAF

SERVES 4 TO 6

¼ cup butter
1 small onion, peeled and
chopped fine
1 clove garlic, peeled and
minced

1 cup long-grain rice
½ cup fine noodles
Salt and pepper to taste
1½ cups chicken stock

In a heavy saucepan, over medium heat, melt the butter, add the onion and garlic and sauté until onion is soft. Stir in the rice and noodles. Season with salt and pepper. Continue to cook over low heat for another 4 minutes, stirring constantly. Add the stock, bring it to a boil and cover quickly. Reduce the heat to low and continue to simmer pilaf another 30 to 45 minutes.

Pastitso, the Greek layered macaroni and meat casserole, is a classic belonging in the same esteemed category as baked lasagne.

PASTITSO

SERVES 12 TO 16

Preheat oven to 375 degrees

2 pounds ziti (or other macaroni), cooked and drained

½ cup melted butter

3 eggs, lightly beaten

2 tablespoons grated Parmesan cheese

½ cup olive oil

3 pounds ground beef

1 pound small eggplants, cubed and salted, (optional)

1 large onion, peeled and chopped fine

2 cloves garlic, peeled and minced

1 tablespoon minced fresh parsley

1 teaspoon cinnamon

½ teaspoon fresh-grated nutmeg

½ teaspoon ground oregano

Salt and pepper to taste

2 cups tomato purée

1 cup dry white wine

1½ quarts favorite Béchamel Sauce (see pages 96–97, 102), heated

¾ pound freshly-grated Parmesan cheese

Place cooked ziti in a bowl and toss with the butter, eggs, and 2 tablespoons grated Parmesan cheese; set aside.

Heat the olive oil in a large, heavy skillet. Sauté the ground beef with the eggplant, onion, garlic, and parsley, breaking up the lumps of meat with the back of a wooden spoon. When everything is nicely browned, add the seasonings. Stir to combine and add the tomato purée and wine. Let sauce simmer, uncovered, for about 30 minutes.

Butter a large casserole (9 x 13 x 2 inches); spoon a very thin layer of meat sauce over the bottom as a protector. Place half the macaroni in the casserole, cover with a layer of the meat-eggplant sauce, and then a layer of the Béchamel sauce. Sprinkle with grated Parmesan cheese. Continue layering until all ingredients are used up. Finish with Béchamel sauce and Parmesan cheese. Bake in the preheated oven for 30 to 45 minutes. Cool for about 15 minutes before cutting.

Another Greek and Middle Eastern classic dish is Kapama, a lovely combination of sweet and spicy flavors, featuring beef, lamb, or chicken.

KAPAMA

SERVES 4

1 to 1½ pounds cubed beef
Salt and pepper to taste
3 tablespoons cooking oil
2 onions, peeled and
*   chopped*
2 cloves garlic, peeled and
*   minced*
One 8-ounce can tomato
*   sauce*
Two 16-ounce cans peeled,
*   whole tomatoes (with*
*   their liquid)*
1 cup white wine (more if
*   additional liquid is*

*   needed)*
½ teaspoon ground cumin
Bouquet garni made with:
*   2 bay leaves, two 2-inch-*
*   long cinnamon sticks, 4*
*   whole cloves, 6 whole*
*   allspice*

12 ounces wide egg noo-
*   dles, cooked and*
*   drained*
½ cup melted butter
½ to ¾ cup grated Parme-
*   san cheese*

Season meat with salt and pepper. In a large stew pot, brown the meat in the oil with the onions and garlic, until the meat and vegetables are golden. Sprinkle with cumin. Add the bouquet garni, tomato sauce, canned tomatoes, and wine. Carefully stir everything together. Bring to a boil. Cover, reduce heat and simmer for about 2 to 3 hours. Meat will be very tender. Check occasionally and stir to be sure meat is covered with liquid. Adjust seasoning.

Return noodles to the pot in which they were cooked. Toss with melted butter and grated Parmesan cheese.

To serve: Use a large platter and place noodles in a ring around the outside of the dish. Spoon meat with some sauce into the center. Serve with a bowl of the remaining sauce and a small bowl with extra grated Parmesan cheese. Or, noodles can be served with some sauce in one bowl and the meat in a second. Garnish with cheese at the table.

Serve butterhead lettuce with lemon dressing as a refreshing salad with this Greek spaghetti and chicken liver casserole.

SPAGHETTI AND CHICKEN LIVERS
SERVES 6

Preheat oven to 350 degrees

1 pound spaghetti, cooked
and drained
¼ cup butter
½ pound chicken livers,
cut into small pieces
¼ cup cooking oil

Sait and pepper to taste
¾ cup Parmesan cheese
3 eggs, lightly beaten
¾ cup grated Gruyère
cheese

Return spaghetti to the pot in which they were cooked and toss with butter.

Sauté the chicken livers in the cooking oil in a medium-size skillet for about 5 minutes. Season with salt and pepper.

Butter a casserole and spread half the spaghetti on the bottom. Sprinkle with half the Parmesan cheese; add the livers. Cover with the remaining spaghetti and Parmesan cheese.

In a small mixing bowl, combine the eggs and the Gruyère cheese. Pour this over the spaghetti casserole. Bake in the preheated oven for about 20 minutes, or until heated through and browned.

Paprika is the dominant seasoning in most Hungarian stews including this veal dish. Guyas (goulash, or *guiyás*) originated as a peasants' "brew." Boiled noodles tossed with butter usually serve as a bed. But in this hearty stew the noodles are cooked with the sauce for added flavor.

VEAL GUYAS WITH NOODLES

SERVES 6

2 *pounds breast of veal,*
   cut into bite-size pieces
¼ *cup flour*
2 *tablespoons melted*
   butter
1 *teaspoon salt*
Dash black pepper
6 *medium onions, peeled*

8 *ounces wide noodles*
1 *cup sliced celery*
1 *tablespoon paprika*
1 *tablespoon chopped fresh*
   parsley
1 *teaspoon grated lemon*
   rind

Dredge meat in flour and brown in melted butter in a Dutch oven. Sprinkle with salt and pepper. Cover with cold water and bring to a boil. Reduce heat and simmer for 1½ hours, adding more water if necessary. Add the onions, noodles, and celery, and cook for another 45 minutes. Turn stew out on a hot platter, garnish with paprika, parsley, and grated lemon rind.

Martel Lovelace, a spirited woman with whom I work on an outdoor-sports program, and I have shared a lot of laughs and inner thoughts. Her German "Mama" makes these croquettes and serves them with applesauce and a light looseleaf or Boston lettuce salad tossed with a delicate sour cream dressing.

SCHINKEN-NUDELKROKETTEN
(Ham-Noodle Croquettes)

SERVES 3 TO 4

8 ounces medium-wide egg noodles
2 cups milk
1 cup fully-cooked fine-diced ham
3 eggs, lightly beaten

1 tablespoon grated Parmesan cheese
1 tablespoon fine-chopped fresh parsley
Salt and pepper to taste
Vegetable oil or shortening to deep-fry

Cook noodles in a large saucepan with the milk until they are very well done and all the milk is absorbed. Let noodles cool. Add ham, eggs, cheese, parsley, salt, and pepper. Form the mixture into croquettes and fry in hot oil, at least ¼-inch deep, until golden yellow.

An Auflauf is a sort of baked pudding, not as fancy as a soufflé. Serve this after a heavy soup, such as bean, lentil, or split-pea. It's a great dessert, too, if you can wait,

MARTEL'S GERMAN APFEL-NUDELAUFLAUF

SERVES 6

Preheat oven to 350 degrees

2 cups egg noodles, cooked and drained
2 cups milk
1 tablespoon butter
½ cup sugar
4 eggs, separated
½ teaspoon vanilla extract
½ teaspoon grated lemon rind
2 cups thin-sliced apples

¼ cup walnuts
¼ cup currants or raisins
1 tablespoon lemon juice
Dash cinnamon
Butter for dotting
Cracker crumbs, (optional)
Whipping cream, as garnish

Combine the noodles and milk in a large mixing bowl. In another bowl, cream the butter; add ¼ cup of the sugar, the egg yolks, vanilla, and lemon rind. Beat until light and fluffy. Beat the egg whites until stiff; fold them into the creamed butter mixture and carefully fold into the milk-noodle mixture.

Line the bottom and sides of a well-buttered deep dish (a 9-inch spring-form pan is best) with half the noodle mixture. Mix the apples with the nuts, currants, the remaining ¼ cup of sugar, the lemon juice, and cinnamon; add to the noodles as a middle layer. Cover with the remaining noodle mixture. Dot with butter and cracker crumbs and bake in preheated oven for 1 hour, or until golden yellow. Serve with whipped cream.

This interesting macaroni is not boiled in water, but cooked first in milk and then in a custard sauce. The macaroni absorbs the liquid. Serve this casserole as an excellent accompaniment to simply prepared meats, especially pork.

FRENCH SWEET MACARONI CUSTARD
SERVES 4 TO 6

Preheat oven to 350 degrees

1½ cups milk

*8 ounces small elbow maca-
roni*

*2 ounces butter, cut into
small pieces*

½ teaspoon salt

2 egg yolks

1 teaspoon cinnamon

Dash fresh-grated nutmeg

*¼ cup golden seedless rai-
sins, plumped in 3
tablespoons sweet Ma-
deira for 30 minutes*

½ cup light cream

1 teaspoon sugar

Carefully bring milk to a boil in a medium saucepan; add the macaroni, butter, and salt, stirring constantly. Cover and reduce heat. Simmer very gently until all the milk has been absorbed, about 10 minutes. Cool slightly. In a small bowl, mix the egg yolks, cinnamon, nutmeg, raisins with Madeira, cream, and sugar and pour this into the noodles. Turn mixture into a buttered, square, baking dish, cover with foil and bake in the preheated oven for 20 to 30 minutes.

SWEETS

Continental noodles appear occasionally as desserts. Some people prepare a simple sweet of egg noodles tossed with butter, poppyseeds, and vanilla, then dusted with sugar.

The Jewish concept of baked noodle puddings (kugels) is popular also in Hungarian cooking, especially where the puddings feature sour cream, raisins, nuts, apricot jam, and grated lemon rind. (See pages 174–80.) Another favorite Hungarian noodle dessert includes butter, walnuts, liqueur, and sugar.

HUNGARIAN NOODLES WITH WALNUTS

SERVES 6

> *8 ounces bowties, cooked and drained*
> *¼ cup sweet butter*
> *¾ cup chopped walnuts*
> *½ teaspoon anisette liqueur*
> *1 teaspoon dark brown sugar*

Return noodles to the pot in which they were cooked and toss with butter until well coated. Add nuts; toss again. Place noodles on warmed serving platter. Sprinkle with anisette and sugar. This is delightful as a light, sweetened dish, especially for a luncheon with a salad.

SWEET VARENIKI

SERVES APPROXIMATELY 10

1 Pelemeni Noodle recipe (see pages 192–94).

FRUIT FILLING:
2 cups favorite preserves

CHEESE FILLING:
1 pound Farmer's cheese   *1 egg*
   (Or pot cheese or   *1 to 2 tablespoons sugar*
   ricotta cheese)   *Dash of vanilla extract*

TOPPING:
1 cup sour cream

Prepare dough according to Pelemeni directions on pages 192–94. Fill with either preserves or cheese mixture. Boil in 1 quart of water for a few minutes, or until they rise to the surface. Place about 10 filled noodles on each serving dish. Top with sour cream.

The American Noodle

MOTHER, apple pie, hot dogs, and baseball have all become symbols of our American heritage. To this list, I'd like to add another item—noodles.

When the colonists first settled in the New World, they brought with them preferences for certain seasonings and tastes, primarily for meat and potatoes. Later, during the American Revolution, the tune "Yankee Doodle" (see page 11) gained great popularity with the soldiers battling for independence. This was the beginning of the importance of noodles in America. But it was not until Thomas Jefferson, the founding father of American noodlery, returned from his European travels that noodles, macaroni, and spaghetti attained their rightful position of culinary respect.

A renowned gourmet, Jefferson traveled abroad from 1784 to 1789, as the American ambassador to France. While in Europe, he visited Italy where he observed the making of macaroni. From Paris, on January 22, 1789, he wrote to a friend in Italy, William Short, requesting his assistance in purchasing a pasta-manufacturing machine. The bill for this item hangs in the Agnesi Historical Museum of Spaghetti (see page 83). When returning to America, Jefferson is reported to have included two cases of macaroni, as well as his beloved machine, among his personal belongings.

The next important boom for American noodlery did not come until the late 19th-century. Though durum wheat used for noodle, macaroni and spaghetti flour was first brought to the United States from Russia in 1853, it did not grow successfully in Kansas soil. Then, with the great Italian emigration from Naples to New York City in the very late 1800s, came several boxes of pasta tucked away in the immigrants' bags and the demand for a lot more when this supply ran out.

Mark Carleton (1866–1925), an agronomist working for the United States Department of Agriculture and a specialist in cereal rusts, traveled to Russia in 1898 to study their wheat. He brought back to the U.S. a variety of durum wheat known as ''kubanka,'' which was resistant to rust disease and would stand up well to drought. Carleton then helped develop the crop by finding which part of the country was best suited to its growth.

From 1900 to 1910 durum wheat production increased successfully. It was first introduced to the central Great Plains. After much trial and error, the climate and soil of northeastern North Dakota were finally determined as the best for the durum.

With World War I (1914–1919) came a sudden drop in the importing of pasta. This resulted in another boost to the domestic manufacture of noodles, macaroni, and pasta products to supply the immigrants' demands.

As mayor of New York City from 1933 to 1941, Fiorello

La Guardia fought for the passage of food control laws. The Pure Food and Drug Act standardized packaging of all foods (including the popular noodle and pasta products) with ingredients and net weight control.

Today, the nineteen-county area of northeast North Dakota which grows most of the noodle and pasta wheat is called the "durum triangle." South Dakota, parts of Montana and Minnesota, and adjacent parts of Canada add to the production. About 30 million bushels are harvested annually to be used exclusively by the American macaroni industry. The development of disease-resistant varieties with shorter straw has helped assure a stable source of supply.

American supermarkets, including health food stores, now carry a vast variety of packaged noodles, macaroni, and spaghetti. In addition to that supply, fast-foods and mixes, boxed, canned, jarred, and frozen, all featuring noodles and pasta, are available. All you need do is tear open a package (or use a can opener), follow the instructions, maybe add your own personal touch, and within seconds to minutes, you will have a delicious, homemade meal.

If you cannot obtain certain specific items, check pages 321–24 for mail order suggestions.

Any of the basic noodle recipes from other chapters of this book can be used for American noodles. Below you will find recipes for country and natural foods–style noodles.

COUNTRY-STYLE THREAD NOODLES
SERVES 4 TO 8

2 eggs
2 to 2½ cups flour

Place eggs in a large mixing bowl and beat lightly. Work enough flour into the eggs to form a firm dough. Divide the dough into four parts and roll each very thin, "until you can see the light through it." According to country tradition: If it is winter, spread the sheets of dough under the stove and dry, though not too long or the dough will crumble or break. Dry just to the stage where there is still enough moisture left to roll the dough up jelly-roll style without its breaking. With a sharp knife, cut noodles as fine as possible.

To cook: Drop noodles very slowly into boiling chicken or beef broth. Do not crowd your soup with them.

To make fried noodles: Prepare dough as above, only cut thicker. Drop noodles into boiling, salted water. Cook for a few minutes, strain and allow to cool. Heat a skillet with sweet butter; when hot, fry noodles in it.

The Pennsylvania Dutch were originally Germans who helped settle William Penn's colony.

PENNSYLVANIA DUTCH NOODLES
SERVES 4 TO 8

2 eggs
½ teaspoon salt
2 to 2½ cups sifted flour

In a large mixing bowl, beat the eggs and add the salt. Work in enough flour to form a stiff dough. Knead thoroughly and divide in half, rolling out each half on a floured board as thin as possible. Cover with a kitchen towel and let rest until slightly dry. Roll up dough and cut into ¼-inch strips. Spread out again to dry a little longer.

To make noodles for stuffing: Cut the dough into 3-inch

strips. Follow instructions on page 235 for Pennsylvania Dutch Stuffed Noodles.

MARTHA JEAN'S WHEAT NOODLES

SERVES 4

> 3 large egg yolks
> 4 teaspoons cold water
> 1 cup whole wheat flour
> ½ teaspoon salt
> ½ teaspoon baking powder

In a large mixing bowl, beat the egg yolks and water together. Sift the dry ingredients together and gradually add to the eggs. (Note: The egg yolks will give the noodles a rich color and the baking powder will add texture.) Knead the dough well until it is smooth. Let it rest for 10 minutes. Roll the dough out thin and cut into desired widths. Boil immediately or dry for later use.

NATURAL FOODS MANICOTTI

SERVES 6 TO 10

> 3 cups cracked wheat flour
> 2 teaspoons sea salt
> 2 eggs
> 2 extra egg whites
>
> 2 tablespoons cooking oil
>   (such as peanut or
>   sunflower)
> 1 to 2 teaspoons water

Combine the flour and salt in a large mixing bowl, and make a well in the center. Put the whole eggs, egg whites, and oil into the well and work with your fingers to mix thoroughly. Add a little water as needed, until you have a smooth dough. Place dough on a floured board; knead for

10 minutes. Cover dough and let it sit for 10 minutes. Divide in half and roll out each piece on a floured board until it is paper-thin. Cut into 5-inch squares. Form the squares into cylinders by pinching two edges together. Drop noodles into rapidly boiling water, and cook for 10 minutes. Remove with a slotted spoon. Allow to cool. Stuff with your favorite filling. See page 236 for a super "healthy" filling.

SNACKS AND STUFFED NOODLES

Leftover noodles are never any problem in our house. Often, I make extras just so I have leftovers. I use them in soups, salads, sometimes with eggs. I've even deep-fried them to use as "croutons" or casserole topping. I think they're best as a snack.

CRUNCHY SNACKS
MAKES $\frac{1}{2}$ CUP, SERVES 2

$\frac{1}{2}$ *cup leftover cooked small noodles (alphabets are super!)*
Cooking oil for deep-frying
1 teaspoon of seasoned garlic salt (or try another seasoning, such as powdered cheese, chili, or smoky flavoring)

In a pot about 3 inches full of oil for deep-frying, cook the noodles, stirring constantly (I like to use a wooden chopstick) until brown. Remove noodles with a soup strainer and drain on paper towels. Toss lightly with seasoned garlic salt.

Often it's not the noodles that are left over but the meat or fowl. After Thanksgiving dinner I'm always trying to come up with interesting ways to use the extra turkey.

STUFFED SHELLS

SERVES 6 TO 8

Preheat oven to 325 degrees

2 cups cooked, cubed
    turkey
1 cup frozen peas, thawed
½ cup mayonnaise
¼ cup fine-chopped onion
12 ounces jumbo shells,
    cooked and drained

One 10¾-ounce can con-
    densed cream of celery,
    mushroom, or aspara-
    gus soup
½ cup milk
3 tablespoons minced fresh
    parsley

In a large mixing bowl, stir together the turkey, peas, mayonnaise, and onion. Fill the shells with this stuffing. Arrange the stuffed shells in a single layer in a baking dish. In a small mixing bowl, blend together the soup and milk; pour over the shells. Cover dish with foil and bake in the preheated oven for 25 to 30 minutes. Garnish with parsley before serving.

The Pennsylvania Dutch stuff their noodles with meat to make a dish that is similar to ravioli.

PENNSYLVANIA DUTCH STUFFED NOODLES

SERVES 6

1 Pennsylvania Dutch Noodle recipe (see   *pages 231–32), cut into 3-inch squares*

MEAT FILLING:

2 tablespoons cooking oil   *1 cup bread cubes*
½ pound ground beef
1 small onion, peeled and   *½ cup dry breadcrumbs*
    chopped fine   *3 tablespoons butter*
Salt and pepper to taste

Prepare the noodle dough.

In a large skillet, heat the oil and brown the meat with the onion. Season with salt and pepper. Soak the bread cubes in water, then squeeze dry; add to the meat. Place a spoonful of meat mixture in the center of each noodle; fold in half like a small pillow and seal the edges. Drop the stuffed noodles into boiling, salted water and cook for 8 to 10 minutes.

Meanwhile, in a small skillet, brown the breadcrumbs in the butter.

When the noodles are done, remove with a slotted spoon to a serving dish and top with buttered breadcrumbs.

You don't have to eat meat to enjoy a protein-rich noodle dish. These "healthy" meatless manicotti are stuffed with nutritious cheeses, raisins, and nuts.

HEALTHY MANICOTTI

SERVES 6

Preheat oven to 350 degrees

1 recipe Natural Foods Manicotti, see page 232

CHEESE, NUTS, AND RAISINS FILLING:

2 cups ricotta cheese

1 cup coarse-grated moz-
zarella cheese

½ teaspoon salt

1 egg, lightly beaten

Few sprinklings fresh-
grated nutmeg

½ cup whole pine nuts

½ cup seedless raisins

1 teaspoon grated lemon
rind

Dash pepper

2 cups your favorite sauce

Prepare the noodles.

Mix all the Filling ingredients in a large bowl and stuff the manicotti. Place in a casserole and cover with 2 cups of your favorite sauce. I like a creamy white or a very light tomato sauce with this. Bake in the preheated oven for 20 to 25 minutes.

My cooking buddy's mother is a most gracious woman with love to spare. During the many afternoons we've spent together, she's always treated me like a daughter.

Rosemary's method of layering this lasagne is unusual and it affects the consistency of the finished dish, making it fairly "custardy."

ROSEMARY MOSES' AMERICAN LASAGNE
SERVES 6

Preheat oven to 350 degrees

1 pound ground beef
round
2 cloves garlic, peeled and
crushed
One 6-ounce can tomato
paste
One 15½-ounce can tomato
sauce
½ cup water

2 bay leaves
1 teaspoon dried parsley
flakes
Salt and pepper to taste
12 lasagne, cooked and
drained
1 cup small-curd style
cottage cheese
1 cup sour cream

To make the sauce: Brown the meat in a large skillet. Add the garlic, tomato paste, tomato sauce, water, bay leaves, parsley flakes, salt, and pepper. Simmer, covered, for one hour. Remove and discard bay leaves.

To assemble lasagne: Place 3 noodles on the bottom of a 9 x 12 x 2-inch baking dish, spread the cottage cheese on top to cover, layer 3 more noodles over the cheese, spread half the meat-tomato sauce to cover, layer 3 more noodles, spread with sour cream to cover, layer the final 3 noodles, and cover with the last half of the sauce. Bake in preheated oven for 20 to 25 minutes. Cut into 3-inch squares and serve.

From the Midwest comes this unique way of preparing filled noodles.

HANNAH PIERSON'S FILLED NOODLES
SERVES 6 TO 8

NOODLE DOUGH:
3 eggs
½ eggshell of vinegar

½ eggshell of water
Flour

MEAT FILLING:
2 pounds ground beef
*2 cups white bread, torn
    into pieces, moistened
    with water*
3 eggs, lightly beaten
*1 cup chopped fresh pars-
    ley*

*2 large onions, peeled and
    chopped*
1 tablespoon flour
1 tablespoon milk
Salt and pepper to taste

BOILING BROTH:
*Boiling beef and/or soup
    bones (enough to make
    a good broth)*
Salt and pepper to taste

*1 large onion, peeled and
    quartered*
Water

To make the noodles: In a large bowl, mix together the eggs, vinegar (this makes the dough extra tender), and the water, adding enough flour to make a stiff dough. Mix and knead, then divide into thirds and roll the dough out.

For the filling, combine all the Meat Filling ingredients in a mixing bowl.

Divide the filling into thirds and spread on the sheets of dough, smoothing it out on top. Roll dough up jelly-roll style. Place stuffed dough on a cookie sheet and put in the refrigerator to chill.

Meanwhile make the broth: In a large kettle with a lot of water, boil the beef and/or bones, seasoned with salt and pepper, and the onion. When the broth is ready (very flavorful), which may take several hours, cut the stuffed dough into serving portions and drop them into the broth. Simmer over low heat for an hour. (Note: If you want to eat the meat off the bones, remove it before adding the noodles.) When noodles are tender, remove them with a slotted spoon to a serving platter or serve them in wide-rimmed soup bowls with the broth.

S O U P S

The American kitchen is blessed to have hundreds of marvelous boxed, canned, and jarred soups readily available. Many of these already contain noodles; if not, add some! In a flash, you can put together a tasty first or main course soup. It can be as simple as chicken or beef broth with noodles. Or with a little ingenuity, you can add a personal touch with a zest of lemon, a dollop of sour cream, a pinch of dried herbs, a dash of wine, or your own favorite extra. You can also try a little mix-and-matching of two or more convenience-style soups.

VEGETABLE NOODLE SOUP

SERVES 6

2 quarts water
One 1⅜-ounce envelope
  onion soup mix
One 1⅜-ounce envelope
  vegetable soup mix
  (or 2 of the same mix)
2 tablespoons chopped
  fresh parsley

Salt and pepper to taste
One 10-ounce package
  frozen mixed vege-
  tables
4 ounces soup noodles

Bring water to a boil in a large soup pot. Add the soup mixes, parsley, salt, pepper, mixed vegetables, and noodles.

Simmer for 20 minutes, stirring occasionally. When noodles and vegetables are tender, remove from the heat and serve.

The Italian—now American—classic minestrone, made with an abundance of fresh vegetables and noodles, is one of the most nutritious of all soups. (See pages 116–17.)

MINESTRONE MY WAY

SERVES 4 TO 6

2 quarts beef stock
½ small head cabbage,
   shredded
2 stalks celery, chopped
2 potatoes, peeled and
   diced
2 carrots, scraped and
   sliced

1 cup shelled fresh peas
1 cup string beans
2 zucchini, diced
1 small onion, peeled and
   chopped
1 to 2 tablespoons tomato
   paste
1 cup cooked soup noodles

GARLIC-HERB PASTE:
3 cloves garlic, peeled and
   mashed
2 tablespoons minced fresh
   basil leaves (If not
   available, use parsley,

but it really won't be
   the same.)
3 tablespoons grated Par-
   mesan cheese
2 to 3 tablespoons olive oil
¼ teaspoon salt

In a large soup pot, bring the stock to a boil. Add all the vegetables and the tomato paste; simmer for 45 minutes. Add the noodles and cook for another 5 minutes.

Make the Garlic-Herb Paste by combining all the ingredients. Add to the soup. Continue to cook soup until everything is well mixed, stirring constantly. Serve in large soup bowls as a main course with lots of crusty sourdough bread.

SALADS

The classic cold noodle, macaroni, or spaghetti dish is, of course, a salad. Many are complete enough—containing meat, seafood, cheese, fruit, and/or vegetables—to serve as the entire meal. Some are festive enough to serve as a dish for a party, buffet, or annual family gathering. These salads are also the perfect "ending" to another day's leftovers.

MACARONI & CHEESE SALAD DELUXE
SERVES 4

SALAD:

1½ cups ditali (small macaroni), cooked, drained, and cooled
1½ cups diced celery
½ cup diced zucchini

3 cups cubed Monterey Jack cheese
½ cup coarse-chopped pecans

DRESSING:

1½ cups mayonnaise
1 teaspoon Worcestershire sauce
Few dashes bottled hot pepper sauce
½ teaspoon cayenne pepper (optional)

3 tablespoons minced fresh parsley
1 teaspoon salt
½ teaspoon fresh-ground black pepper

Large lettuce leaves

Place macaroni in a large mixing bowl; add the celery, zucchini, cheese, and nuts. In a small mixing bowl, combine the mayonnaise,* Worcestershire sauce, pepper sauce, cayenne pepper, parsley, salt, and pepper. Pour this dressing over the macaroni mixture and toss to coat. Refrigerate for 2 to 3 hours (or longer). To serve, line a salad bowl with lettuce leaves and spoon macaroni mixture into it.

NOTE: Use your favorite real mayonnaise, or make your own:

To make homemade mayonnaise, you'll need 3 egg yolks (at room temperature), 2 teaspoons lemon juice, 1 tablespoon tarragon vinegar. (Or substitute your own favorite herb-flavored vinegar.) $\frac{1}{4}$ teaspoon dry mustard, 1 teaspoon salt, $\frac{1}{4}$ teaspoon white pepper, and 2 cups vegetable oil (I use a combination of olive and other oils.) If you own a food processor, use the blending attachment and add the ingredients slowly, one at a time, until each new ingredient is absorbed. Add the oil especially slowly. The machine makes a very creamy, beautiful off-white mayonnaise in practically seconds. Without a food processor, place the egg yolks in a large mixing bowl and beat with a whisk or electric mixer until they are thick and begin to cling. (This takes about 2 to 3 minutes.) Stir in the lemon juice, vinegar, mustard, salt, and pepper. Beat in the oil, slowly, about $\frac{1}{2}$ teaspoon at a time, making sure it is

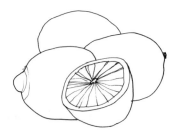

totally absorbed before each new addition. Continue the slow process of adding oil until all is used up. Whichever method you use, taste for seasoning, cover and refrigerate. Homemade mayonnaise should keep for a week or longer —if you don't eat it sooner. This recipe yields 2½ cups.

If you've got a busy day planned, make this salad the night before. You can assemble everything and store it, covered, in the refrigerator to blend the flavors. Then, after your day's activities, you'll have a special treat awaiting.

CHEESY MACARONI SALAD
SERVES 4 TO 6

5 ounces elbow macaroni, cooked, drained, rinsed in cold water, and drained again

4 ounces sharp natural Cheddar cheese, cubed

4 hard-boiled eggs, chopped

1 cup sliced celery

½ cup (or more) mayonnaise (see note pages 242–43)

2 tablespoons minced scallions

¼ teaspoon dry mustard

¼ teaspoon salt

Dash white pepper

2 tablespoons toasted, slivered almonds

Lettuce leaves

In a large bowl, toss together everything except the nuts and lettuce. Chill until serving time. To serve, arrange salad on lettuce leaves. Sprinkle the almonds on top.

Children love macaroni salads, especially when they sneak a taste with their fingers. Here's a yummy one from Skinner's pamphlet "Kids Like Macaroni Salad."

TRADE-WINDS SALAD

SERVES 6

*2 tablespoons butter or
   margarine*
¼ cup dark brown sugar
*1 cup cubed ham or canned
   luncheon meat*
*8 ounces large shells,
   cooked, drained, rinsed
   with cold water, and
   drained again*
*1½ cups pineapple
   chunks, drained and
   juice reserved*

*½ cup grapes or chopped
   apples*
*1 cup cubed Cheddar
   cheese*
*¼ cup mayonnaise (see
   note pages 242–43)*
¼ cup sour cream
*2 tablespoons reserved
   pineapple juice*
½ teaspoon salt

In a medium skillet, melt the butter and brown sugar together. Add the ham and cook until it is brown. Cool. In a mixing bowl, combine the ham, shells, pineapple, grapes or apples, and cheese. In a small bowl, blend the mayonnaise, sour cream, pineapple juice, and salt. Toss macaroni mixture with the mayonnaise dressing and chill.

If you're assigned the salad for the pot luck picnic or backyard barbecue, you'll want to try this one.

PICNIC POT LUCK

SERVES 12 TO 20

*4 cups cooked ditalini or
    other small elbow
    macaroni*
*1 cup mayonnaise (see note
    pages 242–43)*
1 cup chopped celery
¾ cup chopped carrots
⅓ cup thin-sliced radishes
*¼ cup chopped black
    olives*
*6 pimiento-stuffed green
    olives, sliced*

¾ cup chopped scallions
*2 heaping tablespoons
    minced fresh parsley*
*½ teaspoon whole celery
    seeds*
*1 tablespoon Dijon-style
    mustard*
1 tablespoon wine vinegar
2 teaspoons salt
½ teaspoon sugar
Dash pepper

Place macaroni in a large mixing bowl. Add the mayonnaise and toss to coat. Add the remaining vegetables and seasonings. Refrigerate salad for several hours. To make this even more festive, place salad in a pretty bowl and garnish with tomato wedges, hard-boiled egg slices, and sliced sweet pickles.

My cooking buddy, Annie, mixes a super macaroni salad. Since she finds the refrigerator "hardens" the sour cream sauce, she prefers to set the salad out at room temperature before serving.

MACARONI SOUR CREAM SALAD
SERVES 6 TO 10

8 ounces small shell or elbow macaroni, cooked, drained, rinsed with cold water, and drained again

1 cup sour cream

2 hard-boiled eggs, chopped

½ cup chopped celery

⅓ cup chopped dill pickle

½ cup chopped onion

1 pimiento, chopped

½ cup peeled, seeded, and chopped cucumber

2 tablespoons white wine vinegar

1 teaspoon salt

¼ teaspoon pepper

Bottled hot pepper sauce to taste

Place macaroni in a large bowl and combine with all the remaining ingredients, adding hot pepper sauce to taste. Mix gently, but thoroughly. Refrigerate for an hour, then let stand at room temperature for 30 minutes before serving.

Seafood and macaroni team in this salad, tossed with a tangy dressing.

SEAFOOD MACARONI SALAD

16 ounces shells, cooked, drained, rinsed with cold water, and drained again

One 6½-ounce can crabmeat, drained and flaked

1½ cups diced cooked shrimp

4 scallions, chopped

1 large cucumber, peeled and diced

½ cup fine-chopped fresh parsley

1 clove garlic, peeled and minced

2 tablespoons capers

One 2-ounce bottle pimiento-stuffed green olives, cut in half, liquid reserved

TANGY SEAFOOD SALAD DRESSING:

Reserved olive liquid

⅓ cup lemon juice

1½ cups mayonnaise (see note pages 242–43)

½ cup plain yogurt

Salt and pepper to taste

Place all salad ingredients in a large bowl. Mix the dressing ingredients together in another bowl and pour over salad. Blend by tossing gently, but thoroughly. Chill until serving time.

Sweet and spicy are the special touches in this buffet salad.

SOUSED SHELLS

SERVES 8 TO 15

1 cup raisins
1 cup apricot liqueur
12 ounces shells, cooked,
    drained, rinsed with
    cold water, and
    drained again
3 tablespoons lemon juice
¼ teaspoon each cinna-
    mon, fresh-grated nut-

meg, ground cloves,
    powdered ginger,
    and cumin
Dash of curry
1 cup sour cream (or ½
    cup each sour cream
    and mayonnaise)

Place the raisins in a saucepan with the liqueur and let soak for an hour. Place pan on stove and simmer raisins for 1 minute. Turn shells into a large mixing bowl; add the raisins with their liquid, the lemon juice, seasonings, and sour cream. Toss well to coat, and refrigerate until all seasonings blend. Bring to room temperature before serving.

Chili and beans, though spicy, are not always hot.

CHILI SALAD

SERVES 8 TO 10

3 cups cooked elbow maca-
    roni
One 16-ounce can kidney
    beans, drained
½ cup chopped celery
1 small onion, peeled and
    chopped fine
One 1¾-ounce envelope
    chili seasoning mix

1 cup mayonnaise (see
    note pages 242–43)
2 tablespoons ketchup
2 tablespoons vinegar
¼ cup grated Cheddar
    cheese (optional gar-
    nish)

Place macaroni in a bowl with the beans, celery, and onion. In a small bowl, combine the chili seasoning mix, mayonnaise, ketchup, and vinegar; stir into the macaroni mixture. Chill salad thoroughly. Garnish with grated cheese.

Molded salads are excellent for leftovers. The gelatin complements the macaroni's incomplete protein to add nourishment and makes a beautiful showcase as well. For a general guide, you should allow $1\frac{1}{4}$ cup solids for each cup of gelatin or aspic.

MOLDED MACARONI AND CHEESE SALAD
SERVES 6

1 envelope unflavored gelatin
½ cup cold water
¾ cup boiling water
1 teaspoon salt
1 cup grated Cheddar cheese
1 tablespoon lemon juice
1 tablespoon fine-grated onion

8 ounces elbow macaroni, cooked, drained, rinsed with cold water, and drained
½ cup diced celery
3 tablespoons chopped fresh parsley
½ cup mayonnaise (see note pages 242–43)

In a mixing bowl, soften gelatin in cold water, then dissolve it in boiling water. Stir in the salt, cheese, lemon juice, and onion. Place mixture in refrigerator and chill until it begins to set. Add macaroni, celery, parsley, and mayonnaise to gelatin mixture. Lightly oil a 6-cup mold or loaf pan. (The oil will help when turning out mold.) Spoon macaroni mixture into mold. Chill for several hours, until firm. Unmold on a serving platter.

Who said macaroni is fattening? Not I. Here's a salad especially created for dieters by the Creamette Macaroni Company kitchens. There are only 331 calories in each portion.

HAM ICEBOX SALAD

SERVES 6

7 ounces elbow macaroni, cooked, drained, rinsed, and drained again
3 cups diced cooked lean ham or lamb
1 cup diced celery
1 cup low-calorie mayonnaise

¼ cup sweet pickle relish, drained
2 tablespoons chopped onion
2 tablespoons chopped pimiento
1 teaspoon salt
⅛ teaspoon pepper
Lettuce

In a large bowl, combine macaroni with all remaining ingredients except lettuce. Chill. Serve on lettuce leaves.

SAUCED AND SAUTÉED NOODLES (Including Casseroles)

'Twas the week before Christmas and all through the house, everyone was hurrying and hustling about. Hundreds of people were coming to dinner. And what could be better than a spaghetti and sauce feast.

If you're planning to invite a large crowd, you might try, as I did, to keep several pots of different sauces at a slow simmer and one huge pot of water for the spaghetti at a constant boil. Use any of the international favorites from other chapters and one or more of these. But you won't want to wait for a party to try the individual recipes.

SPAGHETTI WITH CREOLE SAUCE
SERVES **6**

¼ cup butter

1 large onion, peeled and chopped

1 green pepper, seeded and chopped

1 sweet red pepper, seeded and chopped

1 clove garlic, peeled and minced

1 cup chopped celery

2 tablespoons flour

One 28-ounce can peeled, whole tomatoes, seeded and chopped (with their liquid)

4 dashes of bottled hot pepper sauce

1 tablespoon Worcestershire sauce

¼ cup tomato paste

1 tablespoon dark brown sugar

Salt and pepper to taste

⅛ teaspoon cayenne pepper

24 large, cooked shrimp

16 ounces of spaghetti, cooked and drained

2 to 4 tablespoons butter

In a large skillet, melt the butter and sauté the onion, peppers, garlic, and celery. When the vegetables are softened, push them aside and stir in the flour; brown lightly. Add the tomatoes with their liquid, the hot pepper sauce, Worcestershire sauce, tomato paste, brown sugar, salt, pepper, and cayenne pepper. Bring to a boil; reduce heat and simmer for about 10 minutes, or until sauce thickens. Taste for seasoning. Stir the cooked shrimp into the sauce and continue to cook for another 10 minutes over very low heat.

Toss hot spaghetti with the butter, top with the sauce and serve.

Here's an easy natural-foods dish. It's excellent for a vegetarian main course dinner. Or enjoy it as a side dish with broiled fresh fish and steamed vegetables.

NATURAL FOODS NOODLES

SERVES 2 TO 4

8 ounces whole wheat fettuccine, cooked and drained (see
*   page 232)*
¼ cup soy sauce
One 8-ounce container plain yogurt, at room temperature
1 scallion, chopped
2 teaspoons sesame seeds

Return drained noodles to a large pot or wok. Add the soy sauce, stirring constantly with wooden chopsticks over medium heat. Add the yogurt, a few tablespoons at a time, until the noodles are well coated. Add the scallions, continuing to toss the noodles. Place noodles on a warm serving platter. Sprinkle with sesame seeds.

The beautiful dots of seeds here add a nice, crunchy texture. Serve this as a fantastic accompaniment to sautéed fresh fish.

SPECKLED NOODLES

SERVES 6 AS A SIDE DISH

6 tablespoons butter
2 tablespoons poppy seeds
1½ tablespoons white sesame seeds
1½ tablespoons black sesame seeds
8 ounces medium egg noodles, cooked and drained

Melt 4 tablespoons of butter in a pot, add the seeds and sauté for a few minutes until they are well coated. Return noodles to the pot in which they were cooked. Toss with the remaining 2 tablespoons of butter. Add the sautéed seeds and toss again.

This is a super-fast vegetable and nut sauté which stands alone for a lunch or light supper.

VEGETABLE AND NUT SAUTÉ
SERVES 4 TO 6

¼ cup cooking oil
¾ cup chopped celery
½ cup sliced fresh mush-
  rooms
½ cup chopped green pep-
  per
½ cup chopped scallions

4 cups cooked noodles (*I
  like fettuccine with
  this.*)
1 teaspoon salt
Dash pepper
⅔ cup chopped lightly
  salted peanuts
Soy sauce

Heat oil in a large skillet or wok and sauté the celery, mushrooms, green pepper, and scallions. When the vegetables are coated with oil and slightly soft, add the noodles. Season with salt and pepper. Heat thoroughly. Stir in the nuts. Serve with a small pitcher of soy sauce for everyone to season to taste.

Living in California, I have been fortunate to enjoy many years of a booming avocado crop. I've used avocados in soups, snacks, and salads. They're great in breads, as garnishes, even in ice cream. I've rubbed the peel on my face and hands as a natural skin conditioner. And I've even planted the pit. So why not toss avocados with noodles as a sauce?

AVOCADO-NOODLE DINNER

SERVES 6

$\frac{1}{4}$ cup butter
$\frac{1}{8}$ teaspoon minced garlic
1 teaspoon salt
8 ounces spiral egg noo-
    dles, cooked and
    drained
1 small avocado, halved,
    pitted, peeled, and
    diced

Lemon juice
6 slices crisp-cooked bacon,
    crumbled
Chopped fresh parsley
Grated American cheese
    (or grated Parmesan
    cheese)

In a skillet, melt the butter and stir in the garlic and salt. Return noodles to the pot in which they were cooked and toss with the garlic butter. Sprinkle avocado with lemon juice (to prevent it from turning color) and gently fold into the noodles. Place on a serving platter. Sprinkle with bacon. Garnish with a border of parsley. Pass bowl of grated cheese separately.

You can bring this noodle dish directly from the stove to the table, so use a pretty skillet.

HAM AND NOODLE SKILLET

SERVES 6

$\frac{1}{4}$ cup butter
$\frac{1}{2}$ cup fine breadcrumbs
1 medium onion, peeled
    and chopped
$\frac{1}{3}$ cup fine-chopped green
    pepper
$\frac{1}{2}$ cup chopped celery
One 4-ounce can sliced
    mushrooms, drained
1 tablespoon flour

$\frac{1}{2}$ teaspoon salt
$\frac{1}{4}$ teaspoon pepper
$2\frac{1}{2}$ cups canned tomatoes
2 cups diced cooked ham
8 ounces medium wide noo-
    dles, cooked and
    drained
$\frac{1}{2}$ cup grated American
    cheese

Melt 2 tablespoons of butter in a large, attractive skillet
and brown the breadcrumbs; remove the crumbs. Add the
remaining butter to the skillet. Sauté the onion, green pepper, celery, and mushrooms until they are tender. Blend in
the flour and season with salt and pepper. Gradually add
the tomatoes, stirring until blended. Add the ham and
noodles. Top skillet with sautéed breadcrumbs and cheese.
Simmer until cheese melts and is bubbly.

Neither a corn croquette nor a noodle pancake—these
patties make a tasty, meatless main dish or a super side
dish to serve with baked ham.

MACARONI AND CHEESE PATTIES
MAKES APPROXIMATELY 16
PATTIES

2 cups cooked shells
1 egg, lightly beaten
One 10¾-ounce can con-
  densed cream of celery
  soup
1 cup milk
1 cup soft breadcrumbs
One 17-ounce can cream-
  style corn

½ pound Cheddar cheese,
  grated coarse
1 tablespoon instant
  toasted onions
1¼ teaspoons salt
Dash pepper
1 cup seasoned bread-
  crumbs
2 to 4 tablespoons cooking
  oil

Combine the macaroni, egg, soup, milk, soft breadcrumbs, corn, cheese, onion, salt, and pepper in a large
mixing bowl. Chill for several hours to make the mixture
more solid and easier to work with.

Place the seasoned breadcrumbs in a dish. Make patties
with about 2 heaping tablespoons of macaroni-corn mixture. Pat into the shape of a hamburger. Coat one at a
time on both sides with the seasoned breadcrumbs. Lift

patties with a spatula to a tray. Place wax paper between layers to store. The patties can be made in advance and refrigerated until cooking time.

When it's time to cook, heat oil in a skillet. Brown patties on both sides until they are golden, about 2 to 3 minutes per side, a little longer if refrigerated.

Cereal, bacon, scrambled eggs, and pancakes may be excellent day-starters. But when I get tired of them all, omelets allow a lot of room for creativity.

HEARTY NOODLE OMELET
MAKES 4 OMELETS

2 to 4 tablespoons butter or margarine	*6 eggs*
½ cup chopped green pepper	*½ teaspoon salt*
	⅛ teaspoon pepper
	⅓ cup mayonnaise
¼ cup sliced scallion	*1 cup cooked noodles*

In a small skillet, melt 1 tablespoon of butter over medium heat. Add the green pepper and scallion and sauté until tender, then remove from pan. In a large mixing bowl, beat together the eggs, salt, pepper, and mayonnaise until smooth. Stir in sautéed vegetables and noodles. In an 8-inch omelet pan, melt about 1 teaspoon of butter over medium heat. Pour ¾ cup of the egg mixture into the omelet pan. Cook over medium heat, tilting pan until mixture covers evenly, about 5 minutes, or until omelet is firm. Fold in half and remove from pan. Repeat 3 more times with remaining egg mixture, adding butter as needed.

One of my more unusual food adventures took place in Mexico. My studies included an exciting week in Leon, the capital of Guanajuato, where I enrolled in the IMLE Mexican Cooking School. My instructor, Sra. Maria Marquez de Merrill prepared a unique omelet which she called a ''Mexican Sunset.''

To make this omelet, Maria used a 12-inch non-stick frying pan. She served it with a salad of cooked greens (cut into ¾-inch pieces), black beans, and chick peas (garbanzos) tossed with a light oil and vinegar dressing and arranged on individual lettuce leaves for a delightful luncheon.

CREPUSCULO MEJICANO (Mexican Sunset)
SERVES 6

3 tablespoons cooking oil
2 cups thin cold cooked noodles (Fideos, broken by hand into small pieces)
1 large fresh tomato, peeled, diced and seeded
½ medium white onion, peeled and diced
2 fresh chilis serrano (small hot green pep-
pers), cut lengthwise, seeds removed and chopped fine
Salt and pepper to taste
3 eggs, beaten to a froth
½ cup evaporated milk or light cream
½ cup shredded cheese: combination of Chihuahua, Monterey Jack, Swiss, and/or Gruyère

Heat the oil in a pan. Add the noodles, tossing lightly until they are heated and begin to brown. Combine the tomato, onion, and chilis (making a Mexican salsa cruda) and pour over the noodles. Toss lightly and season with salt and pepper. Mix together the beaten eggs and milk and pour evenly over the noodles. Sprinkle the shredded cheese over the top, distributing evenly. Let the mixture set for 4 minutes. Cover skillet and reduce heat to a very low simmer for another 5 minutes. The eggs should be set, the cheeses nicely melted, and the tomato-onion-chilis slightly cooked. Cut into wedges and serve immediately.

Macaroni and cheese was once the favorite of England's King Richard II (fourteenth century), and it has remained popular throughout history. Practically every cook has at least one macaroni and cheese recipe in his or her repertoire.

You can start from scratch with noodles, cheese and a sauce. Or you can use a packaged mix and follow the instructions. Short on time? There are several excellent ready-made, frozen macaroni and cheese dishes available at your neighborhood market. If you want to add a home-made touch, place a layer of sliced fresh or canned tomatoes on top. Or you can bake frozen macaroni and cheese according to the package instructions. Then, about 15 minutes before serving, top it with fully cooked smoked sausage links, set it back in the oven, and bake until everything is golden brown. I serve this with soup or salad for a quick, hearty supper.

Cook these noodles in a pretty skillet. Once they're bubbly and hot, serve them directly from the pan.

NOODLES AND CHEESE SKILLET
SERVES 4

8 ounces broad egg noodles, cooked and drained

2 tablespoons grated onion

1 clove garlic, peeled and minced

1 cup cottage cheese

1 cup sour cream

1 teaspoon Worcestershire sauce

Dash bottled hot pepper sauce

Salt and pepper to taste

½ cup minced black olives

¼ cup grated Cheddar cheese

Paprika

In a large mixing bowl, combine the noodles with all the other ingredients except the Cheddar cheese and paprika. Turn mixture into a buttered skillet. Sprinkle with the Cheddar cheese and paprika to color. Simmer over medium heat until everything is hot and bubbly.

This noodle bake is a zesty variation on the macaroni and cheese theme. Egg noodles and cheese combine to make a hearty, wholesome and budget-conscious main dish. The good sauce owes its special flavor to the Worcestershire sauce and prepared yellow mustard.

DEVILED NOODLE BAKE FITZGERALD

SERVES 6

Preheat oven to 400 degrees

DEVILED CREAM SAUCE:

2 tablespoons butter
2 tablespoons flour
½ teaspoon salt
2 cups milk
1½ cups shredded Cheddar cheese
3 ounces cream cheese
2 tablespoons Worcestershire sauce

2 tablespoons prepared yellow mustard

8 ounces egg noodles, cooked and drained
1 green pepper, seeded and chopped
Buttered breadcrumbs or corn flake crumbs

In a medium saucepan, melt the butter; blend in flour and salt. Gradually add the milk. Cook over medium heat, stirring frequently, until cream sauce comes to a boil and thickens. Stir in Cheddar cheese, cream cheese, Worcestershire sauce, and mustard. Turn heat low and continue to cook sauce until cheese melts. Combine noodles and pepper in a 2-quart buttered casserole. Add the Deviled Cream Sauce and top with buttered crumbs. Bake in the preheated oven for 30 to 35 minutes, or until golden brown.

I've always enjoyed attractive ring-shaped molds for company dinners, especially buffets. I fill the centers of

this macaroni and cheese ring with a creamed chicken or
seafood dish.

CHEESE NOODLE RING

SERVES 6

Preheat oven to 350 degrees

*One 10¾-ounce can condensed cream of mushroom soup
   (or other creamed soup)*
1½ cups grated Swiss cheese
Salt and pepper to taste
3 eggs, lightly beaten
8 ounces medium noodles, cooked and drained

In a saucepan, heat the soup with the cheese until the
cheese melts. Season with salt and pepper. Slowly fold in
the eggs. Place noodles in a mixing bowl and carefully fold
sauce into noodles. Turn mixture into a greased 6-cup ring
mold. Set mold in a pan of hot water and bake in the preheated oven for 45 minutes, or until set. Cool for 10 minutes and unmold on a serving platter.

If you don't already have a favorite macaroni and
cheese, you'll especially enjoy this.

ANNIE'S MACARONI AND CHEESE BAKE

SERVES 6

Preheat oven to 375 degrees

*1 small onion, peeled and
   minced*
¼ cup butter
¼ cup flour
1 cup milk
2 teaspoons salt
*1 teaspoon Worcestershire
   sauce*

*2 cups grated sharp Ched-
   dar cheese*
1 cup sour cream
*8 ounces elbow macaroni,
   cooked and drained (or
   substitute spaghetti)*

In a saucepan, sauté the onion in the butter until it is transparent; stir in the flour and cook for 1 minute, stirring constantly. Add the milk and cook, stirring, until the sauce thickens. Add salt, Worcestershire sauce, and 1½ cups of the cheese. Heat, stirring until cheese melts. Empty sour cream into a large bowl. Gradually add the hot cheese sauce, stirring constantly. Fold in the macaroni (or spaghetti). Pour into a buttered 2-quart casserole and sprinkle with the remaining cheese. Bake in the preheated oven for 25 to 30 minutes, or until hot and bubbly.

This noodle soufflé can be prepared in advance and refrigerated until cooking time. Be sure to bring it to room temperature before baking.

KLEIN'S NOODLE SOUFFLÉ
SERVES 3 TO 6

Preheat oven to 350 degrees

½ pound sweet butter
3 ounces cream cheese
Juice of 1 lemon
2 tablespoons sugar
3 eggs, well beaten
1 chopped onion which has been sautéed in 2 tablespoons of butter

Salt and pepper to taste
6 ounces wide flat noodles, cooked and drained
1 cup shredded Swiss cheese
1 cup sour cream

Place the butter, sour cream, and cream cheese in a bowl and beat well with an electric mixer. Gently mix in the lemon, sugar, eggs, onion, salt, pepper, noodles, and cheese (reserving a handful to sprinkle on top of soufflé). Turn mixture into a buttered 2½ quart soufflé dish and bake in the preheated oven for 1 hour.

Instead of using green noodles, you can add spinach to the casserole for the extra color and nutrition.

COTTAGE CHEESE NOODLES FLORENTINE
SERVES 6

Preheat oven to 350 degrees

*One 10-ounce package
  frozen, chopped spin-
  ach, thawed and well
  drained*
*2 cups cream-style cottage
  cheese*
*½ cup grated Parmesan
  cheese*
½ cup sour cream
1 teaspoon salt

*¼ teaspoon dried leaf
  basil, crumbled
  through your fingers*
¼ teaspoon ground thyme
*12 ounces medium egg noo-
  dles, cooked and
  drained*
1 tablespoon melted butter
¼ cup dry breadcrumbs

In a large bowl mix the spinach, cottage cheese, Parmesan cheese, sour cream, salt, basil, and thyme. Stir in the noodles. Turn mixture into a 1½-quart casserole. In a small bowl combine the melted butter and breadcrumbs. Sprinkle them over the top of the buttered casserole. Bake, covered, in the preheated oven for 45 minutes.

The best dinners I've eaten at my mother's house have always included this casserole as a side dish. Sometimes she makes it weeks in advance, freezes it, and then reheats it when she wants to serve it. Once she added a layer of leftover Thanksgiving turkey for a total-meal casserole.

SPINACH NOODLE CASSEROLE
SERVES 4 TO 6 AS A SIDE DISH

Preheat oven to 350 degrees

Two 10-ounce packages frozen chopped spinach, thawed

1 pint sour cream, plus a little extra for topping

One 10¾-ounce can condensed cream of mushroom soup

½ teaspoon salt

½ teaspoon pepper

2 tablespoons grated Parmesan cheese

6 ounces medium egg noodles, cooked and drained

One 6-ounce package sliced Swiss cheese

Dash paprika

Squeeze the excess moisture from the thawed spinach; set the spinach aside. Mix the sour cream, soup, salt, pepper, and Parmesan cheese together in a mixing bowl. In a deep casserole, spread one full tablespoon of sour cream mixture (so the noodles will not stick). Then, alternate in the casserole, layers of noodles, spinach, sour cream mixture and Swiss cheese. Repeat almost to the top of the casserole. Top with a thin layer of sour cream. Sprinkle lightly with paprika. Bake, uncovered, in the preheated oven for 1 hour.

Try this dish for a casual family casserole with lots of dairy goodness.

MALIBU DAIRYLAND CASSEROLE
SERVES 8 TO 10

Preheat oven to 350 degrees

12 ounces ½-inch wide noodles, cooked and drained

3 tablespoons melted butter

1 cup cottage cheese

8 ounces cream cheese

⅓ cup sour cream

1 small onion, peeled and minced

2 tablespoons green pepper, diced

1 tablespoon pimiento, diced

1 tablespoon chives, diced

1 teaspoon salt

1 pound ground beef round

Two 8-ounce cans tomato sauce

½ teaspoon Worcestershire sauce

3 drops bottled hot pepper sauce

Place noodles in a bowl and blend with butter; set aside. In a large bowl, blend thoroughly the cottage cheese, cream cheese, and sour cream. Add the onion, green pepper, pimiento, chives, ½ teaspoon salt; blend well and set aside. In a large skillet, brown the meat, drain fat and add the tomato sauce, the remaining ½ teaspoon of salt, Worcestershire sauce, and hot pepper sauce. Mix skillet ingredients thoroughly. In a buttered 3-quart casserole, layer: meat sauce, noodles, and cheese mixture; repeat, ending with the meat sauce. Bake in the preheated oven for 1 hour.

My friend Jacqueline Perrin adds her French culinary expertise to this "très délicieux" noodle treasure.

MACARONI IMPERIAL

SERVES 8

Preheat oven to 350 degrees

⅔ cup soft breadcrumbs
⅓ cup melted butter
½ cup each sweet red and green pepper, chopped fine (If red is not available, use 1 cup of green.)
2 teaspoons minced onion

1¾ cups grated sharp Cheddar cheese
2 teaspoons salt
2 cups milk, scalded
4 egg yolks, well beaten
6 ounces macaroni, cooked and drained
4 egg whites, stiffly beaten

MUSHROOM-CHEESE SAUCE:

Two 10¾-ounce cans condensed cream of mushroom soup

1 cup grated Cheddar cheese
1 cup milk
¼ teaspoon paprika

Combine the breadcrumbs, butter, peppers, onion, cheese, and salt in a large bowl; add the milk. Then add the egg yolks, stirring to blend. Add the macaroni. Fold in the beaten egg whites. Pour macaroni mixture into two 1-quart greased loaf pans or into one 2-quart casserole. Place loaf pans or casserole in a large pan of hot water and bake in the preheated oven for 1 hour, or until firm. To make the sauce: combine all ingredients in the top of a double boiler. Cook over boiling water until the cheese melts and the mixture is well blended and hot. Unmold the finished casserole onto a serving platter and serve, hot or cold, with the sauce.

Once you've prepared this tetrazzini dish, you'll always look forward to the holidays when you have plenty of leftover roasted turkey or chicken.

BASIC TETRAZZINI

SERVES 4

Preheat oven to 350 degrees

3 tablespoons your favorite brand bottled garlic spread concentrate
¼ cup flour
1 cup milk
¼ cup sherry
Two 4-ounce cans mushroom pieces, drained (liquid reserved)
8 ounces Cheddar cheese, grated

½ teaspoon salt
¼ teaspoon pepper
8 ounces spaghettini, cooked and drained
1 to 2 cups cooked diced turkey, chicken or canned tuna, shrimp, crabmeat, or your own favorite addition
3 tablespoons grated Parmesan cheese

In the top of a large double boiler, melt the garlic spread; gradually stir in the flour, milk and sherry. Add enough water to the reserved mushroom liquid to make ½ cup; add to the sauce. Continue to cook the sauce, stirring constantly with a wire whisk, until it thickens. Gradually add the Cheddar cheese, salt, and pepper. Stir in the spaghettini, mushrooms, and desired seafood or fowl. Pour into a greased shallow casserole. Sprinkle with Parmesan cheese and bake in the preheated oven for 20 to 25 minutes.

Instead of leftover chicken, family friend Irene Giachetto uses pork and veal with her noodles.

MOCK CHICKEN CASSEROLE

SERVES 4 TO 6

Preheat oven to 350 degrees

1 pound ground lean pork   2 pounds ground veal

WHITE MUSHROOM SAUCE:

¼ *cup butter*

¼ *cup flour*

*One 10¾-ounce can con-
densed cream of mush-
room soup*

*One 10½-ounce can beef
bouillon (or milk)*

*10 ounces noodles, cooked
and drained*

*Cracker crumbs, for
topping*

2 tablespoons butter

Cook the pork and veal together over low heat until they are just browned; drain off any excess fat. To make the sauce, melt the butter in a saucepan, add the flour, stirring constantly, the mushroom soup, and beef broth or milk; cook until thick. In a buttered 3-quart casserole alternate layers of noodles, meat, and sauce. Top with cracker crumbs; dot with butter. Bake in the preheated oven for 30 minutes.

On a busy day, there's nothing like a casserole—I make up extras and freeze them ready for the oven.

MOM HOY'S GOOD NOODLE AND GROUND ROUND DELIGHT

SERVES 6 TO 8

Preheat oven to 325 degrees

1 cup cottage cheese

*8 ounces cream cheese,
softened*

1 cup sour cream

⅓ *cup fine-chopped scal-
lions*

*2 tablespoons chopped
green pepper*

*2 pounds ground beef
round*

*One to two 15-ounce cans
tomato sauce*

*8 ounces medium size noo-
dles, cooked and
drained (Or try the
packaged Chinese noo-
dles. They are a bit
daintier.)*

In a large bowl, combine the cottage cheese, cream cheese, sour cream, scallions, and green pepper. In a large skillet, sauté the ground round; drain off any excess fat. Add one can of the tomato sauce. If the mixture appears too dry, add more sauce. Place half the meat on the bottom of a baking dish; add all the noodles, then all the cheese mixture, and top with the remaining meat. Bake in the preheated oven for 40 minutes.

Over 3,000 miles separate the kitchens of fellow game and fish food writer Joan Cone and myself. But our typewriters have helped keep our friendship in bloom. This dish has always been one of her children's favorites. It is great as a "covered dish" meal. I bet that when she has the game the "beef" is venison!

NOODLE BAKE CONE

SERVES 6 TO 8

Preheat oven to 350 degrees

1½ pounds ground beef	*3 ounces cream cheese*
1 teaspoon instant minced onion	*1 tablespoon sugar*
	Salt to taste
Two 10¾-ounce cans condensed tomato soup	*8 ounces noodles, cooked and drained*

Brown the meat in a deep skillet with the onion. Drain off excess fat. Add soup, cream cheese, sugar, and salt. Blend well and simmer for 15 minutes, stirring occasionally. Combine noodles with meat sauce and spoon into a baking dish. Bake in the preheated oven for about 30 minutes, or until hot through.

Cooking for two growing sons and a husband means a lot of hearty meals. A most lovely friend, Brenda Kavert, found this to be her family's favorite.

SUPREME BEEF CASSEROLE

SERVES 4

Preheat oven to 350 degrees

1 teaspoon butter or margarine

1 pound ground chuck

One 16-ounce can peeled whole tomatoes with their liquid

One 8-ounce can tomato sauce

2 teaspoons salt

2 teaspoons sugar

2 garlic cloves, peeled and crushed

5 ounces egg noodles, cooked and drained

1 cup sour cream

3 ounces cream cheese

6 scallions with tops, chopped

1 cup grated Parmesan cheese

Melt the butter in a skillet and sauté the beef, breaking it into pieces with a fork. Cook until lightly browned; drain off excess fat. Stir in the tomatoes, tomato sauce, salt, sugar, and garlic. Simmer for about 10 to 15 minutes.

Place cooked noodles in a bowl; add the sour cream, cream cheese and onions.

In a 2-quart casserole, pour a small amount of meat sauce, cover with a layer of noodles, then with grated cheese. Repeat layers, topping with meat sauce. Bake in the preheated oven for 35 minutes.

Tortilla chips make an interesting topping for this casserole and give it a Mexican flair.

MEXICALI MACARONI

SERVES 4 TO 6

Preheat oven to 350 degrees

½ pound ground beef
1½ cups coarse-grated American or Cheddar cheese
One 8-ounce can stewed tomatoes, broken into small pieces
3 tablespoons chopped green chili peppers

1 teaspoon Worcestershire sauce
½ cup mayonnaise
8 ounces elbow macaroni, cooked and drained
½ cup crumbled tortilla chips

In a large skillet, brown the ground beef; stir in the cheese, tomatoes, chili peppers, and Worcestershire sauce. Cook over medium heat, stirring occasionally, for about 10 minutes, or until the cheese is completely melted. Stir in the mayonnaise. Add the macaroni and toss to coat with sauce. Turn mixture into a buttered 1½-quart casserole; top with tortilla chips. Bake in the preheated oven for 10 minutes, or until warmed through.

A little Southwest U.S.A. and a lot of Mexico are the secrets to this successful dish. Add a tossed green salad, and you've got an excellent party buffet.

CHILI CHEESE NOODLES

SERVES 8 TO 10

Preheat oven to 350 degrees

2 tablespoons cooking oil

1 garlic clove, peeled and minced

2 Spanish onions, peeled and chopped

1 green pepper, seeded and chopped

1 pound ground round, broken into chunks

2 tablespoons chili powder

¼ teaspoon each sage, thyme, oregano, and black pepper

1 teaspoon salt

One 8-ounce can tomato sauce

One 15-ounce can red kidney beans (with their liquid)

8 ounces egg noodles, cooked and drained

1 cup pitted black olives

¾ cup bread cubes, browned in butter

½ cup grated Cheddar cheese

In a large skillet, heat the cooking oil and sauté the garlic, onion, and green pepper until they are limp. Add the ground round and brown the meat. Drain any excess fat and add the chili, sage, thyme, oregano, pepper, salt, tomato sauce, and the liquid from the canned beans. Simmer for 30 minutes, stirring often. Stir in the red beans and noodles; spoon mixture into an oiled 3-quart casserole. Dot the top with the olives, bread cubes and Cheddar cheese. Bake in the preheated oven for 1 hour.

To make this easy seafood-noodle dish especially attractive, try spooning individual portions onto fish shells and baking them as you would a casserole. A simple green salad, tossed with an herb dressing, and a light, fluffy lemon meringue pie complete the menu for a summery supper.

CRAB NOODLE KLAGES
SERVES 4 TO 6

Preheat oven to 350 degrees

12 ounces noodles, cooked and drained
One 16-ounce can crab meat
One 8-ounce can tomato sauce
One 13-ounce package cream cheese, broken into pieces

Toss noodles in a bowl with the crabmeat. In another bowl, blend together the tomato sauce and cream cheese. Place noodle-crab mixture on well-oiled shells or in a well-oiled 3-quart casserole. Top with tomato sauce-cream cheese. Bake in the preheated oven for 20 to 25 minutes. (Cooking time for individual shells will be less than for one casserole.)

Tuna-noodle casseroles are as American as ball-park mustard. One of the first casseroles I ever cooked in college was a combination of canned tuna, canned soup, canned mixed vegetables, canned mushrooms, some milk, salt, pepper, garlic powder, maybe a dash of sherry, all topped with crushed potato chips.

These two casseroles are simple and good.

NUTTY CRUNCHY TUNA CASSEROLE

SERVES 4

Preheat oven to 350 degrees

One 3-ounce can chow mein
    noodles
One 7-ounce can tuna,
    drained and flaked
One 10¾-ounce can con-
    densed cream of celery
    soup

¼ cup milk
1 cup fine-diced celery
½ cup fine-diced onion
¼ pound unsalted cashew
    nuts
Salt and pepper to taste

In a large mixing bowl, combine all the above ingredients, reserving a handful of noodles for topping. Turn mixture into a buttered 2-quart casserole. Sprinkle with reserved noodles. Bake in the preheated oven for about 20 minutes, or until heated through.

EASY, SPECIAL TUNA CASSEROLE

SERVES 6

Preheat oven to 350 degrees

6 ounces macaroni, cooked
    and drained
1 cup sour cream
¼ cup vermouth
½ pound Cheddar cheese,
    grated

One 7-ounce can tuna,
    drained and flaked
Salt and pepper to taste
Grated Parmesan cheese

Combine all ingredients except the Parmesan cheese in a mixing bowl. Spoon into a buttered casserole and sprinkle cheese on top. Bake in the preheated oven for 20 minutes, or until nicely golden.

Restaurants all over the U.S. serve chili con carne (chili with meat) on top of spaghetti with a garnish of cheese and/or onions. Try this easy chili spaghetti dish.

EASY CHILI WITH SPAGHETTI

SERVES 6 TO 8

2 tablespoons butter or cooking oil
½ cup chopped onion
1 clove garlic, peeled and minced
1 pound ground beef
One 16-ounce can peeled whole tomatoes (with their liquid)
One 27-ounce can kidney beans (with their liquid)

1 teaspoon sugar
1 teaspoon salt
1 tablespoon chili powder (If you like it hotter, add more.)
16 ounces spaghetti, cooked and drained
Garnishes of: grated Cheddar, American, or Parmesan cheese and chopped onion

In a large skillet or Dutch oven, melt the butter and sauté the onions and garlic along with the meat. When mixture is browned, add the tomatoes (with their liquid), breaking them up with the back of a wooden spoon. Add the beans (with their liquid). Add seasonings and mix everything together. Cover and simmer for at least an hour. Serve chili over hot spaghetti. Place garnishes in small serving bowls and pass them around the dinner table.

A friend whom I greatly admire is "Mother Earth," Lynn Rapp. There is an aura of beautiful vibrations which encompasses her as well as her daughter Terry and grandson Jeremiah, my son's sweet playmate. Lynn is internationally renowned for her knowledge of plants. Her meatless chili recipe features many ingredients you can grow in your own backyard garden and lots of love. She serves it many ways: on brown rice, stuffed in pita bread, or over eggs for breakfast, lunch, or dinner, with hot tortillas and butter, and of course, over hot macaroni.

MOTHER EARTH'S GROW-YOUR-OWN CHILI

SERVES 8 TO 16, DEPENDING ON
OTHER COURSES

1 pound dried red beans (kidney or pinto), soaked overnight. Throw away the old water, add enough fresh water to cover beans, and then some.

2 large onions, peeled and chopped

3 medium zucchini, chopped

1 pound broccoli, chopped

6 medium tomatoes, parboiled and skinned

1 green chili pepper, seeded and chopped

2 bell peppers, seeded and chopped

One 32-ounce can tomato sauce

One 35-ounce can Italian-style whole, peeled tomatoes with their liquid

Chili powder to taste

Cayenne pepper to taste

2 cloves garlic, peeled and pressed, or garlic powder to taste

Chives, thyme, rosemary (and any other favorite fresh grown herbs), minced together to taste

1 to 2 pounds macaroni (depends on number of people you're feeding), cooked and drained

Grated sharp Cheddar cheese, for topping

Sour cream, for topping

Cook the beans with their water, onions, zucchini, broccoli, tomatoes, chili pepper, the bell peppers, tomato sauce, and Italian tomatoes together in a very large heavy pot for 3 to 4 hours over low to medium flame. The longer the chili cooks, the better it is. Stir frequently. Season to taste with chili powder and cayenne pepper. Add the garlic and fresh herbs, stirring to mix all the ingredients.

Place a layer of cooked hot macaroni on individual plates and top with chili. Then top chili with grated Cheddar cheese and sour cream. You can also add any vegetables you like to this chili. You might also try floating avocados on the top when you serve it.

This recipe serves quite a few, so you might want to cut it in half. It keeps in the refrigerator for up to four days and can be served in many ways.

One of my childhood favorites was my mother's stroganoff, prepared with the finest beef. I learned to cook this in my "swinging" single years. During the first days of dating my husband Bill, I served it to him by candlelight. We were married a few weeks later and I've wondered ever since how much the stroganoff had to do with it.

MOTHER'S BEEF STROGANOFF
(or Stroganoff and the Single Girl)

SERVES 4

2 pounds sirloin tips, sliced 3-inches long and ½-inch thick

2 tablespoons cooking oil

2 teaspoons garlic powder

One 10¾-ounce can condensed cream of mushroom soup

One 4-ounce can whole mushrooms, drained (or sauté in advance about ¼ pound fresh mushrooms, sliced thin)

Dash of Worcestershire sauce

½ cup sherry

1 cup sour cream

8 to 10 ounces broad noodles, cooked, drained, and tossed with 1 to 2 tablespoons melted butter

In a large skillet over medium heat, lightly brown the strips of meat on all sides in the oil, along with 1 teaspoon of the garlic powder. Drain off any excess oil or liquid. Add the soup and remaining garlic powder; stir to blend well. Cover skillet and reduce heat. Simmer for 20 minutes. Remove cover, add mushrooms, Worcestershire sauce, and sherry; stir thoroughly. Remove skillet from heat; add the sour cream. Stir lightly, blending well. Place buttered noodles on a large serving platter. Spoon stroganoff on top of noodles. Serve immediately.

My devoted agent and friend Jane "Auntie Mame" Browne hostessed a party for her teen-aged niece and twenty-one friends. Everything was a great success, especially this stroganoff.

JANE BROWNE'S FAMILY BEEF STROGANOFF

SERVES 12

4 pounds lean round steak, cubed

Instant unseasoned meat tenderizer

¼ pound butter

¼ cup olive oil

4 medium-sized yellow onions, peeled and sliced

2 cloves garlic, peeled and chopped fine

1 pound fresh mushrooms, sliced ¼-inch thick

1½ cups flour

One 6-ounce can tomato paste

One 10½-ounce can condensed beef broth

4 beef bouillon cubes

1½ tablespoons snipped fresh dill

Salt and pepper to taste

1 pint sour cream, slightly warmed

1½ to 2 pounds medium noodles, cooked and drained

Sprinkle meat with tenderizer. In a large skillet, heat one tablespoon of butter and one tablespoon of olive oil. Sear the meat quickly, a small batch at a time, adding butter and oil as needed. As the meat browns, remove it to a large, heavy casserole (5-quart size).

In a second skillet, heat one tablespoon of butter combined with one tablespoon of olive oil and sauté the onion, garlic, and mushrooms until the onions are limp and golden. Stir in the flour. When blended, add the tomato paste. In a saucepan, heat the liquid beef broth and dissolve the bouillon cubes in it. Season with the dill, salt and pepper; stir into the vegetable and sauce mixture and add this to the meat in the casserole. Simmer over very low heat, or cover and place in a 325-degree oven, for 3 hours. Shortly before serving, remove from heat and stir in the slightly warmed sour cream.

This dish should really be prepared the night before, or the morning of the day it is to be served. It is much tastier if prepared ahead and cooked the immediate 3 hours before serving.

Serve over noodles! This recipe can easily be doubled.

Here's a great switch. The meat is the crust and the noodles are the topping!

CORNED BEEF AND MACARONI PIE
SERVES 5 TO 6

Preheat oven to 350 degrees

One 12-ounce can corned beef
½ cup chopped onion
½ teaspoon white cream-style horseradish
½ teaspoon prepared mustard (If you do not like horseradish, use 1 teaspoon of mustard instead.)
1 egg

One 8-ounce can tomato sauce
4 ounces elbow macaroni, cooked and drained
1 cup coarse-grated American or Cheddar cheese
¼ cup evaporated milk
1 teaspoon dried sweet basil
½ teaspoon salt

Combine corned beef, onion, horseradish, mustard, egg and half the tomato sauce. Pat evenly and firmly into the bottom and sides of a 9-inch pie pan. In a mixing bowl, combine the macaroni and cheese; spoon into the meat shell. Combine the remaining tomato sauce with the milk, basil, and salt in a small bowl; pour over the macaroni. Bake in the preheated oven for 40 minutes. If you like this cheesier, sprinkle about ½ cup of grated American or Cheddar cheese over the top of the cooked pie and place it under the broiler until the cheese melts and begins to crisp up.

SWEETS

Cake, candy, ice cream, and pie—oh, we Americans love our desserts.

If you've got any leftover cooked noodles around—bowties are the greatest!—try deep-frying them the Italian or Oriental way. See pages 80, 82 or 158 or follow this recipe:

NOODLE PASTRIES

8 ounces bowties, or extra-wide egg noodles, cooked and drained
Cooking oil for deep-frying
Powdered (confectioners' sugar), cinnamon sugar, or honey, for topping

Allow cooked noodles to cool on paper towels in a single layer so that they do not stick together. Heat cooking oil in a deep pot to about 375 degrees. Drop in a few noodles at a time until they become lightly browned. Drain on paper towels. Continue until all are done. Sprinkle fried noodles immediately with your choice of topping. These are excellent as a sweet snack or to serve along with ice cream.

This is a twist on the classic caramel cereal party nibble, especially popular around the winter holiday season.

WINTER HOLIDAY MIX
MAKES APPROXIMATELY 9 CUPS

Cooking oil for deep-frying

1 cup leftover bowtie noodles (or, cook 4 to 6 ounces of your favorite bite-size noodles)

2 cups spoon-size shredded cereal biscuits (Use your favorite variety; I prefer the wheat biscuits.)

2 cups puffed oat cereal

1 cup puffed rice cereal

2 cups pretzel sticks, broken to the size of the cereal

8 ounces salted peanuts (Spanish peanuts are super!)

1⅓ cups sugar

1 cup butter

½ cup light corn syrup

1 teaspoon vanilla

Heat the cooking oil in a deep pot to 375 degrees. Deep-fry a few noodles at a time until they are a light gold, similar in color to the cereal. Drain noodles on paper towels. Continue until all noodles are golden. When noodles have cooled combine them in a buttered baking pan with the cereals, pretzels, and nuts; set aside.

Combine the sugar, butter, corn syrup, and vanilla in a medium saucepan. (Note: To prevent this caramel sauce from sticking, butter the saucepan in advance.) Cook syrup over low heat, stirring constantly, until it begins to crackle. Pour over the noodle mixture and stir to coat evenly. The mixture should harden very quickly. When it cools, break it into small pieces. Allow to cool fully before eating or putting away for gifts. Store in air tight containers.

These are delicious noodle cookies.

INA GRAVES'S BUTTERSCOTCH NOODLE COOKIES

MAKES 18 TO 24 COOKIES

½ cup peanut butter
One 6-ounce package butterscotch pieces
One 3-ounce can chow mein noodles
2 cups miniature marshmallows
½ cup walnuts

Melt the peanut butter and butterscotch together in the top of a double boiler; cool slightly. Add the noodles, marshmallows, and nuts. Stir gently to coat all the ingredients. Drop by the teaspoonful onto a cookie sheet which has been covered with wax paper; chill.

The Winning Noodle

I N 1971, the first National Pasta Recipe Contest, sponsored by the Durum Wheat Institute, the National Macaroni Institute and the North Dakota State Wheat Commission, was initiated. Its aim was to encourage and reward the creative talent of professional food service people in developing new and practical recipes for pasta products. "A Pasta for Every Palate" brought entries from every part of the United States, from every level of food service.

The competitors vied for recognition and prizes. The sponsors, in turn, sought to emphasize "durum" as the standard for the highest quality noodles, spaghetti, and macaroni.

Hundreds of entries went through a preliminary screening under the direction of a committee of food service specialists at North Dakota State University Extension Service. At the intermediate and final judgings in Chicago, two separate panels of professional food service executives selected the five best recipes in each of three categories— Sauces, Salads and Casseroles. A final judging panel then selected the best recipe in each category and the grand prize winner. Originators of the outstanding three recipes won vacations in San Juan, Puerto Rico and $500 in cash. The grand prize winner, in addition to his category prize, won an expense-paid European holiday for two.

Since its creation, the Pasta Recipe Contest has continued to grow in popularity. It has been held biannually since 1971. In 1975, the rules allowed anyone who owned, managed, or was employed by a quantity food service operation in hotels, restaurants, or institutions, or any student who was enrolled in a Hotel-Restaurant-Institution School in the United States during the contest period, to submit as many entries as he or she wished. Recipes were judged according to four important factors: (1) Practicality—easy and quick to prepare with a minimum of utensils and readily available ingredients, and realistic in cost; (2) Flavor—tastes good, appetizing flavor and texture; (3) Originality—new combination of ingredients, new method of putting everything together; and (4) Appearance—eye appeal.

The 1975 contest was sponsored by the Council on Hotel, Restaurant and Institution Education, Durum Wheat Institute, National Macaroni Institute, North Dakota State Wheat Commission, and The National Restaurant Association. A preliminary judging was done by an independent panel of food experts. Intermediate judging named the 12 best, and final judging named the top three winners. All three won expense-paid vacations in Key Biscayne, plus $500. The ''Grand Champion'' also won an epicurean tour of Italy.

For further information regarding this contest, write to Patricia L. Sparks, Director, Editorial Services, Durum Wheat Institute, 710 North Rush Street, Chicago, Illinois

60611.* Much appreciation is extended to Pat Sparks for her assistance in obtaining the following recipes.

1971 TOP THREE WINNERS

Grand Prize and First Prize Salad

Submitted by Ladell A. Kloek, Supervisor-Manager, Bridgeman Creameries Division of Land O' Lakes, Inc., Duluth, Minnesota, this aptly named "Garden Fresh Salad" combines succulently cooked mixed vegetables, snappy Cheddar cheese cubes, and chewy macaroni rings.

GARDEN FRESH SALAD
SERVES 6

7 ounces macaroni rings, cooked, drained, rinsed, and drained again

One 10-ounce package frozen mixed vegetables, cooked and drained

1 cup diced Cheddar cheese

1 cup mayonnaise

1 teaspoon salt

1 teaspoon onion salt

½ teaspoon pepper

Lettuce leaves

In a large mixing bowl, gently but thoroughly combine the macaroni, vegetables, cheese, mayonnaise, and seasonings. Chill. Serve on lettuce leaves.

First Prize Sauce

Wolf Hanau, Executive Vice-President, Steakthing, Miami, Florida, developed an unusual beef and brandy sauce

* As of November 9, 1976, the contest was in abeyance pending the decision of the supporters of the Durum Hotel-Restaurant-Institutional Program.

as his prizewinner. Select tenderloin tips, fresh mushrooms, and slices of scallion simmer in yogurt.

SPAGHETTI AMERICANA "2000"

SERVES 6

10 tablespoons butter
¼ pound fresh mushrooms,
    sliced
¼ cup sliced scallions
1 pound beef tenderloin
    tips, cubed
⅓ cup water
3 tablespoons brandy
One 8-ounce container
    plain yogurt

1 teaspoon enriched flour
½ teaspoon salt
½ teaspoon sugar
¼ teaspoon powdered nut-
    meg
⅛ teaspoon white pepper
12 ounces spaghetti,
    cooked and drained

Melt 2 tablespoons of the butter in a saucepan or small skillet. Add the mushrooms and onions; cook until just tender. Melt the remaining butter in a large skillet. Add the beef and cook over medium high heat until browned. Remove meat from pan. Add water and brandy to the skillet; boil rapidly for 3 minutes, stirring constantly to loosen the crusty bits from the pan. Combine the yogurt, flour, and seasonings; add to skillet. Cook, stirring constantly for 3 minutes. Add the meat and mushroom-onion mixture; bring to serving temperature. Serve sauce over spaghetti.

First Prize Casserole

The lasagne recipe submitted by Larry G. Gardner, Food Service Manager, Holy Rosary Hospital, Ontario, Oregon, began in the traditional manner—layering broad noodles with a typically Italian sauce of beef, mushrooms, and tomatoes. But for the center layer, he added a spread of chopped spinach, cottage cheese, and eggs. Finally, he sprinkled his top meat layer with sliced olives and American cheese.

TEEN-AGER'S LASAGNE

SERVES 6

Preheat oven to 350 degrees

1 pound ground beef
½ cup chopped onion
1 clove garlic, peeled and minced
1 tablespoon cooking oil
One 8-ounce can tomato sauce
One 6-ounce can tomato paste
One 4-ounce can sliced mushrooms
1 teaspoon salt
½ teaspoon oregano

2 eggs, lightly beaten
One 10-ounce package frozen chopped spinach, thawed and drained
1 cup small curd creamed cottage cheese
12 ounces lasagne noodles, drained, rinsed, and drained again
½ cup sliced, pitted black olives
8 slices (1 ounce each) American cheese

In a large skillet, cook the ground beef, onion, and garlic in the oil until the meat is browned. Stir in the tomato sauce and paste, the mushrooms, salt and oregano. Simmer for 15 minutes. In a mixing bowl, combine the eggs, spinach, and cottage cheese. Layer the ingredients in a 13 x 9 x 2-inch pan as follows: Pour half the tomato sauce in the pan. Cover with half the lasagne. Top with all the spinach-egg mixture. Cover with remaining lasagne. Pour over the remaining tomato sauce. Sprinkle with sliced olives. Cover with foil. Bake in the preheated oven for 45 minutes. Remove the foil. Arrange the cheese slices on top; bake 15 minutes longer.

1973 TOP THREE WINNERS

Grand Prize and First Prize Casserole

For his winning recipe, "Moussaka Romano," Sous Chef Simone "Sam" Billuni, Ten Downing Restaurant, San Diego, California, joined traditional Greek eggplant with the Roman tomato sauce, lasagne noodles, and spices.

MOUSSAKA ROMANO

SERVES 8 TO 10

Preheat oven to 350 degrees

1 pound ground beef
½ cup chopped onion
Two 12-ounce cans tomato
*   paste*
2½ teaspoons salt
½ teaspoon pepper
1 teaspoon garlic powder
1 teaspoon oregano,
*   crushed*
1 teaspoon dried sweet
*   basil, crushed*
4 cups water
¼ cup butter
¼ cup enriched flour
½ teaspoon salt

2 cups milk
One 15-ounce carton
*   ricotta cheese*
½ teaspoon ground cinna-
*   mon*
3 eggs
1 medium eggplant, peeled,
*   sliced ⅜-inch thick*
Cooking oil
1 pound lasagna noodles,
*   cooked, drained, rinsed,*
*   drained and patted dry*
½ cup grated Parmesan
*   cheese*

Brown the ground beef in a large skillet; add the onion and cook for 5 minutes. Add tomato paste, 2 teaspoons of salt, the pepper, garlic powder, oregano, and basil. Stir in the water; simmer for 1 hour. In a medium saucepan, melt the butter; add flour and salt to make a paste. Slowly stir in milk and cook, stirring constantly, until white sauce is thick and smooth. In a small bowl, combine the white sauce, ricotta cheese, cinnamon, and eggs. Fry the eggplant lightly in a skillet with the oil.

Cover the bottom of a $15\frac{3}{8}$ x $10\frac{3}{8}$ x $2\frac{1}{4}$-inch pan with one third of the meat mixture, half the eggplant, one third of the ricotta cheese mixture, and half of the lasagne. Repeat layers. Dot top with remaining ricotta cheese mixture. Ladle 1 cup of the remaining meat mixture around the dots of ricotta mixture; swirl together with a spoon. Sprinkle Parmesan cheese over top. Bake in the preheated oven for 45 minutes. Allow to set about 10 minutes. Cut in squares and serve with remaining sauce.

First Prize Salad

Sister Anna Marie Haiar's prize-winning dish, "Mandarin Chicken Salad," is offered once a month to the staff of the St. Coletta School, Jefferson, Wisconsin, where she is Food Service Supervisor. Assorted crackers, a light dessert and a beverage are served with the salad.

MANDARIN CHICKEN SALAD

SERVES 8

*2 cups cooked cubed
chicken*
1 tablespoon minced onion
1 teaspoon salt
*1 cup seedless grapes,
halved*
1 cup diced celery
*One 11-ounce can manda-
rin orange segments,
drained*
*1 cup salad dressing (oil
and vinegar)*

⅓ cup slivered almonds
1 tablespoon lemon juice
*½ teaspoon grated lemon
peel (optional)*
*4 ounces macaroni rings or
elbow macaroni, cooked,
drained, rinsed and
drained again*
1 cup heavy cream
Lettuce leaves

Combine the chicken, onion, and salt in a bowl; refrigerate for several hours. Add the grapes, celery, orange
segments, salad dressing, almonds, lemon juice, and lemon
peel to the chicken mixture. Stir the macaroni into the
chicken mixture. When ready to serve, whip the cream and
fold into chicken mixture. Serve on lettuce leaves.

First Prize Student Championship

In 1973, for the first time, the contest was opened to
students, as well as professionals in the food service industry. The students, in competition with experienced chefs,
captured three of the top 12 positions. For winner
James W. Young of the Columbus Adult Education Services Center-MOTA, Columbus, Ohio, the contest was a class
project.

In this unusual recipe, the noodles are first cooked in
boiling, salted water, then fried in a mixture of butter,

onion, and garlic. The cabbage is boiled, then fried in bacon fat. To complete the casserole, Young combines the fried noodles and fried cabbage with cottage cheese and seasonings, then sprinkles bacon bits over the top before the dish is baked.

HUNGARIAN FRIED NOODLES AND CABBAGE BUDAPEST STYLE

SERVES 6

Preheat oven to 300 degrees

1 cup minced onion
1 garlic clove, peeled and crushed
½ cup butter
1 pound medium noodles, cooked and drained
1 medium head of cabbage, shredded

10 slices bacon, diced
2 cups large curd cottage cheese
1 cup sour cream
½ teaspoon salt
⅛ teaspoon pepper
1 tablespoon caraway seeds (optional)

In a large skillet, sauté the onion and garlic in butter until tender. Add the noodles. Fry slowly for 5 minutes, tossing the noodles. Boil cabbage in salted water until crisp-tender, 2 to 3 minutes; drain well. In a separate pan, fry bacon until crisp. Remove the bacon; drain. Fry boiled cabbage in bacon fat. Add cottage cheese, sour cream, salt, pepper, caraway seeds and noodles to the cabbage mixture; blend well and turn into a 2-quart baking dish. Sprinkle bacon pieces over the top. Bake in the preheated oven for 20 minutes.

1975 TOP THREE WINNERS

Grand Prize and First Prize Sauce

To create her winning recipe, "Noodle Pudding with Raisin-Nut Sauce," Elizabeth Wyona Irwin, Director of Dietary Services at the Manteno Mental Health Center, Manteno, Illinois, combines a basic custard mixture of eggs, sugar, and milk with egg noodles. But the crowning glory isn't added until it's baked and ready to serve. Then the super-sensational Raisin-Nut Sauce, laced with a hint of rum, raises this down-to-earth classic to epicurean heights.

NOODLE PUDDING WITH RAISIN-NUT SAUCE

SERVES 6

Preheat oven to 300 degrees

2 cups cooked noodles
3 eggs
2 cups milk

⅔ cup sugar
½ teaspoon cinnamon

RAISIN-NUT SAUCE:

1 cup water
½ cup raisins
¼ cup sugar
2 tablespoons butter
2 tablespoons cornstarch
3 tablespoons cold water

⅓ cup English walnut pieces
½ teaspoon grated orange peel
2 tablespoons rum (or ½ teaspoon rum flavoring)

Place noodles in a buttered 8-inch square glass baking dish. Beat eggs; add milk, sugar, and cinnamon. Pour over noodles and mix gently. Bake in the preheated oven for 60 to 70 minutes, or until a knife inserted in the center comes out clean. Cut noodle pudding into squares and serve hot or cold with warm Raisin-Nut Sauce.

To make the sauce: In a small saucepan, bring 1 cup water to a boil. Remove from heat, add raisins and let stand for 10 minutes. Add sugar and butter; cook over medium heat until boiling. Combine cornstarch and cold water; pour into boiling mixture, constantly stirring until thickened. Remove from heat; stir in walnuts, orange peel, and rum.

If desired, garnish sauce-topped pudding with whipped cream.

First Prize First Course

The chowder submitted by Executive Chef Thomas R. Giancoli of The School of Adjustment, Seattle, Washington, is a savory blend of several of the different seafoods from his Northwestern locale. Instead of the usual potato, which tends to melt in the pot, he decided to use enriched durum macaroni shells, which don't get mushy or break apart. Another Giancoli innovation is the use of evaporated milk instead of a cream sauce base.

WORLD'S GREATEST SEAFOOD CHOWDER
MAKES 2 QUARTS

¼ cup butter
½ cup chopped onion
½ cup chopped celery
1 clove garlic, peeled and
    minced
⅓ cup dry white wine
1 teaspoon chicken bouillon
    powder
1 teaspoon salt
½ teaspoon each thyme,
    nutmeg, and pepper
1 bay leaf
5 tablespoons enriched
    flour
⅓ cup cold water
1 pound codfish fillets
    (fresh or frozen and
    thawed), cubed
½ cup diced green pepper

6 oysters (or one 10-ounce
    can frozen oysters,
    drained, liquid re-
    served)
1½ cups small macaroni
    shells, cooked and
    drained
One 13-ounce can
    evaporated milk
One 8-ounce can minced
    clams, drained, liquid
    reserved
One 4-ounce can tiny
    shrimp, drained, liquid
    reserved
¼ cup chopped fresh
    parsley
¼ cup chopped pimiento

In a large saucepan, melt the butter and sauté the onion, celery, and garlic for 5 minutes. Combine the reserved liquid from the clams, shrimp, and oysters and add enough water to measure 3 cups; pour into the saucepan with the vegetables. Add wine, chicken bouillon, and seasonings; cover and simmer for 15 minutes. Mix flour and cold water to a smooth paste. Add to liquid, stirring constantly; cook until thickened. Add codfish, green pepper, and oysters; simmer 10 to 15 minutes. Remove bay leaf. Stir in the macaroni shells, milk, clams, shrimp, parsley and pimiento. Heat to simmering and serve.

First Prize Casserole

"Fettuccelle a la Tunnelli" is a unique recipe prepared in an innovative way. Dietitian at Southern Methodist University, Dallas, Texas, Mildred B. Tunnell's creation combines fettuccelle, Italian sausage, Italian cheeses, black olives, eggs, tomatoes, and seasonings baked in a springform cake pan. When the mold has set, she removes it from the pan and serves it as a main dish pie.

FETTUCCELLE À LA TUNNELLI

SERVES 6

Preheat oven to 375 degrees

10 ounces fettuccelle or narrow noodles, cooked and drained
2 tablespoons butter
1 pound sweet Italian sausage meat *
½ cup chopped onion
½ cup sliced black olives
¼ cup chopped fresh parsley

¼ cup chopped pimiento
1 teaspoon salt
½ teaspoon pepper
3 eggs, well beaten
1 cup coarse-grated mozzarella cheese
1 cup coarse-grated provolone cheese
3 or 4 tomatoes, sliced thin

Return noodles to pot in which they were cooked and toss with butter. In a large skillet, brown the sausage; drain excess fat. Add onion and cook until tender. Combine noodles, sausage mixture, olives, parsley, pimiento, salt, and pepper in a bowl. Pour beaten eggs over noodle mixture; mix thor-

* Note: If using link sausage, remove casings and crumble into skillet.

oughly. Combine mozzarella and provolone cheeses in a bowl. Press half the noodle mixture into a buttered and floured 9-inch spring-form pan. Cover with slices of tomato, overlapping the edges. Sprinkle with half of the cheese mixture. Repeat the layers. Cover with aluminum foil and bake in the preheated oven for 45 to 50 minutes. Remove foil and spring-form; cut the mold into wedges and serve.

The Outdoor Noodle

IN 1971, I married a freezer—a freezer packed with albacore, venison, wild duck, trout, and plenty more fish and game. My husband was, and still is, an avid sportsman. This was just the beginning of a whole new world for me.

Hunting and fishing are his two favorite "escapes." After a day in the field or on the water, Bill has always brought home the fruits of his labor. I've seen these new foods as an outstanding challenge to my culinary hobby.

Having been introduced to the outdoors through his fish and game, I soon grew to love the sports myself. At first it was a way of sharing with my husband, but it soon became a major facet of my professional life. As a freelance writer on assignment, I have ridden horses among the buffalo in Custer State Park, fought (and landed) a 116-pound marlin in the waters near Mazatlan, survived the wilds of snow, cold, and dark in the mountains of Wyoming, built a shelter out of branches as my lone home in New Mexico, cast for bass in the winter rain of Toledo Bend, Louisiana, shivered in the icy duck blinds of Tule, and perspired among the desert cactus trying to photograph flushing bird dogs.

In these six years of outdoor adventures, I have written a fish and game cookbook, hundreds of magazine and newspaper columns, and dozens of newsletters. As the camp-cooking expert for a major food company, I have demonstrated and discussed outdoor cookery on more than two hundred television and radio shows, including several educational films, and have advised newspaper reporters what to say about eating in the outdoors. At national conventions, I have cooked wild game and freeze-dried patties before standing-room-only audiences. It's been great. I've loved every minute of it and thank everyone for their interest, help, and confidence.

In the pages to come, you will find some of my favorite outdoor recipes, several of which have been contributed by friends and business associates. Of course, they all include noodles!

Whether you're planning a day, weekend, or extended trip away from home—backpacking, with a camper, or in a boat—outdoor cooking can be a creative, fun-filled activity. Next time you're shopping at your neighborhood market or sporting goods store, look around at the fantastic display of inexpensive convenience products. There are envelopes of instant, dehydrated soups, sauces, snacks, drinks, and main courses. Small boxes of macaroni and cheese, complete spaghetti dinners, cups of flavored soup and noodles, and cans of already prepared ravioli, spaghetti and meatballs, or hearty soups and stews are among the staples that are ideal for every galley or camp cook.

A package or two of your favorite noodles, macaroni, or spaghetti are a must for every outdoor pantry. They're dehydrated, so there's no need for refrigeration. They're lightweight and take little storage space. In addition, most outdoor noodle recipes require only a few steps for preparation and one pot for cooking (and cleaning!). And, most important, foods high in fats and carbohydrates are the most efficient to supply the energy needed for strenuous activity. (See discussion of Olympic athletes' foods on page 6.)

I must admit that I have found one problem with noodle cooking in the outdoors. Often, these sports—especially backpacking and climbing—are enjoyed in high altitude environments. The higher up, the longer it takes to boil water. I will always remember one hunting trip in Wyoming at 8500 feet when, early in the afternoon, the camp cook put up a huge pot of water to boil for a spaghetti dinner.

Boiling is proportionately lengthened as the altitude increases. Cooking times, therefore, increase with the altitude. So allow more time than at home. Meals that take 30 minutes at sea level will take so long at high altitudes that these recipes are better left at home. If you're camped permanently at these high altitudes, a pressure cooker is practically a necessity.

HIGH-ALTITUDE COOKING

Boiling point of water:

	Degrees F.	Degrees C.	Increase Cooking Time:
Sea Level	212	100	
2,000	208	98	10%
5,000	203	95	40%
7,500	198	92	75%
10,000	194	90	
15,000	185	85	
30,000	158	70	

Outdoor cooking can be a lot of fun, especially if you keep the recipes quite simple. For that special touch, I sprinkle a simmering pot of sauce with some herbs, spices, or wine. After all, I'd rather spend my time enjoying nature than hovering over the campfire.

For a real home-cooked meal in the field, I've found boilable bag sealers do the trick. At home, I always cook large portions so that I can freeze the extras for a second meal. I package such dishes as hearty soups, sauces, and stews in special "boil-in-bags," seal them with the machine, and place them in the freezer. Then, when we're packing for a fishing or camping trip, I place several of these home-made frozen food bags in our cooler where they act like a block of ice and help keep perishables fresh. When it's time for dinner, I simply boil the food right in the bag. The pot stays clean and the water fresh. I use this water later for washing the dishes. A boilable bag sealer machine is an excellent investment for every outdoor kitchen. Besides sealing foods, I use it to seal and protect matches, spices and seasonings, playing cards, camera equipment, cooking utensils, writing supplies and lots more.

Check your spice kit to see what you've brought along. You might add some dehydrated parsley flakes or a dash of hot pepper sauce to the packaged soup. If it is a plain broth, add some small noodles or break up a handful of spaghetti directly into the pot. No spaghetti? Then make these quick outdoor soup noodles.

QUICK OUTDOOR EGG NOODLES
SERVES 3 TO 4

2 eggs
⅛ teaspoon salt
¼ cup flour

In a small bowl, beat the eggs with the salt until they are foamy. Blend in the flour. Pour the batter steadily in a thin stream directly into the 1½ to 2 quarts simmering soup, stirring constantly. Simmer soup with noodles for about 2 minutes. Serve immediately.

S O U P S

The easiest outdoor noodle soup is made by tearing open an envelope or opening a can.*

A vegetable soup is great for camp. You can use fresh celery, carrots, potatoes, onions, and parsley. Or it's a lot easier to use a can with everything already diced and mixed together.

CAMP-STYLE MINESTRONE

SERVES 4

2½ quarts cold water
Two 1½-ounce envelopes onion soup mix (or use your own favorite, such as chicken, vegetable, mushroom, or tomato soup)
8 ounces macaroni or egg noodles
One 15½-ounce can mixed vegetables, liquid reserved

In a large soup pot, bring the water, soup mix and vegetable liquid to a boil; reduce heat and simmer for 20

---

* Before going into wilderness areas, please check food restrictions. Some parks no longer allow glass bottles or cans. If this is the case, you have to repackage all your supplies in plastic containers. Even if there are no prohibitive rules against cans or bottles, please remember to pack out any empties. Do not bury them in the dirt. Animals or children might dig them up.

minutes. Add the noodles and canned vegetables. Continue to simmer about 10 minutes, or until noodles are tender.

I've worked with Kay Berger for several years on magazine food feature ideas. During our last lunch meeting, we talked about her backpacking adventures. Having introduced two children to the sport, she found they enjoyed shopping with her for the food supply. One of their favorite choices is a 3-ounce package of instant, flavored Oriental noodle soup seasoned with some soy sauce and dehydrated shrimp (available in the Oriental section of most markets or Oriental specialty shops). This main dish soup is ready in about 5 minutes. The short cooking time is great for saving valuable propane fuel and for satisfying hungry appetites.

For the first night of backpacking or other outdoor activities, I try to prepare a fresh meat or chicken dish. The trick to handling this perishable without refrigeration is to freeze it at home for several days. Then, prior to departure, wrap it in heavy foil and pack it along. It will defrost slowly during the day and be ready to use for your favorite recipe, such as this soup, in the evening.

LUMBERJACK SOUP

SERVES 4

1 pound ground beef
Two ¾-ounce envelopes onion gravy sauce mix
3 cups water
One 16-ounce can peeled whole tomatoes with their liquid
8 ounces elbow macaroni

Brown the meat in a large skillet or Dutch oven. Stir in the onion gravy mix. Add the water, tomatoes, and macaroni; stir well and bring to a boil. Cover and simmer for 15 minutes, or until macaroni is tender, stirring occasionally. If you brought some grated Parmesan cheese along, you might want to sprinkle some on top of the individual soup bowls.

SAUCED AND SAUTÉED NOODLES (Including Camp-Style Casseroles)

It's not that difficult to make a sauce from scratch in the outdoors. Melted butter or hot olive oil, seasoned to please and tossed with noodles and lots of grated cheese is always our favorite. If you want a more complicated sauce, you can make a basic roux and then add canned evaporated milk or canned broth and your choice of seasonings. Or to be really quick, you can forget the butter and flour and just use canned or packaged sauce mixes. A can of condensed soup can also be transformed into a delicious sauce.

OUTDOOR SAUCE MAGIC

Try these ideas. Or mix your own creation:

1. Cheese Sauce: Thin one 11-ounce can condensed Cheddar cheese soup with a little milk (can be evaporated). Add a dash of mustard or hot pepper sauce.
2. Cream Sauce: Thin a 10¾-ounce can condensed cream of celery, chicken, mushroom, onion, shrimp, or potato soup with a little milk (can be evaporated). Add a sprinkling of dried parsley flakes.

3. Mushroom Sauce: Thin a 10¾-ounce can condensed golden mushroom soup with a little water. Add a few drops of wine.

4. Tomato Sauce: Thin one 10¾-ounce can condensed tomato soup with a little water. Add your favorite herbs and/or spices.

A most successful southern gentleman-businessman-sportsman, Walter S. McIlhenny, shared with me several outdoor sauce suggestions, adding a few drops of his Tabasco sauce. These are ideal for camp or galley kitchens to serve over your favorite cooked noodles:

1. Add Tabasco, grated Parmesan cheese, and evaporated milk to melted butter.

2. Combine fine-chopped garlic, canned anchovy fillets, olive oil, and Tabasco. Serve grated cheese as garnish.

3. Heat canned kidney beans with olive oil, Tabasco, lemon juice, fine-chopped garlic, and shredded salami. Toss with grated cheese and parsley.

When the hunters bring some pheasant, grouse, or other upland game bird back to camp, we often use it to make this sauce.

PHEASANT SPAGHETTI SAUCE

MAKES APPROXIMATELY
3 TO 4 CUPS
SERVES 4 TO 6

1 to 2 pheasants, cleaned and cut into small serving portions
2 tablespoons cooking oil or bacon fat
1 large clove garlic, peeled and minced
½ cup chopped onion
1 cup diced celery

One 32-ounce can peeled whole tomatoes, drained and mashed
½ cup diced green pepper
1½ teaspoons salt
½ teaspoon pepper
Dash sugar
1½ pounds spaghetti, cooked and drained

Brown the pheasant pieces in a Dutch oven in the hot oil or bacon fat with the garlic and onion. When onion softens and pheasant is golden add the remaining ingredients. Simmer sauce for 2 to 3 hours over very low heat. Pour over spaghetti.

A dear friend and fellow writer, Kathy Farmer was also introduced to the outdoors by her husband. Having lived in a log cabin in the wilds of Wyoming for many years, their winter meals used elk, deer or antelope instead of store-bought beef. One day while we talked, she was in the process of making spaghetti sauce. The aroma of the simmering ''gravy,'' as she called it, was life to the spirit.

Whenever she and her husband returned from a trip in the woods, Charlie would always want this dish to welcome them home. Any leftover spaghetti was refrigerated in its sauce. The next day, Charlie would melt some butter in a pan, sauté the spaghetti with a bit of the sauce. And then sprinkle this "crispy" spaghetti with grated Parmesan cheese.

Although I've never had the privilege of tasting Kathy's spaghetti with game meat sauce, I had a similar Wyoming dish, prepared by camp cook Lannie Merritt.

I once spent two weeks in the Merritt's hunting camp— a few hours drive by four-wheel and a horseback ride from Jackson Hole, Wyoming. Though the weather wasn't on our side, the eating was. One evening, our guide, Kevin, my husband, Bill, and I returned to camp after 11 hours of hard horseback riding and hunting. Weary and hungry, we quickly downed a most delicious and warming dinner of spaghetti and game meatballs.

LANNIE'S SPAGHETTI AND GAME MEATBALLS

SERVES 14

CAMP SPAGHETTI SAUCE:

1 tablespoon olive oil

2 large cloves garlic, peeled and minced

1 large onion, peeled and chopped fine

Three 15-ounce cans stewed tomatoes

Eight 15-ounce cans tomato sauce with mushrooms

Two 4-ounce cans whole mushrooms, drained

1 cup red wine (Burgundy)

1 teaspoon oregano

1 teaspoon mixed Italian seasonings

1 teaspoon sweet basil

1 heaping tablespoon sugar

Salt and pepper to taste

WILD GAME MEATBALLS:

2 pounds ground moose or
    elk meat
1 pound sweet sausage,
    (optional; if not add-
    ing, increase ground
    meat to 3 pounds)
2 tablespoons minced dried
    onion
1 large clove garlic, peeled
    and minced

1 cup cracker crumbs or
    breadcrumbs (or ½
    cup whole wheat
    cereal)
1 egg
Canned milk
Salt and pepper to taste
Olive oil
Grated Parmesan cheese

To make the sauce: Heat the oil in a 6 to 8 quart (or larger) saucepan. Add the garlic and onion and sauté. When they soften, add the tomatoes, tomato sauce, and mushrooms. Rinse the sauce cans out with the wine as you add it to the sauce. Add the remaining ingredients and allow sauce to simmer for an hour while preparing meatballs.

To make the meatballs: In a large bowl, combine all the ingredients, adding just enough milk to bind the mixture until it appears moist. Form into 20 to 24 medium-size balls and brown on all sides in a little hot olive oil in an iron skillet. After browning, place meatballs in the sauce and simmer everything together for 4 to 8 hours, the longer the better. Serve meatballs and sauce over spaghetti with grated cheese.

During the season, you might be able to dig for fresh clams for a tomato sauce. But if none are available, use the canned to make this in about 10 minutes.

CLAMS AND TOMATO SAUCE

SERVES 3 TO 4

*1 clove garlic, peeled and
    minced*
1 tablespoon olive oil
*One 10½-ounce can
    minced clams, liquid
    reserved*

*One 10-ounce can spa-
    ghetti sauce with mush-
    rooms*
*8 ounces vermicelli,
    cooked and drained*
*Grated Parmesan cheese
    for topping*

In a medium saucepan, sauté the garlic in the olive oil.
Add the liquid from the canned clams and continue cooking over high heat for about 5 minutes to reduce some of
the liquid. Add the clams and spaghetti sauce. Continue to
heat another 5 minutes. Pour sauce over cooked vermicelli.
Serve with plenty of grated Parmesan cheese. (Variation:
Use one 6½-ounce can of clams and one 4½-ounce can of
shrimp.)

CREAMY OYSTER SAUCE

SERVES 4 TO 6

2 tablespoons cooking oil
*1 medium onion, peeled
    and chopped fine*
*10 pimiento-stuffed green
    olives, sliced in half*
*One 10¾-ounce can con-
    densed cream of celery
    soup (or other favorite
    creamed soup)*

*Two 8-ounce cans whole
    oysters, liquid reserved*
*10 ounces noodles, cooked
    and drained*
*Salt, white pepper, and
    cayenne pepper to taste*
*2 tablespoons grated Par-
    mesan cheese*

Heat the oil in a large saucepan; sauté the onion and
olives. When they are softened, add the soup and oyster

liquid, stirring well. Cover and cook at a low simmer for 10 minutes. Add the cooked noodles; stir in the oysters and season to taste. Stir frequently for 3 to 5 minutes. Sprinkle with cheese and serve.

ORIENTAL CHICKEN STEW
SERVES 3 TO 4

*Two 15¼-ounce cans
chicken stew
One 16-ounce can Oriental
chow mein vegetables,
drained
2 teaspoons soy sauce*

*½ teaspoon instant minced
onion
One 3-ounce can chow
mein noodles
2 tablespoons toasted
slivered almonds*

In a saucepan, combine the chicken stew, vegetables, soy sauce, and onion. Heat, stirring occasionally. Place chow mein noodles on a serving dish; pour chicken mixture on top. Garnish with almonds.

What could be more outdoorsy than chili! You can make a quick, simple chili-macaroni, by combining canned chili with macaroni. Or, if you've got the time and the supplies, try making the more deluxe chili-spaghetti.

CHILI-ETTI
SERVES 4 TO 5

*1 pound lean ground beef
1 onion, peeled and
chopped
Two 8-ounce cans tomato
sauce with mushrooms
One 16-ounce can kidney
beans*

*1 cup water
4 ounces spaghetti, broken
into 1-inch pieces
1 teaspoon chili powder
1 teaspoon salt
1 cup shredded Cheddar
cheese*

Brown the ground beef and onion in a large skillet; drain excess fat. Add the sauce, beans, water, spaghetti, chili powder, and salt. Cover and simmer for 12 to 15 minutes, or until spaghetti is tender. Stir in the cheese and heat until it melts. Serve immediately.

Though not a chili, this dish, created by my husband, is quite similar. Every outdoors person loves it. Originally, we did not make it with macaroni, but we knew something was missing. Then, one day we had some cooked macaroni left over from the previous evening and tossed it in during the last few minutes of simmering. Wow! Our recipe was complete.

GREEN'S GRAND GROUDO

SERVES 2 TO 4

1½ *pounds ground veni-*
son (If you don't have
any, substitute ground
beef and add a little
pepperoni to simulate
the extra bite of game
meat.)
Cooking oil
1 large clove garlic, peeled
and chopped
1 onion, peeled and
chopped coarse
Salt and pepper
One 8-ounce can tomato
sauce

3 medium tomatoes, peeled
and chopped
One 15-ounce can pinto or
red kidney beans
One 3-ounce can chopped
chili peppers or 4 small
fresh yellow chili
peppers, diced
½ *teaspoon chili powder*
3 stalks celery, chopped
coarse (optional)
4 to 6 ounces elbow maca-
roni or small shells,
cooked and drained

Crumble the venison with your hands and sauté it in oil with the garlic and onion until the onion is golden. Season with salt and pepper. Add the tomato sauce, tomatoes, beans, chili peppers, and chili powder. Stir thoroughly to mix all the ingredients. Simmer, covered, for 45 minutes, stirring occasionally. Add the celery for a crunchy texture and simmer, uncovered, for 6 minutes more. If the sauce is too thick, add a small amount of water. Add the cooked macaroni; stir. Simmer another 5 minutes to blend all ingredients. Serve piping hot with Mexican flour or corn tortillas. I like a sprinkle of grated Parmesan or Cheddar cheese on top. Every time we make this it is somehow different. Once I added carrots. Another time canned pitted black olives.

Macaroni and cheese, rich in both proteins and carbohydrates for energy, is popular as well as at home.

CAMPERS' MACARONI AND CHEESE WITH VEGETABLES

SERVES 6

One 1½-ounce envelope cheese sauce mix
1 cup milk (We use powdered milk reconstituted with water.)
One 16-ounce can mixed vegetables, drained
8 ounces elbow macaroni, cooked and drained

In a large saucepan, combine the sauce mix and milk, stirring to blend. Continue to cook over medium heat for 5 minutes until thickened. Add the vegetables; heat thoroughly. Add the cooked macaroni. You can also add canned seafood for a complete one-pot meal. Or, if you're lucky, serve this as an accompaniment to fresh caught trout.

For several years during the summer camping months, I traveled around the United States making television and radio guest appearances for the R. T. French Company as their Outdoor Living and Cooking Consultant, demonstrating simple one-pot dishes for which all the seasonings were pre-mixed in one small envelope.

You can make this spaghetti within minutes. Instead of using fresh meat, I usually crumble beef jerky (dried beef) into the sauce while it's cooking.

ONE-POT SPAGHETTI

SERVES 4

One 1½ ounce envelope spaghetti sauce mix
One 6-ounce can tomato paste
6 cups water

2 tablespoons cooking oil or butter
8 ounces spaghetti, broken into small pieces
1 to 2 sticks beef jerky, crumbled

Combine the sauce mix and tomato paste in a large saucepan. Add the water and oil or butter; bring to a boil. Add spaghetti and beef jerky to sauce. Cook for 10 minutes, or until spaghetti is tender, stirring often. If you wish to add fresh meat instead of jerky: Brown ½ to 1 pound ground meat in oil or butter. Stir the sauce mix into the meat and continue to follow preceding directions. Canned hamburgers can also be used instead of fresh meat.

After a day of active sports in the fresh air, I like a quick skillet dish like this hearty casserole.

GREGORY LARSEN'S FAMILY SPAGHETTI CASSEROLE

SERVES 4

1 pound ground beef
¾ cup chopped onion
1 tablespoon cooking oil
One 16-ounce can mixed
   vegetables

One 15-ounce can spa-
   ghetti in tomato sauce
   with cheese
One 3-ounce can French-
   fried onion rings

Brown the beef and onion in cooking oil in a large skillet. Stir in the mixed vegetables and canned spaghetti. Simmer everything for 10 minutes or until heated through. Top with onion rings and serve.

Here's a quick and easy way to stretch just a half pound of ground beef into a main dish for campers.

BEEF ORIENTAL

SERVES 4 TO 5

½ pound ground beef
One 5-ounce can bamboo
   shoots, drained
One 16-ounce can mixed
   Oriental chow mein
   vegetables

One ¾-ounce envelope
   gravy mix
1 cup water
2 tablespoons soy sauce
1 teaspoon sugar
8 ounces spaghetti, cooked
   and drained

Brown the ground beef in a large skillet, stirring to crumble. Pour off any excess fat. Add the bamboo shoots and canned mixed Oriental vegetables; cook and stir for 2 or 3 minutes. Add the gravy mix, water, soy sauce, and sugar. Heat just to boiling. Add the spaghetti, stirring occasionally until hot. Or substitute one to three 3-ounce cans of chow mein noodles for the spaghetti and use them as a bed for the beef skillet dish.

Before I left on our two-week hunting trip to Wyoming, I bought several bags of nuts, dried fruits, and candies. I expected we'd horseback ride, hike and hunt all day only to return to camp to cook our own dinners. Not so at the Merritt's camp.

PAT'S ELK STROGANOFF
WITH CAMP NOODLES

SERVES 5 TO 8

CAMP NOODLES:

2+ cups flour

2 teaspoons salt

5 eggs

Boiling salted water

Salt

Butter or margarine

ELK STROGANOFF:

3 to 4 pounds elk loin,
sliced into thin, short
strips

2 cups cooking oil

Two 1⅜-ounce envelopes
onion soup mix

2 to 3 cups hot water

One 6-ounce can button
mushrooms

Two 1½-ounce envelopes
Sour Cream Sauce mix,
prepared with water
according to package
directions

To make the noodles: Put 2 cups of the flour, salt, and eggs in a bowl. Stir mixture with a fork, leaving it sticky. Scoop a pile of flour onto the board or table top; place the egg-flour mixture on it and knead until the mixture is no longer sticky. Roll the dough until it is ⅛-inch thick. Cut into strips ¼-inch wide and 4-inches long. These noodles will swell up to about three times their size in cooking. Bring a 6-quart pot of water to a boil. (Note: At our 8500 foot altitude with a wood-burning stove, the water took over 1 hour to boil.) Add enough oil to the water to make a thin film on the surface. Salt the water generously.

After the noodles have dried in a hot tent for 15 to 20 minutes, drop them into the boiling water; stir occasionally. Cook the noodles to taste, about 15 minutes. Place them in a serving bowl and toss with butter or margarine.

To make the Stroganoff: Allow ½ pound meat per person. Heat the cooking oil in a large cast iron skillet. When it starts to smoke, drop the meat to the hot oil and cook until it browns. Add the soup mix and enough hot water (about 2 to 3 cups) to cover the meat. Simmer, covered, for 2 hours. Fifteen minutes before serving, add the mushrooms and prepared sour cream sauce. Serve on top of noodles.

As an outdoor writer, I meet many outstanding people professionally, several of whom have become close personal friends. One of these special people is Sheila Link. A spirited woman with a very pretty smile and a twinkle in her eye, Sheila has many outdoor specialties, including canoeing, kayaking, survival, backpacking, fishing, and hunting. When Sheila's children were young, she camped with them from the East to the West Coast and back. One of their staple dinners was this camp-style casserole. The beauty of this recipe is that it requires no fresh ingredients.

TUNA CAMP CASSEROLE

SERVES 3 TO 4

*16 ounces broad egg
    noodles, cooked and
    drained*
*One 7-ounce can tuna,
    drained and flaked*
*One to two 4-ounce cans
    sliced mushrooms,
    drained*

*One 4-ounce can peas,
    drained*
*One 10¾-ounce can con-
    densed cream of celery
    soup*
2 to 4 tablespoons butter
Salt and pepper to taste

Place all the ingredients (except the noodles) in a large pot over medium to low flame; heat through. Add the noodles and stir everything to mix thoroughly. Serve with a salad and crusty bread.

Although Mexican cuisine favors beans, rice, and tortillas, occasionally macaroni makes an appearance. Shirley Miller and her husband, Tom, experts on the Baja Peninsula, have enjoyed this dish while camp traveling.

MILLER'S MEXICAN MACARONI AND CHEESE

SERVES 4

*1 onion, peeled and
chopped*
½ green pepper, chopped
2 tablespoons butter
*One 10-ounce can mild
enchilada sauce*
1 teaspoon salt

*10 ounces macaroni shells,
cooked and drained*
*1 pound grated Cheddar
cheese*
*One 8-ounce can pitted
black olives*

Sauté the onions and pepper in butter. Add the enchilada sauce and sprinkle with salt; simmer another 5 minutes. Add cooked macaroni to sauce; stir. Add grated cheese and olives. Simmer for 15 minutes, stirring occasionally.

Hot dogs have become synonymous with cooking outdoors. They go together like sugar and spice.

FRANKS 'N BEANS 'N MACARONI

SERVES 6

1 tablespoon cooking oil
*6 frankfurters, sliced into
1-inch pieces*
*½ cup chopped green
pepper*
½ cup chopped onion
*One 15½-ounce can
tomato sauce*
*One 16-ounce can kidney
beans*

½ cup water
1 teaspoon chili powder
1 teaspoon salt
*Dash bottled hot pepper
sauce*
*16 ounces wagon wheels,
twisties, or other fun-
shaped noodles, cooked
and drained*

In a large skillet, heat the oil and brown the hot dog pieces, green pepper, and onion. Add remaining ingredients, including macaroni. Simmer, stirring occasionally, for 15 minutes.

MACARONI-CHEESE-HOT DOGS AMERICANA

SERVES 6

8 ounces macaroni, cooked
  and drained
1 pound frankfurters, cut
  into 1-inch pieces
1 cup mayonnaise
½ cup American cheese,
  sliced into julienne-
  style strips

½ cup diced scallions
2 tablespoons prepared
  mustard
½ teaspoon salt
Pepper to taste

Heat all ingredients together in a large saucepan.

We always take a can of tuna fish along on our camping expeditions. If the fishing isn't good, we still have dinner. In a couple of minutes, we stir together a great one-pot noodle dish.

TUNA DINNER DELUXE

SERVES 5

12 ounces thin noodles
1 small onion, peeled and
chopped
2 tablespoons cooking oil,
butter, or margarine
One 16-ounce can whole
peeled tomatoes with
their liquid
One 4-ounce can mush-
rooms with liquid

One 7-ounce can tuna,
drained and flaked
½ cup chopped green pep-
per (optional)
Salt and pepper to taste
Few drops bottled hot pep-
per sauce
Grated Parmesan cheese,
for garnish

In a large skillet, sauté the noodles and onion in the cooking oil until they are golden. Add all the remaining ingredients, except the cheese. Bring to a boil; cover and simmer for 15 minutes. Stir; sprinkle with cheese. Cover and continue cooking another 5 minutes, until the noodles are cooked and the cheese has melted. Serves 5.

This one is a twist on the usual bacon, eggs, and toast for camp breakfast.

BACON, EGGS, AND NOODLES

SERVES 4

12 strips bacon, diced
16 ounces leftover cooked medium wide noodles
4 eggs, lightly beaten (If you have more people, add more
eggs.)
Salt and pepper to taste

Fry the bacon until browned. Add the noodles and coat well with bacon fat. Add the eggs and season with salt and pepper. Toss mixture until eggs set, about ½ minute.

Leftover noodles can also be used for patties.

NOODLE PANCAKES

SERVES 4

4 eggs
Salt and pepper to taste
½ teaspoon instant minced
  onion

4 ounces grated American
  or Parmesan cheese
2 cups leftover cooked
  noodles
2 to 4 tablespoons butter

In a large mixing bowl, beat eggs until foamy; season with salt, pepper and onion. Fold in the cheese. Fold in the noodles, mixing everything gently. Fry small "pancakes" in hot melted butter until they are golden on both sides. Or, for an innovative way to prepare them in camp: Melt butter in a skillet and spread entire noodle mixture evenly on top. When first side is browned, use a spatula to turn it over carefully onto the second side to brown. Remove entire patty to a platter and top with crumbled crisp bacon or cooked sausage links.

Hungry for dessert? Sweets are important in camp, too. Use your leftover noodles—deep-fry them and sprinkle with sugar or dip them in honey. (See pages 82, 158.)

How to Buy a Noodle
(And Other Cooking Necessities)

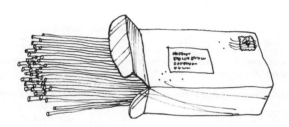

I F   Y O U are trying to locate specific cooking supplies, utensils, or ingredients, my first suggestions are to:

1. Check your local telephone directory for gourmet cookware stores and specialty markets in your area.

2. Contact your local newspaper's food editor or local radio station's food show host.

3. Check with your local major department store's houseware and cooking supplies department.

4. Check the mail order companies' catalogues you have received for their cookware specialties.

In addition to these local sources, you might write to the following stores which accept mail orders. Do check first to find out if they have a minimum order and for the lowest mail or delivery costs. Several of these companies print catalogues.

INTERNATIONAL GOURMET COOKWARE AND SUPPLIES

Hammacher Schlemmer, 147 East 57th Street, New York, New York 10022

Heidi's Around The World Food Shop, 1149 S. Brentwood Boulevard, St. Louis, Missouri 63117

Kitchen Bazaar, 4455 Connecticut Avenue, N.W., Washington, D.C. 20008

Maid of Scandinavia Co., 3244 Raleigh Avenue, Minneapolis, Minnesota 55416

Maison Glass, 52 East 58th Street, New York, New York 10022

Paprikas Weiss, 1546 Second Avenue, New York, New York 10028

H. Roth and Son (Lekvar-By-The-Barrel), 1577 First Avenue, New York, New York 10028

Williams-Sonoma, Mail Order Department, P.O. Box 3792, San Francisco, California 94119

THE ORIENTAL NOODLE

Eastern Trading Company, 2801 Broadway, New York, New York 10025

Ginza Market, 2600 W. Jefferson Boulevard, Los Angeles, California 90018

Granada Fish, 1919 Lawrence Street, Denver, Colorado 80202

Japan Food Corporation, 900 Marin Street, San Francisco, California 94124

Katagiri and Company, 224 E. 59th Street, New York, New York 10022

Kwong Hang Company, 918 Grant Avenue, San Francisco, California 94108

Min Sun Trading Company, 2222–2228 South La Salle Street, Chicago, Illinois 60616

New China Supply Company, 709 H Street, N.W., Washington, D.C. 20001

New Frontier Trading Corporation, 2394 Broadway, New York, New York 10024

Rafu Bussan Company, 344 E. First Street, Los Angeles, California 90012

Wing Fat Company, 33–35 Mott Street, New York, New York 10013

THE ITALIAN NOODLE

Acropolis Food Market, 1206 Underwood Street, N.W., Washington, D.C. 20015

Manganaro Foods, 488 Ninth Avenue, New York, New York 10018

Paul Urbani, 130 Graff Avenue, Trenton, New Jersey, 08638

Rino Gnesi Company, Inc., Mail Order Department, 415 Shirley Street, Winthrop, Massachusetts 02152

Trinacria Importing Company, 415 Third Avenue, New York, New York 10016

THE CONTINENTAL NOODLE

Acropolis Food Market, 1206 Underwood Street, N.W., Washington, D.C. 20015

Antone's Import Company, P.O. Box 3352, Houston, Texas, 77019

Bremen House, Inc., 200 E. 86th Street, New York, New York 10028

C & K Importing Company, 2771 West Pico Boulevard, Los Angeles, California 90006

European Grocery Store, 520 Court Place, Pittsburgh, Pennsylvania 15219

Greek Importing Company, 2801 West Pico Boulevard, Los Angeles, California 90006

Ideal Bakery, 2436 Ursulines Avenue, New Orleans, Louisiana 70119

Kassos Brothers, 570 Ninth Avenue, New York, New York 10036

Main Importing Company, Inc., 1188 St. Lawrence, Montreal 126, Quebec

Mediterranean and Middle East Import Company, 233 Valencia Street, San Francisco, California 94103

Nick Carras, 422 North 48th Street, Seattle, Washington 98103

Progress Grocery Company, 915 Decatur Street, New Orleans, Louisiana 70016

Schaller and Weber, 1654 Second Avenue, New York, New York 10028

THE AMERICAN NOODLE

Mother's General Store, 101 North Church Street, Hendersonville, North Carolina 28789

THE OUTDOOR SPORTS NOODLE

Eddie Bauer, P.O. Box 3700, Third and Virginia, Seattle, Washington 98130

L. L. Bean, Inc., Freeport, Maine 04033

Index

~~~~~~~~~~~~~~~~~~~~